史上最经典的美国中学生文史读本

最好的美国历史书，引导孩子领悟一个国家的成长

# 哈佛教授写给中学生的美国历史

下

[美] 爱德华·帕金斯·钱宁 著　杨东龙 / 主编　陈赓拓 / 译

英汉对照注释版

A STUDENT'S HISTORY OF THE UNITED STATES

人民东方出版传媒

東方出版社

**图书在版编目(CIP)数据**

哈佛教授写给中学生的美国历史 : 英汉对照 / (美)钱宁著 ; 陈赓拓译. -- 北京 : 东方出版社, 2015

书名原文: A STUDENT'S HISTORY OF THE UNITED STATES

ISBN 978-7-5060-8688-2

Ⅰ. ①哈… Ⅱ. ①钱… ②陈… Ⅲ. ①英语－汉语－对照读物②美国－历史 Ⅳ. ①H319.4 : K

中国版本图书馆CIP数据核字(2015)第259244号



**哈佛教授写给中学生的美国历史（下）**

［美］爱德华·帕金斯·钱宁 著　杨东龙 主编　陈赓拓 译

---

责任编辑：杜丽星　杨朝霞
出　　版：東方出版社
发　　行：人民东方出版传媒有限公司
地　　址：北京市东城区东四十条113号
邮政编码：100007
印　　刷：北京富达印务有限公司
版　　次：2017年5月第1版　2017年5月北京第1次印刷
开　　本：710毫米×1000毫米　1/16
印　　张：43.5
字　　数：561千字
书　　号：ISBN 978-7-5060-8688-2
定　　价：99.00元（上下册）
发行电话：（010）85924663　85924644　85924641

---

# 第九篇 PART IX

# 1812—1829年，战争与和平

## WAR AND PEACE, 1812~1829

## Books for Study and Reading
## 研究和阅读用书

**References.**—Higginson's *Larger History*, 365~442; Scribner's *Popular History*, IV; Lossing's *Field–Book of the War of 1812*; Coffin's *Building the Nation*, 149~231.

**Home Readings.**—Barnes's *Yankee Ships*; Roosevelt's *Naval War of 1812*; Seawell's *Midshipman Paulding*; Holmes's *Old Ironsides*; Goodwin's *Dolly Madison*.

## CHAPTER 25

# 1812—1815年，第二次独立战争

## THE SECOND WAR OF INDEPENDENCE, 1812~1815

260．公元1812年，作战计划——美军的作战计划是让赫尔将军（William Hull，1753~1825）从底特律进军加拿大。随后，他可以向东进军，在伊利湖北部与另一支渡过尼亚加拉河的军队会师。这两支军队将继续向东进军，与来自纽约的第三支部队会师。这三支军队随后将夺取蒙特利尔和魁北克，进而攻占整个加拿大。这是一个宏伟的计划。但是，有三个问题阻碍了它的实施：（1）美国没有受过正规训练的军队；（2）就算要让一支军队集合并受训，也没有补给可以供应它；（3）加拿大有一小股受过良好训练并且给养充足的军队。

261．公元1812年，赫尔将军在底特律投降——在那个时期，底特律和俄亥俄已开发地区之间隔着200英里的荒野。为了把军队和给养带到底特律，赫尔首先开辟了一条穿越森林的道路。英军在赫尔之前得知了美国对

1815年的底特律

英宣战的消息①。他们冲向他的各个涣散的小分队，夺走了美军的给养。赫尔派出一支又一支的远征军去收集给养，招募当地散居的移民。特库姆斯和其他英国的印第安人盟军俘虏了一支又一支的美国远征军。英军向底特律进军，赫尔投降。这次惨败使英军控制了上游的湖泊。他们甚至一度入侵了俄亥俄州。

262. 公元1813年，佩里的伊利湖大捷——但是，英军的胜利没有持续多久。1812年与1813年之间的冬天，奥利弗·哈泽德·佩里（Oliver Hazard Perry，1785~1819）在伊利湖组建了一支舰队。这些军舰是用专门为此砍伐的新木材制造的。它们虽然看起来很简陋，但是与英国军舰一样棒。1813年9月，佩里起航去搜寻英国军舰。找到英国军舰之后，他在桅顶挂了一面巨大的蓝旗，旗上写着劳伦斯②不朽的名言——“不要弃船”。这场战斗非常激烈。不久，佩里的旗舰“劳伦斯号”失去了战斗能力，只有九个船员没有受伤。划船登上了另一艘军舰之后，佩里继续作战。又过了不到15分钟，所有英国军舰都投降了。于是，伊利湖的控制权落在了美国人手中。英军从湖的南面撤走

佩里的战旗

① 战争开始前，赫尔奉命前往底特律担任西北准州的州长。美国对英国宣战的同一天，美国战争部通过不同的途径向赫尔发出了两封信，其中只有一封提到了对英宣战的事，然而这封信却没有按时送到赫尔的手中。因此，赫尔的失利其实是美国政府没有做好战争准备所导致的。

② 指在1813年6月4日阵亡的美国海军将领詹姆斯·劳伦斯（James Lawrence，1781~1813），他是佩里的好友。佩里在伊利湖战役开始前请当地妇女缝制了一面旗，将劳伦斯牺牲前最后的命令“不要弃船”缝在了旗上，以表示继承好友的坚定勇敢的战斗精神。“不要弃船”也从此成为一句著名的战斗口号，今天仍然被美国海军使用。

了。哈里逊将军[①]夺回了底特律。他随后侵入了加拿大，并在泰晤士河畔打败了一支英军（1813年10月）。

**263. “宪法号”护卫舰**—— “宪法号”是美国第一批投入使用的军舰之一。它的指挥官是艾萨克·赫尔（Isaac Hull，1773~1843）。它从切萨皮克海湾驶往纽约，并将作为一艘护卫舰在纽约服役。它在航行中偶然遇到了一个英国海军中队。“宪法号”在整个英国舰队的穷追不舍下继续航行。不久，风开始变小。“宪法号”的船员用水把船帆打湿，以便更好地利用风力。后来，风完全停止了。赫尔船长下令放下小船。船员们开始划小船来拖拽“宪法号”。但是英军也放下了小船。他们用许多小船来拖拽他们最快的军舰。这艘军舰开始要赶上“宪法号”了。这时，赫尔船长发现他们是在浅水中航行。尽管看不见陆地，他还是在一只小船的前面抛下了一个小锚。锚放下之后，舰上的人就用力拖拽锚链。他们这样反复做了很多次。于是，“宪法号”的速度开始超过英国舰队。随后，一阵突发的风暴向舰船袭来。赫尔船长意识到了暴雨的来临，于是做好了充分利用它的准备。当雨停下来的时候，“宪法号”已经摆脱了追逐的威胁。但是，它已经无力前往纽约了，于是赫尔船长把它开到了

“宪法号”

这是一幅早期绘画作品，它表现的是“宪法号”逃离英国舰队追逐的情景。船上的人们正准备放下小锚。

① 即蒂珀卡努之战中的美军主将威廉·亨利·哈里逊。他随后在泰晤士河之战（这条泰晤士河并非英国的泰晤士河，它位于今天的加拿大安大略省查塔姆肯特地区）中消灭了印第安人联盟，联盟首领特库姆斯也在此役中阵亡。

波士顿。联邦政府立即命令他原地待命，但是在命令传到波士顿之前，“宪法号”已经走远了。

**264. 公元1812年，“宪法号”与“女战士号”**——赫尔船长指挥“宪法号”在圣劳伦斯湾巡航了一段时间。一天，他发现了一艘英国护卫舰——“女战士号”——它是之前追击“宪法号”的军舰之一。不过这一次，赫尔发现只有它一条船，于是就指挥“宪法号”径直朝它驶去。在离第一次开炮不到三十分钟的时间里，“女战士号”就变成了一堆残骸。它所有的桅杆和帆桁都被打落，大部分船员非死即伤。“宪法号”只受到轻微的损伤，不久就做好了攻打另一艘英国护卫舰的准备——要是还有这样一艘英国护卫舰要打的话。事实上，“宪法号”上的外科医生登上了“女战士号”去帮助英国海员包扎伤口。“女战士号”比“宪法号”稍小一些，火力配备也比“宪法号”稍差一些。但是，这次大获全胜的真正原因是“宪法号”在船只和火力的操控方面远远胜于“女战士号”。

“宪法号”与“女战士号”

**265. 公元1812年，“黄蜂号”与“佛罗里克号”**——几乎与此同时，美国军舰“黄蜂号”捕获了英国双桅船“佛罗里克号”。“黄蜂号”有三根桅杆，而“佛罗里克号”只有两根。但是这两艘船在规模上其实几乎是一样的，因为美国军舰只比它的敌人长5英尺，并且火力装备要差一些。战斗刚打响几分钟，“佛罗里克号”就被打成了一艘废船，它的甲板上只剩下一个安然无恙的船员。这场冲突结束之后不久，一艘英国战舰就赶来捕获了“黄蜂号”及其战利品。“黄蜂号”和“宪法号”的那些胜利所产生的影响是巨大的。战争开始之前，英国海军军官们把“宪法号”称为“一捆木棍”。这时，他们认为，对于英国护卫舰来说，单独出海已经不再是安全的了。它们必须成对地行动，以保护彼此免遭“老铁甲”[1]的袭击。没过多久，“宪法号”在新任指挥官班布里奇船长（William Bainbridge，1774~1833）的指挥下俘获了英国护卫舰“爪哇号”，而迪凯特船长[2]指挥的“合众国号”护卫舰则俘获了英国军舰“马其顿号”。另一方面，美军的“切萨皮克号”[3]被英军的“香农号”俘获。这一胜利给了英国人极大的满足。但是，劳伦斯船长的遗言“不要弃船”从此成为一句光荣的口号，一直激励着美国的船员们。

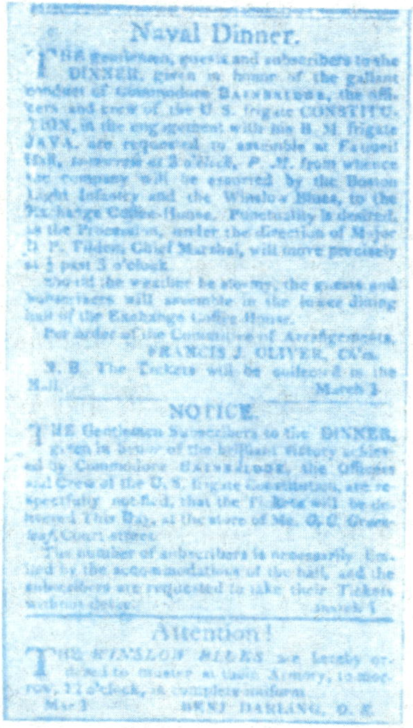
Naval Dinner.
THE Gentlemen, guests and subscribers to the DINNER, given in honor of the gallant conduct of Commodore BAINBRIDGE, the officers and crew of the U. S. frigate CONSTITUTION, in the engagement with his B. M. frigate JAVA, are requested to assemble at Faneuil Hall, to-morrow at 2 o'clock, P. M. from whence the company will be escorted by the Boston Light Infantry and the Winslow Blues, to the Exchange Coffee-House. Punctuality is desired, as the Procession, under the direction of Major B. P. Tilden, Chief Marshal, will move precisely at ½ past 3 o'clock.

Should the weather be stormy, the guests and subscribers will assemble in the lower dining hall of the Exchange Coffee-House.

Per order of the Committee of Arrangements,
FRANCIS J. OLIVER, Ch'n.

N. B. The Tickets will be collected in the Hall. March 1

NOTICE.
THE Gentlemen Subscribers to the DINNER, given in honor of the brilliant victory achieved by Commodore BAINBRIDGE, the Officers and Crew of the U. S. frigate Constitution, are respectfully notified, that the Tickets will be delivered This Day, at the store of Mr. [illegible], Court street.

The number of subscribers is necessarily limited by the accommodations of the hall, and the subscribers are requested to take their Tickets without delay. March 1

Attention!
THE WINSLOW BLUES are hereby ordered to muster at their Armory, to-morrow, 11 o'clock, in complete uniform.
Mar 1 BENJ DARLING, O. S.

美国海军部为庆祝“宪法号”在班布里奇的指挥下取得胜利而举行宴会的通知

266. 公元1814年，布朗入侵加拿大——战争打响后的最初两年，驻守在纽约的各支美国陆军并没有采取任何行动。不过这时，一些更有能

① 指“宪法号”。
② 即在打击北非海盗中扬名的美国海军将领斯蒂芬·迪凯特。
③ “切萨皮克号”当时的船长就是詹姆斯·劳伦斯，他在与“香农号”的战斗中阵亡。

力的人在指挥这些军队。这些人当中，雅各布·布朗将军（Jacob Jennings Brown，1775~1828）、麦科姆将军（Alexander Macomb，1782~1841）、温菲尔德·斯科特上校（Winfield Scott，1786~1866）和里普利上校（Eleazer Wheelock Ripley，1782~1839）都值得被后人铭记。美军的作战计划是：布朗、斯科特和里普利一起渡过尼亚加拉河，然后入侵加拿大；麦科姆将军则和麦克多诺（Thomas MacDonough, Jr.，1783~1825）率领的海军一起守住尚普兰湖战线。英军的计划是经由尚普兰湖入侵纽约。布朗渡过了尼亚加拉河，并在奇佩瓦和伦迪巷打了两场漂亮仗。第二场战役尤其辉煌，因为美军缴获了英军的武器，并用这些武器击退了那些经验丰富的英国兵发动的多次进攻。尽管如此，布朗将军最后还是被迫撤退了。

**267. 公元1814年，麦克多诺的普拉茨堡大捷**——普雷沃斯特将军（Sir George Prevost，1767~1816）率领一支装备精良、经验丰富的陆军从加拿大向南进军，与此同时，一支英国舰队溯流而上[①]进入尚普兰湖。尚普兰湖的西面是普拉茨堡，麦科姆将军率军驻扎于此。普拉茨堡的前面停泊着麦克多诺的舰队。普雷沃斯特攻击了麦科姆的军队但被击退。英国舰队攻击了麦克多诺的舰队却被消灭。这一结果终结了普雷沃斯特的入侵。他尽可能快地撤回了加拿大。

**268. 公元1814年，切萨皮克地区的英军**——除了在加拿大边境的行动，英军还曾试图占领新奥尔良以及切萨皮克湾周边的城市。英军在华盛顿市的南面登陆。他们向首都进军。他们进入了华盛顿。他们烧毁了国会大厦、白宫以及其他几个公共建筑。随后，他们丢下受伤人员匆忙离开

① 这里的“流”是指黎塞留河，它从尚普兰湖的北部流向圣劳伦斯河，所以这里的“溯流而上”从地理方位上来说也即是南下。

麦克亨利堡

麦克亨利堡的星条旗

上面有十五颗星和十五道横条，每一颗星和条代表美国当时的一个州。

了。过了一些时候，英军攻打了巴尔的摩，但被击退而且损失惨重。就在这个时候，弗朗西斯·斯科特·凯伊（Francis Scott Key，1779~1843）创作了《星条旗》。战斗期间，凯伊被扣押在一艘英国军舰上。他透过浓烟热切地注视着位于港口的麦克亨利堡上方的星条旗。那天早上，旗帜依然在那里飘扬。这次败北结束了英军在切萨皮克地区的行动。

269. 克里克战争——克里克族印第安人生活在亚拉巴马。他们对白人居住地的日益扩张感到不安。美国这时正忙于对英战争。这将是消灭他们的大好时机。于是，克里克人袭击了白人，并杀死了大约四百人。田纳西州的安德鲁·杰克逊将军（Andrew Jackson，1767~1845）掌管着美国西南部的陆军。一得知到克里克人正在袭击居民，他立即召集起士兵，追到了印第安人的大本营。他对他们的要塞发动了猛攻并杀死了大部分守卫。

270. 公元1814—1815年，杰克逊防卫新奥尔良——杰克逊刚忙完这项工作，就得知一支英国大军来到了密西西比河的入海口。他立即赶去防卫新奥尔良。新奥尔良南面的地区对于防御方非常有利。因为除了河岸沿线，那里几乎没有坚实的地面。杰克逊挑选了一个特别狭窄的地方，用棉花包和垃圾修建了一个防御工事。他在防御工事前面挖了一条深沟。英军匆忙发起了进攻。他们的大部分将领非死即伤，损失极其惨重。稍后，他们再次发起了进攻，又再次被击退。

新奥尔良保卫战

这幅画出自杰克逊将军的一名部下之手。

**271. 公元1814年，海上之战**——大约只有战争的第一年，美英两国的军舰之间展开了许多战斗。从那以后，美国军舰再也无法到达海上，因为英国人把所有的舰队都安置在了美国主要港口的入口处。但是，仍有一些美国军舰冲破了英国舰队的封锁，并且获得了累累战果。比如，"宪法号"船长查尔斯·斯图尔特（Charles Stewart，1778~1869）曾一次性俘获了两艘英国军舰。不过，大部分到达海上的美国军舰迟早都被英军俘获。

查尔斯·斯图尔特

**272.武装民船**——任何英国舰队都没能阻止武装民船离港。它们一窝蜂地冲到海上，俘获了数以百计的英国商船，有些武装民船还到达了能看到大不列颠海滨的地方。它们总共俘获了超过2500艘英国船只。它们甚至和敌人的小型军舰战斗过。

**273. 公元1814年，《根特条约》**——战争刚刚爆发，合众国与大不列颠双方就都派出了专员去进行和谈。但是，他们没有取得任何进展，直到1814年的战败让英国人明白了他们根本攻不下合众国的任何地方。这时，英国人才完全做好了准备来讲和，于是，两国于1814年12月在根特签订了一个条约。条约的签订是在新奥尔良的英军惨败的两周前，而这个战败的消息又过了数月才传到欧洲。条约中只字未提这场战争的缘由。但是这些事提与不提真的没什么区别。因为在美国对英宣战的消息传到伦敦之前，英国人就已经取消了他们针对美国船只的命令。至于“强行征用”，“宪法号”的炮火早已使之寿终正寝。

**274. 公元1814年，哈特福德会议**——当新任专员正在商讨和平条约的时候，另一些争论者正在康涅狄格的哈特福德谈论这场战争。他们是新英格兰联邦党人的主要成员。他们认为，位于华盛顿的联邦政府已经做了许多合众国宪法不允许它做的事情。他们起草了一套决议案，其中的一些

共和党讽刺哈特福德会议的漫画

旧州议会大厦

哈特福德会议就是在这里召开的。

读起来就像杰斐逊和麦迪逊于1789年起草的决议案。这些哈特福德的辩论家还认为，联邦政府没有完全做到保护新英格兰的海岸免受英国人攻击，因此，他们提出，联邦应该退还它向新格兰各州征的税，以供它们保卫自身之用。事实上，当杰克逊取得新奥尔良大捷和《根特条约》签订的消息传到华盛顿时，这些专员们正在华盛顿提议以这种方式瓜分国家的税收。得知这两个消息后，他们就匆忙赶回到各自的州去了。于是，共和党重新获得了广大选民的支持。

275. 战争的收获——经过所有这些海陆战役，合众国没有获得任何领土。它甚至也没得到停止“强制征用”的明确承诺。但有件事相对来说更为重要，即美国人民开始认为美利坚本身是一个民族。美国人不再把英国人或法国人看作效仿的榜样。他们变成了美利坚人。获得这种独立和民族的意识是一个巨大进步。因此，我们不妨把这场战争看作是第二次独立战争。

## 【Original Text】

**260. Plan of Campaign, 1812.**—The American plan of campaign was that General Hull should invade Canada from Detroit. He could then march eastward, north of Lake Erie, and meet another army which was to cross the Niagara River. These two armies were to take up the eastward march and join a third army from New York. The three armies then would capture Montreal and Quebec and generally all Canada. It was a splendid plan. But there were three things in the way of carrying it out: (1) there was no trained American army; (2) there were no supplies for an army when gathered and trained; and (3) there was a small, well-trained and well-supplied army in Canada.

**261. Hull's Surrender of Detroit, 1812.**—In those days Detroit was separated from the settled parts of Ohio by two hundred miles of wilderness. To get his men and supplies to Detroit, Hull had first of all to cut a road through the forest. The British learned of the actual declaration of war before Hull knew of it. They dashed down on his scattered detachments and seized his provisions. Hull sent out expedition after expedition to gather supplies and bring in the scattered settlers. Tecumthe and the other Indian allies of the British captured one expedition after another. The British advanced on Detroit, and Hull surrendered. By this disaster the British got control of the upper lakes. They even invaded Ohio.

**262. Perry's Victory on Lake Erie, 1813.**—But the British triumph did not last long. In the winter of 1812~13 Captain Oliver Hazard Perry built a fleet of warships on Lake Erie. They were built of green timber cut for the purpose. They were poor vessels, but were as good as the British vessels. In September, 1813, Perry sailed in search of the British ships. Coming up with them, he hoisted at his masthead a large blue flag with Lawrence's immortal words, "Don't give up the ship," worked upon it. The battle was fiercely fought. Soon Perry's flagship, the Lawrence, was disabled and only nine of her crew were uninjured. Rowing to another ship, Perry continued the fight. In fifteen minutes more all the British ships surrendered. The control of Lake Erie was now in American hands. The British retreated from the southern side of the lake. General Harrison occupied Detroit. He then crossed into Canada and defeated a British army on the banks of the river Thames (October, 1813).

**263. The Frigate Constitution.**—One of the first vessels to get to sea was the

*Constitution*, commanded by Isaac Hull. She sailed from Chesapeake Bay for New York, where she was to serve as a guard-ship. On the way she fell in with a British squadron. The *Constitution* sailed on with the whole British fleet in pursuit. Soon the wind began to die away. The *Constitution's* sails were soaked with water to make them hold the wind better. Then the wind gave out altogether, Captain Hull lowered his boats and the men began to tow the ship. But the British lowered their boats also. They set a great many boats to towing their fastest ship, and she began to gain on the *Constitution*. Then Captain Hull found that he was sailing over shoal water, although out of sight of land, so he sent a small anchor ahead in a boat. The anchor was dropped and men on the ship pulled in the anchor line. This was done again and again. The *Constitution* now began to gain on the British fleet. Then a sudden squall burst on the ships. Captain Hull saw it coming and made every preparation to take advantage of it. When the rain cleared away, the *Constitution* was beyond fear of pursuit. But she could not go to New York, so Captain Hull took her to Boston. The government at once ordered him to stay where he was; but, before the orders reached Boston, the *Constitution* was far away.

**264. *Constitution* and *Guerrière*, 1812.**—For some time Hull cruised about in the Gulf of St. Lawrence. One day he sighted a British frigate—the *Guerrière*—one of the ships that had chased the *Constitution*. But now that Hull found her alone, he steered straight for her. In thirty minutes from the firing of the first gun the *Guerrière* was a ruinous wreck. All of her masts and spars were shot away and most of her crew were killed or wounded. The *Constitution* was only slightly injured, and was soon ready to fight another British frigate, had there been one to fight. Indeed, the surgeons of the *Constitution* went on board of the *Guerrière* to help dress the wounds of the British seamen. The *Guerrière* was a little smaller than the *Constitution* and had smaller guns. But the real reason for this great victory was that the American ship and the American guns were very much better handled than were the British ship and the British guns.

**265. The *Wasp* and the *Frolic*, 1812.**—At almost the same time the American ship *Wasp* captured the British brig *Frolic*. The *Wasp* had three masts, and the *Frolic* had only two masts. But the two vessels were really of about the same size, as the American ship was only five feet longer than her enemy, and had the lighter guns. In a few minutes after the beginning of the fight the *Frolic* was a shattered hulk, with only one sound man on her deck. Soon after the conflict a British battleship came up and captured both the *Wasp* and her prize. The effect of these victories of the *Constitution* and the *Wasp* was tremendous. Before the war British naval officers had called the *Constitution* "a bundle of sticks." Now it was thought to be no longer safe for British frigates to sail the seas alone. They must go in pairs to protect each other from "Old Ironsides." Before long the *Constitution*, now commanded by Captain Bainbridge, had captured the British frigate *Java*, and the frigate *United States*, Captain Decatur, had taken the British ship *Macedonian*. On the other hand, the *Chesapeake* was captured by the *Shannon*. This victory gave great satisfaction to the British. But Captain Lawrence's last words, "Don't give up the ship," have always been a glorious inspiration to American sailors.

**266. Brown's Invasion of Canada, 1814.**—In the first two years of the war the American armies in New York had done nothing. But abler men were now in command. Of these, General Jacob Brown, General Macomb, Colonel Winfield Scott, and Colonel Ripley deserve to be remembered. The American plan of campaign was that Brown, with Scott and Ripley, should cross the Niagara River and invade Canada. General Macomb, with a naval force under McDonough, was to hold the line of Lake Champlain. The British plan was to invade New York by way of Lake Champlain. Brown crossed the Niagara River and fought two brilliant battles at Chippewa and Lundy's Lane. The latter battle was especially glorious because the Americans captured British guns and held them against repeated attacks by British veterans. In the end, however, Brown was obliged to retire.

267. McDonough's Victory at Plattsburg, 1814.—General Prevost, with a fine army of veterans, marched southward from Canada, while a fleet sailed up Lake Champlain. At Plattsburg, on the western side of the lake, was General Macomb with a force of American soldiers. Anchored before the town was McDonough's fleet. Prevost attacked Macomb's army and was driven back. The British fleet attacked McDonough's vessels and was destroyed. That put an end to Prevost's invasion. He retreated back to Canada as fast as he could go.

**268. The British in the Chesapeake, 1814.**—Besides their operations on the Canadian frontier, the British tried to capture New Orleans and the cities on Chesapeake Bay. The British landed below Washington. They marched to the capital. They entered Washington. They burned the Capitol, the White House, and several other public buildings. They then hurried away, leaving their wounded behind them. Later on the British attacked Baltimore and were beaten off with great loss. It was at this time that Francis Scott Key wrote "The Star-Spangled Banner." He was detained on board one of the British warships during the fight. Eagerly he watched through the smoke for a glimpse of the flag over Fort McHenry at the harbor's mouth. In the morning the flag was still there. This defeat closed the British operations on the Chesapeake.

**269. The Creek War.**—The Creek Indians lived in Alabama. They saw with dismay the spreading settlements of the whites. The Americans were now at war. It would be a good chance to destroy them. So the Creeks fell upon the whites and murdered about four hundred. General Andrew Jackson of Tennessee commanded the American army in the Southwest. As soon as he knew that the Creeks were attacking the settlers, he gathered soldiers and followed the Indians to their stronghold. He stormed their fort and killed most of the garrison.

**270. Jackson's Defense of New Orleans, 1814~15.**—Jackson had scarcely finished this work when he learned of the coming of a great British expedition to the mouth of the Mississippi River. He at once hastened to the defense of New Orleans. Below the city the country greatly favored the defender. For there was very little solid ground except along the river's bank. Picking out an especially narrow place, Jackson built a breastwork of cotton bales and rubbish. In front of the breastwork he dug a deep ditch. The British rushed to the attack. Most of their generals were killed or wounded, and the slaughter was terrible. Later, they made another attack and were again beaten off.

**271. The War on the Sea, 1814.**—It was only in the first year or so of the war that there was much fighting between American and British warships. After that the American ships could not get to sea, for the British stationed whole fleets off the entrances to the principal harbors. But a few American vessels ran the blockade and did good service. For instance, Captain Charles Stewart in the *Constitution* captured two British ships at one time. But most of the warships that got to sea were captured sooner or later.

**272. The Privateers.**—No British fleets could keep the privateers from leaving port. They swarmed upon the ocean and captured hundreds of British merchantmen, some of them within sight of the shores of Great Britain. In all, they captured more than twenty-five hundred British ships. They even fought the smaller warships of the enemy.

**273. Treaty of Ghent, 1814.**—The war had hardly begun before commissioners to treat for peace were appointed by both the United States and Great Britain. But they did nothing until the failure of the 1814 campaign showed the British government that there was no hope of conquering any portion of the United States. Then the British were ready enough to make peace, and a treaty was signed at Ghent in December, 1814. This was two weeks before the British disaster at New Orleans occurred, and months before the news of it reached Europe. None of the things about which the war was fought were even mentioned in the treaty. But this did not really make much difference. For the British had repealed their orders as to American ships before the news of the declaration of war reached London. As for impressment, the guns of the *Constitution* had put an end to that.

**274. The Hartford Convention, 1814.**—While the New commissioners were talking over the treaty of peace, other debaters were discussing the war, at Hartford, Connecticut. These were leading New England Federalists. They thought that the government at Washington had done many things that the Constitution of the United States did not permit it to do. They drew up a set of resolutions. Some of these read like those other resolutions drawn up by Jefferson and Madison in 1798. The Hartford debaters also thought that the national government had not done enough to protect the coasts of New England from British attacks. They proposed, therefore, that the taxes collected by the national government in New England should be handed over to the New England states to use for their defense. Commissioners were actually at Washington to propose this division of the national revenue when news came of Jackson's victory at New Orleans and of the signing of the Treaty of Ghent. The commissioners hastened home and the Republican party regained its popularity with the voters.

**275. Gains of the War.**—The United States gained no territory after all this fighting on sea and land. It did not even gain the abolition of impressment in so many words. But what was of far greater importance, the American people began to think of itself as a nation. Americans no longer looked to France or to England as models to be followed. They became Americans. The getting of this feeling of independence and of nationality was a very great step forward. It is right, therefore, to speak of this war as the Second War of Independence.

CHAPTER 26

# 1815—1824年，和睦时代

## THE ERA OF GOOD FEELING, 1815~1824

276. 从整体来看这一时期——1815年至1824年这几年被称为“和睦时代”，因为这段时间内没有任何尖锐的政治斗争——至少最后一两年之前是这样的。1816年，门罗在没有遭到太多反对的情况下当选为总统。1820年，他连任总统时仍然没有遇到任何异议。比起政治斗争，人们这时正忙于在西部的广大地区发展种植业，在东部发展大型制造业。他们还在忙着修建道路与运河，以便将西部的农场与东部的城市和工厂连接起来。这一时期的后半段是一个无比繁荣的时期。时不时会出现某个需要讨论的难题，人们会将其搁置，或者就其麻烦之处达成妥协。这几年间，联邦党销声匿迹了，而共和党则分裂成若干派系。到1824年之前，共和党内部的差异已经变得非常大了，这使得“和睦时代”迅速地走到了尽头。

詹姆斯·门罗

第五任美国总统（1817~1825）

277. 移民西部——这个时期的最初几年间，沿海原始州的人民感到非常贫穷。船主们再也不能获得高额利润。因为欧洲当时处于和平状态，于是欧洲船就和美国船展开了竞争。大量英国商品被运到美国，并以非常低

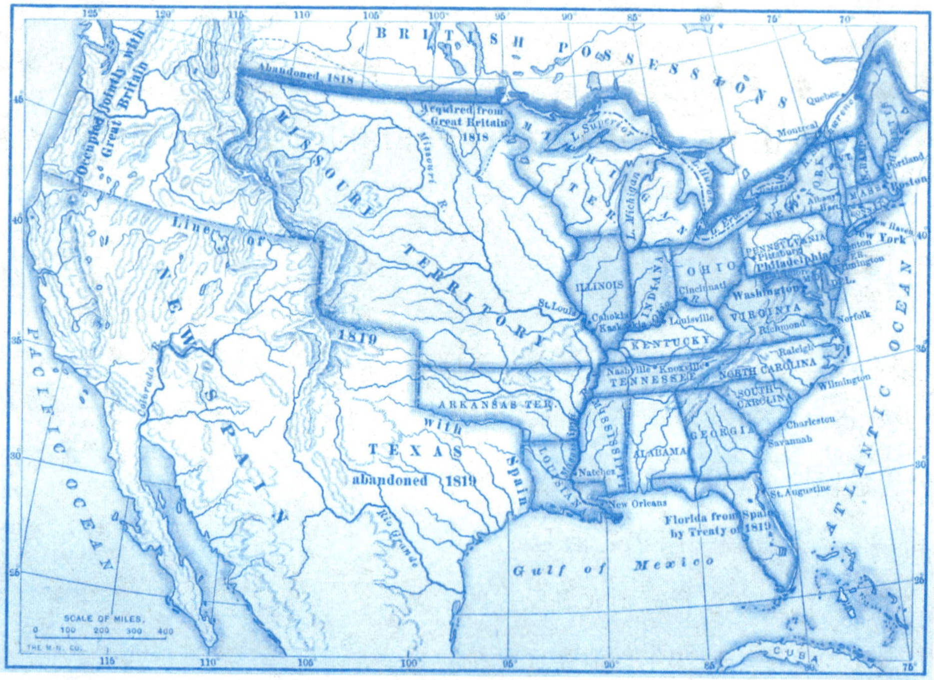


1819年的美国

的价格出售。美国商品的需求量大大降低了。作坊主关闭了他们的作坊。男女工人都找不到工作了。结果，美国国内兴起了一股从东部沿海的原始州向西部新居住地移民的巨大浪潮。在西部，移民可以用极低的价格从政府手中买到土地，而辛勤的劳动也能够让他们养家糊口。这种西进运动在1817年达到了高潮。1816年至1819年，又有四个新州加入了联邦。它们分别是印第安纳州（1816年）、密西西比州（1817年）、伊利诺伊州（1818年）和亚拉巴马州（1819年）。有些移民甚至渡过密

1818年的星条旗

每一颗星和条代表美国当时的一个州。

西西比河到密苏里和阿肯色定居。1819年，密苏里和阿肯色的居民申请作为密苏里州加入联邦，或以“阿肯色”为名建立准州政府。缅因人也请求国会允许他们作为“缅因州”加入联邦。

**278. 反对密苏里加入联邦**——许多北方人反对允许密苏里加入联邦，因为提出申请的这个“州”的那些移民是奴隶主。密苏里将会成为蓄奴州，而这些北方人不想再增加任何蓄奴州了。一开始，奴隶制曾存在于所有的原始十三州。但是马里兰州以北的各州已经在1819年之前废除了奴隶制，或采纳了某个将逐渐终结奴隶制的方案。而西北地区早已通过著名的《1787法令》将奴隶制拒之门外。这些方法已经使奴隶制在马里兰州和肯塔基州以北的地方不再是必不可少的制度。那么凭什么要让奴隶制在密西西比河以西得到许可呢？路易斯安那已经作为蓄奴州加入了联邦（1812年）。但是，接纳路易斯安那是美国和法国签订购买路易斯安那的条约时做出的规定。而南方人则以同样坚定的态度提出了相反的意见。他们说，他们的奴隶是他们的财产，他们有充分的权利携带自己的财产住在属于这个国家的土地上。既然一个蓄奴州已经建立起来了，唯一正确的做法就是允许它加入联邦。

**279. 公元1820年，《密苏里妥协案》**——当接纳缅因和密苏里的问题摆在国会面前时，参议院中支持蓄奴州和自由州的参议员数完全相同。但是，自由州拥有众议院的多数席位。自由州比蓄奴州发展得快，而且可能将以更快的速度继续发展。因此，众议院中被自由州占据的席位也很可能继续增加。如果自由州在参议院也获得了多数席位，南方人就会在政府中完全失势。出于这些理由，南方人不同意缅因作为自由州加入联邦，除非密苏里同时作为蓄奴州加入联邦。经过长期的努力，缅因和密苏里都加入了联邦——一个作为蓄奴州，一个作为自由州。不过，国会还达成了共识：密苏里州南部边界以北所有的通过路易斯安那购地案获得的土地，除密苏里州外，应当永远是自由的土地。这项约定被称为《密苏里妥协案》。它是亨利·克莱的杰作。这是一个十分重要的事件，因为它把关于奴隶制的不可避免的冲突推迟了25年。

**280. 公元1819年，《佛罗里达条约》**——在这场争论持续期间，美国从西班牙手中买来了一大块非常适合建立黑人奴隶制的土地。这就是佛罗里达。它原来属于西班牙，是各色人等的避难所。这些人包括逃亡的黑人、亡命的印第安人、走私贩子，以及各种罪犯。一旦到了佛罗里达，亡命之徒通常就安全了。但是，他们并非一直安全无虞。例如，1818年，杰克逊将军曾越过国界追捕逃跑的印第安人。他们向一个西班牙要塞寻求庇护，于是杰克逊被迫消灭了这个要塞和那些印第安人。这一战绩让西班牙人更愿意卖掉佛罗里达，价格是500万美元。但是，到了要放弃这个地区的时候，西班牙人发现他们很难信守自己的承诺。条约于1819年签订，但直

位于佛罗里达州圣奥古斯丁的老房子

到1821年，杰克逊才以佛罗里达总督的身份占领了这个新准州。甚至到了这个时候，西班牙总督还拒绝交出档案，因此，在他变得相对理智一些之前，杰克逊不得不把他关进监狱。

281. “神圣同盟”——大多数其他西属殖民地的人民都在反抗西班牙，西班牙国内也发生了叛乱。其他欧洲国家和西班牙一样也发生了叛乱。事实上，造反精神几乎蔓延到了世界各地。这给欧洲的皇帝们和国王们敲响了警钟。除英国国王外，他们联合起来共同镇压叛乱。他们把他们的联盟称为“神圣同盟”①。他们不久就让西班牙国王重新回到了他的王座上。他们随后认为必须派遣军舰和军队渡过大西洋去镇压西属殖民地上的叛乱。这时，合众国的人民同情那些渴望独立的西属殖民地人。他们也不喜欢欧洲人干涉美洲事务的想法。“美洲是美洲人的美洲”是当时的口号。碰巧英国人也希望西属殖民地人能获得自由。因为作为西班牙的国民，他们不允许购买英国的商品。但是，如果他们获得了自由，他们就可以随心所欲地购买各国的商品了。英国政府因此提议合众国与大不列颠联合发布一个宣言，宣布各西属殖民地是独立的国家。约翰·亚当斯的儿子约翰·昆西·亚当斯（John Quincy Adams，1767~1848）当时是门罗总统的国务卿。他认为接受这个做法是不明智的，因为这将让美洲事务受到欧洲的控制。当俄国沙皇准备在北美洲的西海岸建立殖民地时，亚当斯越发想要避免陷入这一纠葛，以便能腾出手来对付俄国。

282. 公元1823年，门罗主义——在这种情况下，门罗总统向国会递

① “神圣同盟”成立于1815年9月26日，由俄国沙皇亚历山大一世发起，除了他之外，最初的成员还有奥地利皇帝弗兰茨一世和普鲁士国王腓特烈·威廉三世。后来，欧洲的大多数基督教国家加入了这个组织。

交了一个咨文[①]。他在该咨文中陈述了美国的如下政策：（1）美洲不再向任何欧洲政权的殖民活动开放；（2）美国过去未曾干涉，将来也不会干涉欧洲的事务；（3）美国把“神圣同盟”组织向美洲的扩张视为对美国的威胁；（4）美国将把“神圣同盟”对美洲事务的干涉看成是一种“不友好行为”。咨文的这一部分是亚当斯执笔的。他长期从事外交工作，经验丰富。他使用“不友好行为”这样的字眼，是因为外交家们在使用它们的时候通常是在暗示：一个“不友好行为”将成为引发战争的一个诱因。英国政府也告知“神圣同盟”，后者对美洲事务的干涉将招来不满。于是“神圣同盟”放弃了镇压西属殖民地的整个想法。而俄国沙皇也同意不在北纬54度40分以南[②]建立殖民地。

**283. 门罗主义的意义**——门罗总统向国会提交的那个著名的咨文中所包含的思想一直被称为“门罗主义”。其中大多数观点并非门罗或亚当斯首创。它们中的许多内容可以在华盛顿的《中立宣言》和《告别演说》、杰斐逊的《就职演说》以及其他文献中找到。门罗咨文的创新之处在于声明了欧洲对美洲事务的干涉会被美国视为导致战争的“不友好行为”。欧洲的国王们可以在欧洲镇压独立，他们可以瓜分亚洲和非洲。但是，他们不得干涉美洲事务。

① 《美利坚合众国宪法》的第二条第三款规定，总统应不定期地向国会报告国情，并就国家重大措施的审议向国会提供必要且适当的建议。第一任总统华盛顿将这种报告以演讲的形式公开发表，不过从第三任总统杰斐逊开始，就改为向国会提交的形式发表，1913年，威尔逊总统又恢复了以演讲的形式发表国情报告，直至今天。这种报告，就是国情咨文（State of the Union Message）。美国法律并未对国情咨文的发布时间做出规定，但是国情咨文每年都会发布。

② 当时，北纬54度40分以南至北纬42度以北的俄勒冈地区，是英美之间的争议地区。19世纪初期，两国经过一系列谈判，决定搁置争议，共同管理该地。所以，所谓“北纬54度40分以南”，在当时也就是指除了英国单独控制的殖民地之外，包含英美共治领土在内的整个美洲地区（含南美洲）。

## 【Original Text】

**276. The Era as a Whole.** —The years 1815~24 have been called the Era of Good Feeling, because there was no hard political fighting in all that time—at least not until the last year or two. In 1816 Monroe was elected President without much opposition. In 1820 he was reëlected President without any opposition whatever. Instead of fighting over politics, the people were busily employed in bringing vast regions of the West under cultivation and in founding great manufacturing industries in the East. They were also making roads and canals to connect the Western farms with the Eastern cities and factories. The later part of the era was a time of unbounded prosperity. Every now and then some hard question would come up for discussion. Its settlement would be put off, or the matter would be compromised. In these years the Federalist party disappeared, and the Republican party split into factions. By 1824 the differences in the Republican party had become so great that there was a sudden ending to the Era of Good Feeling.

**277. Western Emigration.**—During the first few years of this period the people of the older states on the seacoast felt very poor. The shipowners could no longer make great profits. For there was now peace in Europe, and European vessels competed with American vessels. Great quantities of British goods were sent to the United States and were sold at very low prices. The demand for American goods fell off. Mill owners closed their mills. Working men and women could find no work to do. The result was a great rash of emigrants from the older states on the seaboard to the new settlements in the West. In the West the emigrants could buy land from the government at a very low rate, and by working hard could support themselves and their families. This westward movement was at its height in 1817. In the years 1816~19, four states were admitted to the Union. These were Indiana (1816), Mississippi (1817), Illinois (1818), and Alabama (1819). Some of the emigrants even crossed the Mississippi River and settled in Missouri and in Arkansas. In 1819 they asked to be admitted to the Union as the state of Missouri, or given a territorial government under the name of Arkansas. The people of Maine also asked Congress to admit them to the Union as the state of Maine.

**278. Opposition to the Admission of Missouri.**—Many people in the North opposed the admission of Missouri because the settlers of the proposed state were slaveholders. Missouri would be a slave state, and these Northerners did not want any more slave states. Originally slavery had existed in all the old thirteen states. But every state north of Maryland had before 1819 either put an end to slavery or had adopted some plan by which slavery would gradually come to an end. Slavery had been excluded from the Northwest by the famous Ordinance of 1787. In these ways slavery had ceased to be a vital institution north of Maryland and Kentucky. Why should slavery be allowed west of the Mississippi River? Louisiana had been admitted as a slave state (1812). But the admission of Louisiana had been provided for in the treaty for the purchase of Louisiana from France. The Southerners felt as strongly on the other side. They said that their slaves were their property, and that they had a perfect right to take their property and settle on the land belonging to the nation. Having founded a slave state, it was only right that the state should be admitted to the Union.

**279. The Missouri Compromise, 1820.**—When the question of the admission of Maine and Missouri came before Congress, the Senate was equally divided between the slave states and the free states. But the majority of the House of Representatives was from the free states. The free states were growing faster than were the slave states and would probably keep on growing faster. The majority from the free states in the House, therefore, would probably keep on increasing. If the free states obtained a majority in the Senate also, the Southerners would lose all control of the government. For these reasons the Southerners would not consent to the admission of Maine as a free state unless at the same time Missouri was admitted as a slave state. After a long struggle Maine and Missouri were both admitted—the one as a free state, the other as a slave state. But it was also agreed that all of the Louisiana Purchase north of the southern boundary of Missouri, with the single exception of the state of Missouri, should be free soil forever. This arrangement was called the Missouri Compromise. It was the work of Henry Clay. It was an event of great importance, because it put off for twenty-five years the inevitable conflict over slavery.

**280. The Florida Treaty, 1819.**—While this contest was going on, the United States bought of Spain a large tract of land admirably suited to negro slavery. This was Florida. It belonged to Spain and was a refuge for all sorts of people: runaway negroes, fugitive Indians, smugglers, and criminals of all kinds. Once in Florida, fugitives generally were safe. But they were not always safe. For instance, in 1818 General Jackson chased some fleeing Indians over the boundary. They sought refuge in a Spanish fort, and Jackson was obliged to take the fort as well as the Indians. This exploit made the Spaniards more willing to sell Florida. The price was five million dollars. But when it came to giving up the province, the Spaniards found great difficulty in keeping their promises. The treaty was made in 1819, but it was not until 1821 that Jackson, as governor of Florida, took possession of the new territory. Even then the Spanish governor refused to hand over the record books, and Jackson had to shut him up in prison until he became more reasonable.

**281. The "Holy Alliance."**—Most of the people of the other Spanish colonies were rebelling against Spain, and there was a rebellion in Spain itself. There were rebellions in other European countries as well as in Spain. In fact, there seemed to be a rebellious spirit nearly everywhere. This alarmed the European emperors and kings. With the exception of the British king, they joined together to put down rebellions. They called their union the Holy Alliance. They soon put the Spanish king back on his throne. They then thought that they would send warships and soldiers across the Atlantic Ocean to crush the rebellions in the Spanish colonies. Now the people of the United States sympathized with the Spanish colonists in their desire for independence. They also disliked the idea of Europeans interfering in American affairs. "America for Americans," was the cry. It also happened that Englishmen desired the freedom of the Spanish colonists. As her subjects Spain would not let them buy English goods. But if they were free, they could buy goods wherever they pleased. The British government therefore proposed that the United States and Great Britain should join in a declaration that the Spanish colonies were in dependent states. John Quincy Adams, son of John Adams, was Monroe's Secretary of State. He thought that this would not be a wise course to follow, because it might bring American affairs within European control. He was all the more anxious to prevent this entanglement, as the Czar of Russia was preparing to found colonies on the western coast of North America and Adams wanted a free hand to deal with him.

**282. The Monroe Doctrine, 1823.**—It was under these circumstances that President Monroe sent a message to Congress. In it he stated the policy of the United States as follows: (1) America is closed to colonization by any European power; (2) the United States have not interfered and will not interfere in European affairs; (3) the United States regard the extension of the system of the Holy Alliance to America as dangerous to the United States; and (4) the United States would regard the interference of the Holy Alliance in American affairs as an "unfriendly act." This part of the message was written by Adams. He had had a long experience in diplomacy. He used the words "unfriendly act" as diplomatists use them when they mean that such an "unfriendly act" would be a cause for war. The British government also informed the Holy Allies that their interference in American affairs would be resented. The Holy Alliance gave over all idea of crushing the Spanish colonists. And the Czar of Russia agreed to found no colonies south of fifty-four degrees and forty minutes north latitude.

**283. Meaning of the Monroe Doctrine.**—The ideas contained in Monroe's celebrated message to Congress are always spoken of as the Monroe Doctrine. Most of these ideas were not invented by Monroe or by Adams. Many of them may be found in Washington's Neutrality Proclamation, in Washington's Farewell Address, in Jefferson's Inaugural Address, and in other documents. What was new in Monroe's message was the statement that European interference in American affairs would be looked upon by the United States as an "unfriendly act," leading to war. European kings might crush out liberty in Europe. They might divide Asia and Africa among themselves. They must not interfere in American affairs.

CHAPTER 27

# 1824~1829年，新政党与新政策

## NEW PARTIES AND NEW POLICIES, 1824~1829

284.“和睦时代”的终结——1824年，“和睦时代”突然结束了。门罗总统的第二任期将于1825年结束。他拒绝了再次被提名为总统候选人。就这样，门罗遵从了华盛顿、杰斐逊、麦迪逊所树立的榜样，以此巩固了总统任期限为八年的惯例。继任他总统这一要职的候选人并不少。

285. 约翰·昆西·亚当斯——第一个重要的总统候选人是来自马萨诸塞州的约翰·昆西·亚当斯。他曾是门罗的国务卿，而这个职位已成为通往总统宝座的一个台阶。门罗曾是麦迪逊的国务卿；麦迪逊曾是杰斐逊的国务卿；而杰斐逊曾是华盛顿的国务卿——尽管他在成为总统之前的职位是副总统。约翰·昆西·亚当斯是一个经验丰富、卓有才干的政治家。他是一个受人敬仰、学识渊博的人。他获得了马萨诸塞州和新英格兰其他州的议会的提名。

286. 威廉·H. 克劳福德——除了亚当斯，门罗内阁的其他两名成员也想成为总统。他们是约翰·C. 卡尔霍恩和威廉·H. 克劳福德（William Harris Crawford，1772~1834）。卡尔霍恩不久就退出了竞争，接受了所有派别的提名而当选为副总统。克劳福德来自佐治亚州，当时是财政部长。作为这个庞大部门的首脑，他有权任命的职位比其他内阁成员有权任命的总和还要多。利用公职报答政治盟友的习惯开始于宾夕法尼亚州。华盛顿在

他的第二任期内，亚当斯和杰斐逊在他们的第一任期内都只任命自己派系的成员担任公职。杰斐逊还撤掉了一些政治对手的职务。但是撤换职务的过程困难重重。克劳福德突然产生了一个想法，提出了任命的官员任期只有四年的方案。国会立即对这个想法表示赞成，并通过了《官员任期法》，把官员的任期限定为四年。克劳福德立即用这个新的权力在财政部组建了一个强大政治机器并让其为他的个人晋升服务。国会的核心成员提名他为总统候选人，于是他就成为了“固定的”总统候选人。

约翰·考德威尔·卡尔霍恩

**287. 克莱与杰克逊**——还有两个非内阁成员被推举出来竞选总统。他们是田纳西州的安德鲁·杰克逊和肯塔基州的亨利·克莱。克莱和卡尔霍恩几乎是同时进入政界的。他们当时也怀有相同的政治主张。卡尔霍恩后来放弃了他早期的思想。然而，克莱始终坚持着“国家主义”政策。克莱也支持用政府的开支来进行内部改进。他是伟大的“调解者”，并试图通过妥协的手段把联邦的所有部分联合起来。克莱热爱国家，而且无比相信美国人民。肯塔基州和其他几个州的议会提名他为总统候选人。在所有候选人当中，最有实力的是“新奥尔良的英雄”安德鲁·杰克逊。他在政治上从不突出。但是他

亨利·克莱

的战绩让选民们——尤其是西部的选民——对他的名字和实力十分熟悉。他是人民中的一员，在这一点上，他的竞争对手没有一个能望其项背。他代表着民主与联邦。田纳西州和其他几个州的议会提名他为总统候选人。

288. 公元1824年，亚当斯当选总统——大选开始了。总统选举人在他们各自的州集合，投票选举总统和副总统。选票被送到华盛顿清点。没有一个总统候选人获得了多数的总统选举人票。杰克逊得票比其他任何一名候选人都多。第二名是亚当斯，然后是克劳福德，最后一名是克莱。众议院通过各州投票提出必须从前三名中选出一人担任总统。因此，克莱出局。克莱及其支持者与亚当斯及其支持者信奉相同的观点，而这两派几乎都不认同杰克逊与克劳福德的观点。因此，克莱派加入了亚当斯的阵营，选择让亚当斯担任总统。杰克逊派愤怒不已。他们宣称众议员使“民众的意愿”落空了。

约翰·昆西·亚当斯

第六任美国总统（1825~1829）

289. 亚当斯政府的厄运——亚当斯的第一个错误是任命克莱担任国务卿。这是一个错误，因为这让杰克逊派有机会宣称亚当斯与克莱之间进行了一场“交易”。他们把克莱称为“西部的犹大”。他们声称“民众的意愿”被“腐败的交易”打败了。他们一再重复这些指控，致使许多人真的开始相信必定有什么理由才产生这些指责。杰克逊派还极不公正地指责亚当斯偷了国家的钱。英国政府抓住亚当斯政府软弱的机会，禁止美国船舶进入英属西印度群岛的港口。

290. 早期的关税——自从1789年以来，制造业就得到了保护。最初的关税税率很低。但《禁运法》《互不通商法》，以及1812年战争终止了外国商品的进口。资本家把大量的钱投资到棉花作坊、羊毛作坊和铁作坊上。随着和平于1815年的到来，英国商人的廉价商品如潮水一样涌进了美国市场。制造商请求国会给予更多的保护，于是国会立即通过了一项新的关税法案。它提高了早期法律所规定的关税。但是它并没有给制造商带来他们想要的全部保护。1824年，国会起草了另一项法案。它进一步提高了关税。南方人反对通过这项法案。因为他们很明白这种贸易保护对他们是没有好处的。但是，北方人及西部人衷心地拥护提高关税，于是，这项法案获得了通过。

291. 公元1828年，令人深恶痛绝的关税——1828年，新一届总统大选就要举行了。制造商们认为，这是要求更高的保护性关税的好机会，因为政治家们会因害怕失去选票而不敢对这部法律的通过提出反对意见。杰克逊派想出了一个计划。这个计划能让他们看起来是支持提高关税的，实际上却是在反对提高关税。因此，他们提议对制成品征收高关税，这将取悦北方的制造商；他们又提议对原料征收高关税，这将取悦西部的生产者。但是，他们认为制造商会反对这个法案的最终通过，因为对原料征收高关税会严重伤害到他们。所以这项法案将不会获得通过，而这又将取悦南方的棉花种植者。这是一个十分精明的小计划。但是，它没能发挥作用。制造商认为，无论如何，只要提高制成品关税就行了——也许他们要不了多久就能设法取消对原料征收的关税。北方的国会议员投票赞同这个法案，于是它获得了通过。

292. 公元1828年，杰克逊当选总统——在外交事务和这种关税引发的纷争等诸如此类的不顺期间，1828年的总统大选开始了。亚当斯和杰克逊是仅有的两名总统候选人。杰克逊获得多数选票而成功当选。不过，亚当斯得到的选票只比他在1824年得到的选票少一张。两人在宾夕法尼亚州和纽约州这两个大州中的支持率非常接近。要是这两个州中再多出数千个选民把票投给亚当斯，这些州的总统选举人票就会全部投给他，那么他就会当选。幸运的是，杰克逊当选了。因为一场各州和联邦政府之间的巨大冲突正在到来。一个像杰克逊这样有领导实力而且广受欢迎的人做政府首脑是非常合适的。

## 【Original Text】

**284. End of the Era of Good Feeling.**—The Era of Good Feeling came to a sudden ending in 1824. Monroe's second term as President would end in 1825. He refused to be a candidate for reëlection. In thus following the example set by Washington, Jefferson, and Madison, Monroe confirmed the custom of limiting the presidential term to eight years. There was no lack of candidates to succeed him in his high office.

**285. John Quincy Adams.**—First and foremost was John Quincy Adams of Massachusetts. He was Monroe's Secretary of State, and this office had been a kind of stepping-stone to the presidency. Monroe had been Madison's Secretary of State; Madison had been Jefferson's Secretary of State; and Jefferson had been Washington's Secretary of State, although he was Vice-President when he was chosen to the first place. John Quincy Adams was a statesman of great experience and of ability. He was a man of the highest honor and intelligence. He was nominated by the legislatures of Massachusetts and of the other New England states.

**286. William H. Crawford.**—Besides Adams, two other members of Monroe's cabinet wished to succeed their chief. These were John C. Calhoun and William H. Crawford. Calhoun soon withdrew from the contest to accept the nomination of all the factions to the place of Vice-President. Crawford was from Georgia and was Secretary of the Treasury. As the head of that great department, he controlled more appointments than all the other members of the cabinet put together. The habit of using public offices to reward political friends had begun in Pennsylvania. Washington, in his second term, Adams, and Jefferson had appointed to office only members of their own party. Jefferson had also removed from office a few political opponents. But there were great difficulties in the way of making removals. Crawford hit upon the plan of appointing officers for four years only. Congress at once fell in with the idea and passed the Tenure of Office Act, limiting appointments to four years. Crawford promptly used this new power to build up a strong political machine in the Treasury Department, devoted to his personal advancement. He was nominated for the presidency by a Congressional caucus and became the "regular" candidate.

**287. Clay and Jackson.**—Two men outside of the cabinet were also put forward for Monroe's high office. These were Andrew Jackson of Tennessee and Henry Clay of Kentucky. Clay and Calhoun had entered politics at about the same time. They had then believed in the same policy. Calhoun had abandoned his early ideas. But Clay held fast to the policy of "nationalization." He still favored internal improvements at the national expense. He still favored the protective system. He was the great "peacemaker" and tried by means of compromises to unite all parts of the Union. He loved his country and had unbounded faith in the American people. The legislatures of Kentucky and other states nominated him for the presidency. The strongest man of all the candidates was Andrew Jackson, the "Hero of New Orleans." He had never been prominent in politics. But his warlike deeds had made his name and his strength familiar to the voters, especially to those of the West. He was a man of the people, as none of his rivals were. He stood for democracy and the Union. The legislatures of Tennessee and other states nominated Jackson for the presidency.

**288. Adams chosen President, 1824.**—The election was held. The presidential electors met in their several states and cast their votes for President and Vice-President. The ballots were brought to Washington and were counted. No candidate for the presidency had received a majority of all the votes cast. Jackson had more votes than any other candidate, next came Adams, then Crawford, and last of all Clay. The House of Representatives, voting by states, must choose one of the first three President. Clay, therefore, was out of the race. Clay and his friends believed in the same things that Adams and his friends believed in, and had slight sympathy with the views of Jackson or of Crawford. So they joined the Adams men and chose Adams President. The Jackson men were furious. They declared that the Representatives had defeated the "will of the people."

**289. Misfortunes of Adams's Administration.**—Adams's first mistake was the appointment of Clay as Secretary of State. It was a mistake, because it gave the Jackson men a chance to assert that there had been a "deal" between Adams and Clay. They called Clay the "Judas of the West." They said that the "will of the people" had been defeated by a "corrupt bargain." These charges were repeated over and over again until many people really began to think that there must be some reason for them. The Jackson men also most unjustly accused Adams of stealing the nation's money. The British government seized the opportunity of Adams's weak administration to close the West India ports to American shipping.

**290. Early Tariffs.**—Ever since 1789 manufactures had been protected. The first tariff rates were very low. But the Embargo Act, the non-intercourse law, and the War of 1812 put an end to the importation of foreign goods. Capitalists invested large amounts of money in cotton mills, woolen mills, and iron mills. With the return of peace in 1815, British merchants flooded the American markets with cheap goods. The manufacturers appealed to Congress for more protection, and Congress promptly passed a new tariff act (1816). This increased the duties over the earlier laws. But it did not give the manufacturers all the protection that they desired. In 1824 another law was drawn up. It raised the duties still higher. The Southerners opposed the passage of this last law. For they clearly saw that protection did them no good. But the Northerners and the Westerners were heartily in favor of the increased duties, and the law was passed.

**291. The Tariff of Abominations, 1828.**—In 1828 another presidential election was to be held. The manufacturers thought that this would be a good time to ask for even higher protective duties, because the politicians would not dare to oppose the passage of the law for fear of losing votes. The Jackson men hit upon a plan by which they would seem to favor higher duties while at the same time they were really opposing them. They therefore proposed high duties on manufactured goods. This would please the Northern manufacturers. They proposed high duties on raw materials. This would please the Western producers. But they thought that the manufacturers would oppose the final passage of the bill because the high duties on raw materials would injure them very much. The bill would fail to pass, and this would please the Southern cotton growers. It was a very shrewd little plan. But it did not work. The manufacturers thought that it would be well at all events to have the high duties on manufactured goods—perhaps they might before long secure the repeal of the duties on raw materials. The Northern members of Congress voted for the bill, and it passed.

**292. Jackson elected President, 1828.**—In the midst of all this discouragement as to foreign affairs and this contest over the tariff, the presidential campaign of 1828 was held. Adams and Jackson were the only two candidates. Jackson was elected by a large majority of electoral votes. But Adams received only one vote less than he had received in 1824. The contest was very close in the two large states of Pennsylvania and New York. Had a few thousand more voters in those states cast their votes for Adams, the electoral votes of those states would have been given to him, and he would have been elected. It was fortunate that Jackson was chosen. For a great contest between the states and the national government was coming on. It was well that a man of Jackson's commanding strength and great popularity should be at the head of the government.

# QUESTIONS AND TOPICS
# 问题与论题

## CHAPTER 25

§§ 260-262.—a. Explain by a map the American plan of campaign and show its advantages and disadvantages.

b. Describe Perry's victory. How did this turn the scale of war?

§§ 263-265.—a. Describe the escape of the *Constitution* from the British fleet. Describe the destruction of the *Guerrière* and of the *Frolic*. What was the reason for the American successes?

b. Why was the effect of these victories so great?

c. Why did the capture of the *Chesapeake* cause so much delight in England? Why are Lawrence's words so inspiring?

§§ 266, 267.—a. Compare the second plan for the invasion of Canada with the earlier one.

b. Discuss the events of Brown's campaign and its results.

c. Compare Prevost's campaign with Burgoyne's. Why was it unsuccessful?

d. What do Perry's and McDonough's victories show?

§ 268.—a. Why were the British attacks directed against these three portions of the country?

b. Describe the attack on Washington. Was the burning of the public buildings justifiable?

c. Read the "Star-Spangled Banner" and explain the allusions.

§§ 269,270.—a. Describe Jackson's plans for the defense of New Orleans. Why were they so successful?

b. Why did not this success of the Americans have more effect on the peace negotiations?

§§ 271,272.—a. Why were most of the naval conflicts during the first year of the war? What is a blockade? What is a privateer?

b. What work did the privateers do?

§ 273. —a. Why was so little advance made at first toward a treaty of peace?

b. Why was the news of the treaty so long in reaching Washington?

c. What was settled by the war?

§ 274.—a. Were the Federalists or the Republicans more truly the national party?

b. What propositions were made by the Hartford Convention? If such proposals were carried out, what would be the effect on the Union?

c. Compare the principles underneath these resolutions with those of the Kentucky and Virginia Resolutions.

§ 275. —a. Note carefully the effect of this war.

b. Why is it called the Second War of Independence?

## CHAPTER 26

§§ 276, 277.—a. What is meant by the Era of Good Feeling? Is this period more important or less important than the period of war which preceded it? Why?

b. What matters occupied the attention of the people?

c. What shows the sudden increase in Western migration?

§§ 278, 279.—a. State carefully the objections to the admission of Missouri on the part of the Northerners. Why did the Southerners object to the admission of Maine?

b. Trace on a map the line between the free states and the slave states. Why was slavery no longer of importance north of this line? Why was it important south of this line?

c. Why were the free states gaining faster than the slave states?

d. Explain the Missouri Compromise. How did the Compromise postpone the conflict over slavery?

§ 280.—a. Why was Florida a danger to the United States?

b. What people in the United States would welcome the purchase of Florida?

c. What does this section show you as to Jackson's character?

§ 281.—a. Why was the Holy Alliance formed? What did the allies propose as to America?

b. How was this proposal regarded by Americans? Why?

c. How was it regarded by Englishmen? Why?

§§ 282, 283.—a. Explain carefully the four points of Monroe's message.

b. Were these ideas new? What is an "unfriendly act"?

c. What action did Great Britain take? What was the result of the declarations of the United States and Great Britain.

d. What was the new point in Monroe's message?

e. Do we still keep to the Monroe Doctrine in all respects?

## CHAPTER 27

§§ 284-288.—a. Who were the candidates for President in 1824? Describe the qualities and careers of each of them. For whom would you have voted had you had the right to vote in 1824?

b. How were these candidates nominated? What is a caucus?

c. Describe the Tenure of Office Act. Should a man be given an office simply because he has helped his party?

d. In what respects was Jackson unlike the early Presidents?

e. What was the result of the election? Who was finally chosen? Why? If you had been a Representative in 1824, for whom would you have voted? Why?

f. What is a majority? A plurality?

§ 289.—a. Why was the appointment of Clay a mistake?

b. What charges were made against Adams?

c. Describe the misfortunes of Adams's administration.

§§ 290, 291.—a. How are manufactures protected?

b. Why were the protective tariffs of no benefit to the Southerners?

c. Why was an attempt for a higher tariff made in 1828?

d. Explain the plan of the Jackson men. Why did the plan fail?

§ 292.—a. Describe the election of 1828.

b. How was Jackson fitted to meet difficulties?

## GENERAL QUESTIONS
## 综合性问题

a. Why was the navy better prepared for war than the army?

b. Why did slaveholders feel the need of more slave territory in the Union?

c. Jackson has been called "a man of the people." Explain this title.

# SUGGESTIONS TO THE TEACHER
# 给教师的建议

The results of the War of 1812 should be carefully studied and compared with the proposals of the Hartford Convention. These last can be taught by comparison with the Kentucky and Virginia Resolutions.

To the Missouri Compromise much time and careful explanation should be given. Touch upon the economic side of slavery, and explain how the continued supremacy of the slave power was threatened.

The Monroe Doctrine is another difficult topic; but it can be explained by recent history.

The election of 1824 can be carefully employed to elucidate the mode of electing President, and the struggle over the tariffs can be illustrated by recent tariff contests.

# 第十篇
# PART X

## 1829—1844年，国家民主

## THE NATIONAL DEMOCRACY, 1829~1844

## Books for Study and Reading
## 研究和阅读用书

**References.**—Scribner's *Popular History*, IV; Lodge's *Webster*; Coffin's *Building the Nation*, 251-313.

**Home Readings.**—Roosevelt's *Winning of the West*; Hale's *Stories of Inventions*; Wright's *Stories of American Progress*.

## CHAPTER 28
# 1830年的美国人民
## THE AMERICAN PEOPLE IN 1830

293. 一个新的民族——在杰斐逊当选总统和杰克逊当选总统期间，美国发生了巨大的变化。老一辈的革命政治家全都下台了。新人们取代了他们的位置。过去毫无生机的生活消失了。这时，到处都是喧嚣和忙碌。在1800年，联邦党人喜欢英国人，而共和党人则喜欢法国人。这时，似乎没人关心英国人和法国人。终于，人民变成了美国人。联邦党消失了。每个人这时要么是投票支持亚当斯的国家共和党人，要么是投票支持杰克逊的民主共和党人。

294. 人口与面积——1800年，整个美国只有550万人。这时，美国有接近1300万人。而且这些人也有一个比过去大得多的国家可以居住。1800年，美国的面积大约为80万平方英里。但是随后美国就买下了路易斯安那和佛罗里达。这时（1830年），美国的面积大约是200万平方英里。原始州的人口已经大幅增长，而城市人口的增长尤为显著。1800年，纽约市大约有6万人；而它这时有20万人。但人口增长最快的是西部。1800年以来，俄亥俄、伊利诺伊、亚拉巴马、密西西比、路易斯安那与密苏里全都被许可加入了联邦。

295. 国家道路——蒸汽船这时已经运行于五大湖和西部所有的重要河流上。这种新型交通方式所产生的第一个结果是缩短了东西部之间的距

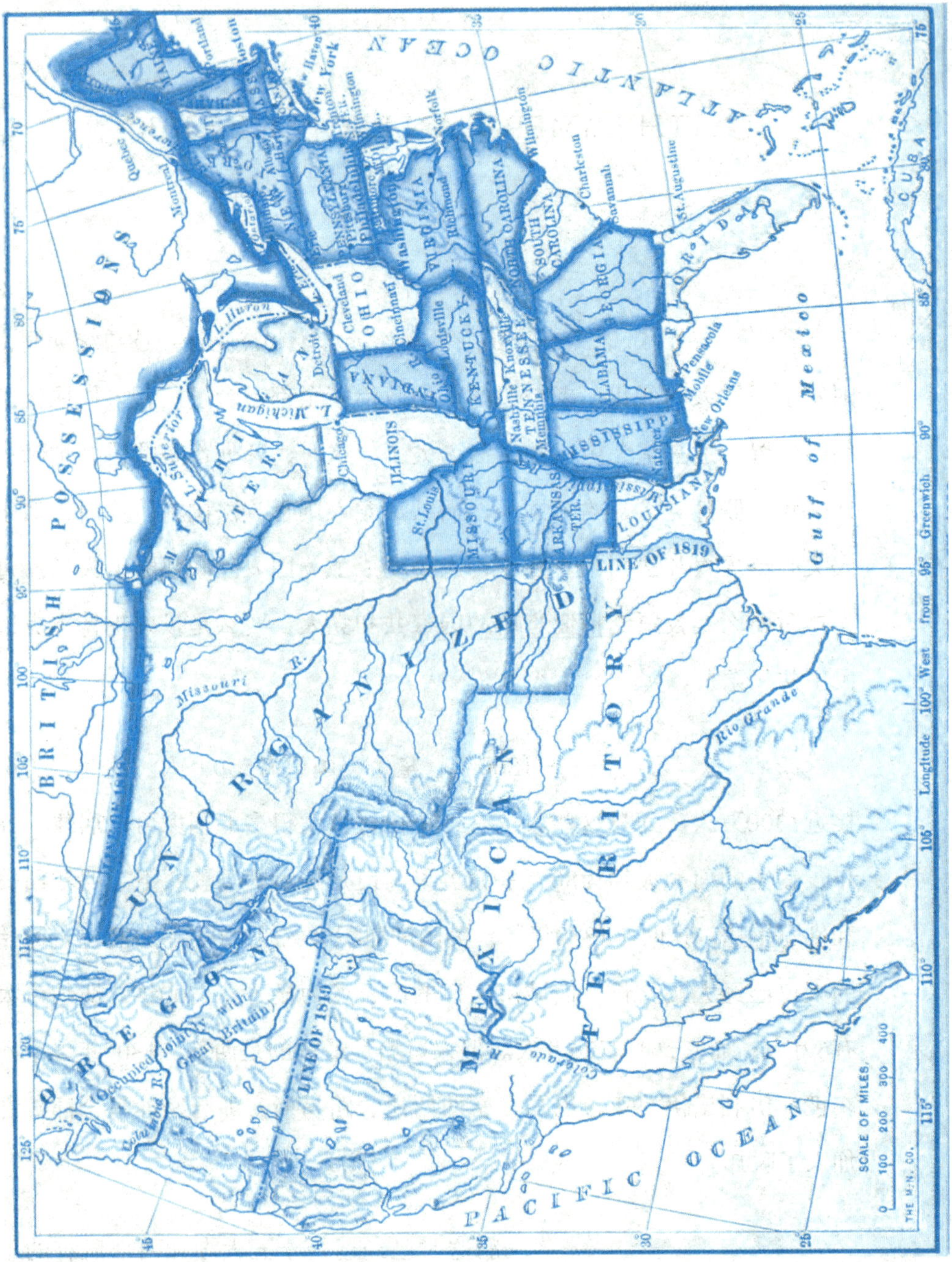
ATLANTIC OCEAN
PACIFIC OCEAN
Gulf of Mexico
BRITISH POSSESSIONS
UNORGANIZED TERRITORY
MEXICAN TERRITORY
OREGON
Occupied jointly with Great Britain
LINE OF 1819
OHIO
INDIANA
ILLINOIS
KENTUCKY
TENNESSEE
VIRGINIA
NORTH CAROLINA
SOUTH CAROLINA
GEORGIA
ALABAMA
MISSISSIPPI
LOUISIANA
MISSOURI
ARKANSAS TER.
FLORIDA
CUBA
L. Michigan
L. Superior
L. Huron
Missouri R.
Rio Grande
Colorado R.
St. Louis
New Orleans
Charleston
Savannah
Richmond
Washington
Cincinnati
Cleveland
Detroit
Chicago
Nashville
Knoxville
Louisville
Pensacola
Mobile
Natchez
Wilmington
Norfolk
St. Augustine
Boston
Portland
New York
Montreal
Quebec
Memphis
SCALE OF MILES
0 100 200 300 400
Longitude 100° West from 95° Greenwich
THE M-N. CO.

1830年的美国

离。蒸汽船可以载着乘客和商品在密西西比河及其各支流来回航行，而且比通过翻越阿勒格尼山脉运输乘客与商品便宜、舒服。因此，许多人建议修建一条良好的马车道以连接波托马克河和俄亥俄河。这条大道的东端是马里兰州波托马克河畔的坎伯兰。因此，它通常被称为“坎伯兰大道”。1811年，政府出资[①]开始修建这条路。到1820年，这条路修到了俄亥俄河畔的惠灵。蒸汽船可以从那里驶往匹兹堡、辛辛那提、圣路易斯和新奥尔良。稍后，这条路修到了更远的西部，直到伊利诺伊。随后，铁路的出现使得进一步的修筑变得没有必要。

19世纪美国西部拓荒者使用的宽轮大篷车

296. 伊利运河——把两条蒸汽船航线连接起来的最好方式是挖掘一条运河。这些运河中，最著名的当属连接哈德逊河与伊利湖的伊利运河。人们于1817年开始挖掘这条运河，到1825年完工通航。德维特·克林顿[②]

① 在此之前，公路的修建都是各地州政府负责的，坎伯兰大道是第一条由联邦政府出资修建的公路，因此，它是美国第一条真正意义上的国道。它从1811年开始修建，至1852年才全部竣工，全长834英里。

② 德维特·克林顿曾担任美国参议院议员和纽约州第六任州长。他还曾以联邦党总统候选人的身份参加1812年总统选举，虽不敌麦迪逊，但他是自1800年以来总统大选中得票最多的联邦党候选人。

（DeWitt Clinton，1769~1828）认为这样一条运河会让纽约市从中获益，因为人们可以通过这条运河把纽约州西北部和西部的农产品运到纽约市。同时，这条河还会让那些地区的农场主从中获益，因为经水路运送农产品比经陆路横穿宾夕法尼亚州便宜。又因为水运比陆运的运费率要低得多，所以这条河还能让这些农场主买到便宜得多的商品，从而使他们进一步获益。人们并没有像德维特·克林顿一样把事情看得这么清楚。他们用非常轻蔑的口吻谈论这项事业，并把这条运河称为“克林顿的大沟”。不久，事实就证明了克林顿是正确的。没过一年，把一吨谷物从伊利湖运到哈德逊河的运费就从100美元降到了15美元。纽约市很快就超越所有竞争对手，成为美国贸易与财富的中心。其他运河，比如切萨皮克—俄亥俄运河，都是技术的非凡杰作。但是，它们都不像伊利运河拥有如此优越的地理位置，也就无法成功地与它竞争。

德维特·克林顿

297. 早期的铁路——即便是最好的石铺路也往往有某些地方非常难走。有人想出了更好的办法：把木轨铺在路上，然后给马车的车轮装上轮圈或轮缘，以使它们能保持在木轨上。1807年，美国第一条这样的道路在波士顿建成。这是一个非常粗糙简陋的玩意儿，并且只用于从一座山丘的顶部向港口运送泥土。这些木轨不久就损坏了，因此下一步是在这些木轨的上面钉上铁条。不久，这种轨道路（railroads）连成的长距离线路就建好了。它们既能运送乘客又能运载货物。它们中的一些是私人或企业出资建的。有些则是某个城镇或某个州修建的。只要付少许钱，任何拥有马匹和带轮缘马车的人都可以使用这种铁路。这就是蒸汽机车发明时的情况。

298. 蒸汽机车——蒸汽已经被用来驱动船只在水上航行。那么它为什么不可以用来拉动铁路上的马车呢？这是一个很容易提出却很难解答的问题。过了一年又一年，发明家们一直在对此进行研究。大约1830年，突然之间，几个地方的几个人几乎同时解决了这个问题。然而，此后又过了几年，蒸汽机车的使用才得到普及。早期的铁路列车都是非常简陋的东西。那些车厢和带轮缘的公共马车相差无几。人们用链条把它们拴在一起，当车头发动或熄火的时候，会产生一阵可怕的撞击和震动。车头的烟囱非常高，并且以铰链固定，这是为了在遇到低矮的桥梁或隧道时能将它放下来。这种时候，浓烟和煤渣就会直接喷到乘客的脸上。但是这些火车比运河上的船只或蒸汽船跑得都要快。很快，铁路就成了最重要的交通方式。

一个早期的蒸汽火车头

一个20世纪初的火车头

299. 其他发明——蒸汽机车的到来，加快了1830年各方面已经显现的变化。一段时间之前，人们就已经在宾夕法尼亚州发现了大量的硬煤或无烟煤[①]。但是，这种煤太硬了，以至于它在老式的火炉和壁炉里都无法燃烧。这时，可以烧无烟煤的火炉被发明了出来，完全改变了室内取暖方

① 美国煤炭行业根据煤炭的煤化程度从高到低将煤分为四类：无烟煤、烟煤、次烟煤、褐煤。其中，无烟煤和烟煤统称为硬煤。煤化程度越高，这种煤燃烧所提供的热量也就越多。无烟煤的煤化程度最高，但其密度和硬度也相对较大，燃点高，不易燃烧。美国的东部、中部和西部都有煤炭资源，但无烟煤只产于宾夕法尼亚东部。

一辆早期的马拉轨道车

式。随后，人们找到了用无烟煤炼铁的方法。整个钢铁产业焕发了新的生机。接着，煤气在城市中得到了广泛的应用。制造业的巨大增长和交通方式的巨大变化，导致人们纷纷涌入城市和城镇。这些发明，使解决聚集在小区域内的大批人口的温饱问题成为可能。城市开始高速发展，人们再也不用靠近他们工作和购物的地方居住了。公共马车路线建立了起来，不久，街道中就铺设了铁轨，行驶于其上的马拉轨道车就取代了传统的四轮马车。

300. 文化进步——人们在教育方面也取得了巨大的进步。学校系统不断得到改善。西部更是如此，那里的政府专门拨出三十六分之一的公共土地兴办教育。人们建立了高中，不久又建立了师范学校。甚至大学在经历了长期的停滞之后也焕发了新的生机。更多的学生走入了校园。教学方法也得到了改进。关于科学的教育也得到了少量关注。1828年，诺亚·韦伯斯特（Noah Webster, Jr.，1758~1843）出版了他的大辞典的第一个版本。遗憾的是，他试图改变许多单词的拼写。但是从其他方面来说，他的字典是一个巨大的进步。他定义了单词以帮助人们理解。他还给出了许多单词的美国含义，例如“国会”。这时，美国作家也开始蜚声世界。库珀（James

诺亚·韦伯斯特

Fenimore Cooper，1789~1851）、欧文（Washington Irving，1783~1859）和布莱恩特（William Cullen Bryant，1794~1878）已经扬名海外。不久，又有一批出色的作家加入了其中，他们迅速使美国闻名于世界。他们是爱默生（Ralph Waldo Emerson, 1803~1882）、洛威尔（James Russell Lowell, 1819~1891）、朗费罗（Henry Wadsworth Longfellow，1807~1882）、霍姆斯（Oliver Wendell Holmes，1809~1894）、霍桑（Nathaniel Hawthorne，1804~1864）、普雷斯科特（William Hickling Prescott，1796~1859）、莫特利（John Lothrop Motley，1814~1877）、班克罗夫特（George Bancroft，1800~1891）和斯帕克斯（Jared Sparks，1789~1866）[①]。在科学界，也有一批名人正在开始他们的研究工作，如皮尔斯（Benjamin Peirce，1809~1880）、格雷（Asa Gray，1810~1888）、西利曼[②]（Benjamin Silliman，1779~1864; Benjamin Silliman, Jr.，1816~1885）、达纳（James Dwight Dana，1813~1895）。不久，路易斯·阿加西斯（Louis Agassiz，1807~1873）开始了他精彩的系列讲座，它们极大地促进了科学的普及。总之，杰克逊政府标志着美国人进入了现代生活的新时代。

路易斯·阿加西斯的科普讲座

① 这句话提到的九个人当中，只有前五位是文学家，后四位其实都是历史学家。这里之所以把他们都归为作家，是因为在19世纪时，美国史学家的作品往往具有文史不分的特点。

② 这一时期有两位名叫本杰明·西利曼的化学家，他们是父子，都毕业于耶鲁大学并在耶鲁大学执教。其中，老西利曼是下文提到的詹姆斯·德怀特·达纳的老师。这段文字所提到的所有人物中，除了这三位毕业于耶鲁大学的科学家以及一开始提到的三位文学家（即库珀、欧文和布莱恩特），其他人都毕业于哈佛学院（即后来的哈佛大学）。

## 【Original Text】

**293. A New Race.**—Between the election of President Jefferson and the election of President Jackson great changes had taken place. The old Revolutionary statesmen had gone. New men had taken their places. The old sleepy life had gone. Everywhere now was bustle and hurry. In 1800 the Federalists favored the British, and the Republicans favored the French. Now no one seemed to care for either the British or the French. At last the people had become Americans. The Federalist party had disappeared. Every one now was either a National Republican and voted for Adams, or a Democratic Republican and voted for Jackson.

**294. Numbers and Area.**—In 1800 there were only five and one-half million people in the whole United States. Now there were nearly thirteen million people. And they had a very much larger country to live in. In 1800 the area of the United States was about eight hundred thousand square miles. But Louisiana and Florida had been bought since then. Now (1830) the area of the United States was about two million square miles. The population of the old states had greatly increased. Especially the cities had grown. In 1800 New York City held about sixty thousand people; it now held two hundred thousand people. But it was in the West that the greatest growth had taken place. Since 1800 Ohio, Indiana, Illinois, Alabama, Mississippi, Louisiana, and Missouri had all been admitted to the Union.

**295. National Roads.**—Steamboats were now running on the Great Lakes and on all the important rivers of the West. The first result of this new mode of transport was the separation of the West from the East. Steamboats could carry passengers and goods up and down the Mississippi and its branches more cheaply and more comfortably than people and goods could be carried over the Alleghanies. Many persons therefore advised the building of a good wagon road to connect the Potomac with the Ohio. The eastern end of this great road was at Cumberland on the Potomac in Maryland. It is generally called, therefore, the Cumberland Road. It was begun at the national expense in 1811. By 1820 the road was built as far as Wheeling on the Ohio River. From that point steamboats could steam to Pittsburg, Cincinnati, St. Louis, or New Orleans. Later on, the road was built farther west, as far as Illinois. Then the coming of the railroad made further building unnecessary.

**296. The Erie Canal.**—The best way to connect one steamboat route with another was to dig a canal. The most famous of all these canals was the one connecting the Hudson River with Lake Erie, and called the Erie Canal. It was begun in 1817 and was completed so that a boat could pass through it in 1825. It was De Witt Clinton who argued that such a canal would benefit New York City by bringing to it the produce of the Northwest and of western New York. At the same time it would benefit the farmers of those regions by bringing their produce to tide water cheaper than it could be brought by road through Pennsylvania. It would still further benefit the farmers by enabling them to buy their goods much cheaper, as the rates of freight would be so much lower by canal than they were by road. People who did not see these things as clearly as DeWitt Clinton saw them, spoke of the enterprise most sneeringly and called the canal "Clinton's big ditch." It very soon appeared that Clinton was right. In one year the cost of carrying a ton of grain from Lake Erie to the Hudson River fell from one hundred dollars to fifteen dollars. New York City soon outstripped all its rivals and became the center of trade and money in the United States. Other canals, as the Chesapeake and Ohio Canal, were marvels of skill. But they were not so favorably situated as the Erie Canal and could not compete with it successfully.

**297. Early Railroads.**—The best stone and gravel roads were always rough in places. It occurred to some one that it would be better to lay down wooden rails, and then to place a rim or flange on the wagon wheels to keep them on the rails. The first road of this kind in America was built at Boston in 1807. It was a very rude affair and was only used to carry dirt from the top of a hill to the harbor. The wooden rails soon wore out, so the next step was to nail strips of iron on top of them. Long lines of railroads of this kind were soon built. Both passengers and goods could be carried on them. Some of them were built by private persons or by companies. Others were built by a town or a state. Any one having horses and wagons with flanged wheels could use the railway on the payment of a small sum of money. This was the condition of affairs when the steam locomotive was invented.

**298. The Steam Locomotive.**—Steam was used to drive boats through the water. Why should not steam be used to haul wagons over a railroad? This was a very easy question to ask, and a very hard one to answer. Year after year inventors worked on the problem. Suddenly, about 1830, it was solved in several places and by several men at nearly the same time. It was some years, however, before the locomotive came into general use. The early railroad trains were rude affairs. The cars were hardly more than stagecoaches with flanged wheels. They were fastened together with chains, and when the engine started or stopped, there was a terrible bumping and jolting. The smoke pipe of the engine was very tall and was hinged so that it could be let down when coming to a low bridge or a tunnel. Then the smoke and cinders poured straight into the passengers' faces. But these trains went faster than canal boats or steamboats. Soon the railroad began to take the first place as a means of transport.

**299. Other Inventions.**—The coming of the steam locomotive hastened the changes which one saw on every side in 1830. For some time men had known that there was plenty of hard coal or anthracite in Pennsylvania. But it was so hard that it would not burn in the old-fashioned stoves and fireplaces. Now a stove was invented that would burn anthracite, and the whole matter of house warming was completely changed. Then means were found to make iron from ore with anthracite. The whole iron industry awoke to new life. Next the use of gas made from coal became common in cities. The great increase in manufacturing, and the great changes in modes of transport, led people to crowd together in cities and towns. These inventions made it possible to feed and warm large numbers of persons gathered into small areas. The cities began to grow so fast that people could no longer live near their work or the shops. Lines of stagecoaches were established, and the coaches were soon followed by horse cars, which ran on iron tracks laid in the streets.

**300. Progress in Letters.**—There was also great progress in learning. The school system was constantly improved. Especially was this the case in the West, where the government devoted one thirty-sixth part of the public lands to education. High schools were founded, and soon normal schools were added to them. Even the colleges awoke from their long sleep. More students went to them, and the methods of teaching were improved. Some slight attention, too, was given to teaching the sciences. In 1828 Noah Webster published the first edition of his great dictionary. Unfortunately he tried to change the spelling of many words. But in other ways his dictionary was a great improvement. He defined words so that they could be understood, and he gave the American meaning of many words, as "congress." American writers now began to make great reputations. Cooper, Irving, and Bryant were already well known. They were soon joined by a wonderful set of men, who speedily made America famous. These were Emerson, Lowell, Longfellow, Holmes, Hawthorne, Prescott, Motley, Bancroft, and Sparks.

In science, also, men of mark were beginning their labors, as Pierce, Gray, Silliman, and Dana. Louis Agassiz before long began his wonderful lectures, which did much to make science popular. In short, Jackson's administration marks the time when American life began to take on its modern form.

CHAPTER 29

# 1829—1837年，安德鲁·杰克逊时期

## THE REIGN OF ANDREW JACKSON, 1829~1837

301. 杰克逊将军——杰克逊出生于卡罗来纳的边远地区。他年轻时就越过阿勒格尼山脉到田纳西定居。无论西部人何时遇到麻烦，无论他们何时需要勇敢的气魄和钢铁般的意志，杰克逊都会挺身而出。他一直在履行自己的义务，而且履行得很好。杰克逊为人正直、真诚。他相信自己，也相信美国人民。作为总统，他带领人民进入了我们历史上变化最剧烈的时期之一。他的身边聚集了很多能人。但是，他主要只听从几个朋友的建议。这些人和他一起抽烟袋，组成了他的“厨房内阁”[①]。他很少召开常规的内阁会议，即使召开一次，也常常只是通知内阁成员他做出了什么决定。

302. “政党分肥制”——来自纽约州的范布伦（Martin Van Buren，1782~1862）和马尔西（William Learned Marcy，1786~1857）与来自宾夕法尼亚州的布坎南（James Buchanan, Jr.，1791~1868）都为杰克逊当选总统立下了汗马功劳。他们在各自的州建立了强大的政党机器。对他们而言，“战利品属于胜利者这一原则没有任何错误”。因此，当他们“获胜”时，他们就用

威廉·勒尼德·马尔西
“战利品属于胜利者。”

① “厨房内阁”的成员其实相当于总统的私人顾问和助理，虽然他们不一定有正式官职，却在许多国家重大事务上影响着总统的决策。美国总统有“厨房内阁”的传统也从杰克逊这里产生。

官职来酬谢为他们的党派出过力的人。这时，政党分肥制开始在联邦政府流行起来。那些曾为杰克逊效力的人纷纷涌进华盛顿。宾馆和寄宿公寓都住满了人。有些人甚至露宿在首都的公园和公共广场上。撤换官员这时也“愉快地”进行着。“轮流当官”①是当时的口号。不久，杰克逊就撤了将近一千个官员的职，并任命自己政治上的追随者接替他们。

303. 北方和南方——南方这时成为主要的棉花生产区。这里的棉花由黑人奴隶种植。而北方这时是主要的制造业和商业区。它还是一个很大的农耕区。但是，北方的作坊里、田野间和船上的劳动力都是自由的白人劳动力。因此，美国实际上分成了两个部分：一部分盛行奴隶制并致力于发展几种主要原料产业，比如棉花；另一部分则盛行自由白人劳动力并致力于发展各种工业产业。

304. 公元1829年，政治形势——南方一直在逐渐变得富足；而北方在致富之路上的速度比南方快得多。卡尔霍恩和其他南方人认为这种发展速度的差异是由保护性制度②造成的。1828年，国会通过了一项关税。这项关税如此糟糕以至于被称为“可憎的关税”。南方人没能阻止它的通过。在这种情况下，卡尔霍恩写了一份关于宪法原则的“说明”。这篇文章被南卡罗来纳州议会当作参考意见采纳。卡尔霍恩在该文章中宣称：合众国宪法是一个契约；每个州都是一个拥有自主权的州，都可以宣布国会通过的

① 杰克逊撤换官员的幅度是美国建国以来最大的，而委派官员的“民主”作风也大大超过了杰斐逊时代的民主。杰克逊认为，政府公职的工作是简单的，任何具有一般能力的民众皆可担任；同时，这种频繁进行人事变动的“官员轮换制”有利于防止官员对民众产生傲慢作风，是一种合理的民主式制度。

② 从1816年起，美国就开始对进出口商品征收关税以保护本国工业。1824年、1828年以及下文提到的1832年，关税税率一再提高，最后达到了47%的税率。保护性关税对北方制造业和南方原材料业（主要是棉花种植业）造成了完全相反的结果。制造业需要抑制国外产品进口以保护本国市场，而棉花需要出口。因此，保护性关税大大地打击了南方的种植业，加深了南北之间的矛盾。

任何法律无效。保护性制度在效果上不公正，也不平等。它会造成“南方的贫穷和完全颓败”。因此，南卡罗来纳州和其他南方各州应拒绝执行这项关税法案。

**305. 公元1830年，韦伯斯特和海恩**——卡尔霍恩当时是副总统，他主持了参议院的辩论。因此，由南卡罗来纳州的参议员海恩（Robert Young Hayne，1791~1839）代为阐述卡尔霍恩的主张。他以一篇非常有力的演讲完成了这项工作。而马萨诸塞州的丹尼尔·韦伯斯特（Daniel Webster，1782~1852）以国会历史上最精彩的演讲回应了他。韦伯斯特宣称，宪法是“人民的宪法，人民的管理原则；它由人民制定并适合人民。人民早已宣布了这部宪法……是至高无上的法律”。只有联邦最高法院可以宣布一项联邦法律违宪；任何州都不能这样做。

丹尼尔·韦伯斯特

罗伯特·杨·海恩

他用一句令人难忘的话结束了这次伟大的演讲：“从现在到永远，自由与联邦，始终是一体，永远不可分。”

**306. 公元1832~1833年，拒绝执行联邦法律**——1832年，国会通过了一项新的关税法。南卡罗来纳人决定尝试运用卡尔霍恩所说的“拒绝执行联邦法律”这个武器。他们召开了一次大会，宣布这项法律无效，禁止南卡罗来纳人遵守这项法律。他们可能以为杰克逊不会反对他们。但是，

安德鲁·杰克逊
第七任美国总统（1829~1837）

他们本应该对他的反对确信无疑。因为杰克逊早在杰斐逊诞辰纪念日就提出过他著名的祝酒词："我们联邦的统一，必须得到维护。"① 这时，他告诉卡罗来纳人他会强制执行这些法律，于是他开始用他全部的旧式精神来做这件事。他向查尔斯顿派遣了军舰和士兵，并命令该港口的收税员征收关税。他随后请求国会授予他更大的权力。于是，国会通过了《强制法案》，授予了他想要的权力。至于南卡罗来纳人，他们则废除了宣布联邦法令无效的条例，因而避免了一场与"老山核桃"②——杰克逊的仰慕者这样称呼他——的军事冲突。

**307. 公元1833年，妥协关税**——那些宣布联邦法律无效的人事实上赢得了这场斗争的一部分胜利，因为1832年的关税法被废除了。国会通过了所谓的《妥协关税》取而代之。它是调解人亨利·克莱的成就。根据这一法案，关税会逐渐降低，到1842年，它们会降低到《1816年关税法》规定的水平。

**308. 合众国第二银行③**——现今，任何拥有足够资金的人都可以在政

① 杰克逊说这句话的时候，当时身为副总统的卡尔霍恩也在场，他马上接下去举杯说道："联邦：次于我们最宝贵的自由！"（The Union: next to our liberty, the most dear.）

② 杰克逊带兵打仗时期与士兵风餐露宿，同行的将士赞叹他"像老山核桃一般坚毅"，因此杰克逊就获得了这个绰号。

③ 这里提到的合众国第二银行是当时美国唯一的国家银行，第一银行已不复存在。1790年汉密尔顿的方案被华盛顿批准后成立的第一银行，其授权书至1811年到期，之后国会没有批准再授权。1816年，国会表决通过了重新成立国家银行，此时成立的就是第二银行。

府的保护下在华盛顿开办一家联邦银行。然而在那个时候，只有一家大型的合众国银行。它的总部设在费城，而其分行遍布全国。和杰斐逊一样，杰克逊对联邦政府是否有权建立一家这样的银行抱有极大的怀疑。它的规模和兴旺让他担心。况且，它的股东和经理人大多数都是他的政敌。合众国银行也严重妨碍了州立银行的运行——这些州立银行中，有一部分是杰克逊的支持者经营的。这些友人力劝杰克逊“毁掉”合众国银行，于是他决定“毁掉”它。

**309. 围绕银行特许状展开的斗争**——这家银行的特许状直到1836年才到期，而1828年当选为总统的杰克逊到1833年任期就结束了。但是，在向国会提交的第一篇咨文中，杰克逊已经预先通知了他不会同意颁发新的特许状。克莱和他的支持者立即接受了挑战。他们通过了一项颁布新的特许状的法案。杰克逊否决了这项法案。克莱派没能得到足够的票数以推翻他的否决。因此，第二银行问题成为1832年大选的议题之一。杰克逊获得的选票大大超过了克莱。民众明显站在了他这一边，于是他立即着手“毁掉”这家银行。

**310. 转移存款**——在那个时候，华盛顿还没有建立合众国国库，只有一些用来储藏黄金、白银和纸币的大型地下室。各个重要的商业城市也没有国库分库。合众国银行及其分行接受了联邦政府的货币存款，并依据特定的联邦政府官员签署的支票来支出它们。1833年，合众国银行中属于联邦政府的钱大约有九百万美元。杰克逊下令，这些钱必须按要求提取出来以支付联邦政府的开支，而且联邦政府的钱不得再存入这家银行。将来，联邦政府的钱必须存到某些州立银行。那些被选中的银行是由杰克逊的政治盟友掌控的，因此被称为“宠儿银行”。

**311. 公元1836年，杰克逊的《使用金属通货公告》**——转移存款产生的第一个结果大大出乎杰克逊的预料。这一时期，西部的土地投机买卖非常活跃。但凡手上有一点闲钱的人都购买了西部土地。那些手中没钱的人就向银行贷款购买西部土地。这时，碰巧许多"宠儿银行"也设立在西部。政府的钱存到这些银行，诱使他们的经营者更随意地把钱贷出去。这相应地使人们更容易从事投机活动。杰克逊发现，要是不做点什么来遏制这种投机行为，灾难必然降临。因此，他向合众国土地官员发布了一项通告。这项通告被称为《使用金属通货公告》，因为总统在这个通告中禁止土地官员在出售公共土地时接受黄金、白银和某些有价证券以外的任何东西。

一间西部拓荒者的小屋

**312. 公元1837年，偿还国债**——这时，国债已经全部还清。政府得到的钱除了用于联邦政府开支外，还有盈余。联邦政府还被迫征收超出它的开支更多的钱，因为《妥协关税》使得削减关税每年只能以某个确定的数目进行，不能更快。没人敢中断实施《妥协关税》，因为这样做会招致一场最尖锐的政治斗争。联邦政府在"宠儿银行"存的钱已经多到不安全了。它不能把更多的钱存入这些银行了。

313. 公元1837年，分配盈余——这时，有人想出了一个古怪的方案。那就是把盈余的税款按照总统选举人的比例贷给各州。各州可以用三种方式偿还这些贷款。随后，1837年大恐慌降临，于是联邦政府不得不借钱支付必要的开支。然而，杰克逊在这之前已经卸任总统了。当时担任总统的是他的国务卿马丁·范布伦。范布伦于1836年11月当选总统。

马丁·范布伦

第八任美国总统（1837~1841）

## 【Original Text】

**301. General Jackson.**—Born in the backwoods of Carolina, Jackson had early crossed the Alleghanies and settled in Tennessee. Whenever trouble came to the Western people, whenever there was need of a stout heart and an iron will, Jackson was at the front. He always did his duty. He always did his duty well. Honest and sincere, he believed in himself and he believed in the American people. As President he led the people in one of the stormiest periods in our history. Able men gathered about him. But he relied chiefly on the advice of a few friends who smoked their pipes with him and formed his "kitchen cabinet." He seldom called a regular cabinet meeting. When he did call one, it was often merely to tell the members what he had decided to do.

**302. The Spoils System.**—Among the able men who had fought the election for Jackson were Van Buren and Marcy of New York and Buchanan of Pennsylvania. They had built up strong party machines in their states. For they "saw nothing wrong in the principle that to the victors belong the spoils of victory." So they rewarded their party workers with offices—when they won. The Spoils System was now begun in the national government. Those who had worked for Jackson rushed to Washington. The hotels and boarding-houses could not hold them. Some of them camped out in the parks and public squares of the capital. Removals now went merrily on. Rotation in office was the cry. Before long Jackson removed nearly one thousand officeholders and appointed political partisans in their places.

**303. The North and the South.**—The South was now a great cotton-producing region. This cotton was grown by negro slaves. The North was now a great manufacturing and commercial region. It was also a great agricultural region. But the labor in the mills, fields, and ships of the North was all free white labor. So the United States was really split into two sections: one devoted to slavery and to a few great staples, as cotton; the other devoted to free white labor and to industries of many kinds.

**304. The Political Situation, 1829.**—The South was growing richer all the time; but the North was growing richer a great deal faster than was the South. Calhoun and other Southern men thought that this difference in the rate of progress was due to the protective system. In 1828 Congress had passed a tariff that was so bad that it was called the Tariff of Abominations. The Southerners could not prevent its passage. But Calhoun wrote an "Exposition" of the constitutional doctrines in the case. This paper was adopted by the legislature of South Carolina as giving its ideas. In this paper Calhoun declared that the Constitution of the United States was a compact. Each state was a sovereign state and could annul any law passed by Congress. The protective system was unjust and unequal in operation. It would bring "poverty and utter desolation to the South." The tariff act should be annulled by South Carolina and by other Southern states.

**305. Webster and Hayne, 1830.**—Calhoun was Vice-President and presided over the debates of the Senate. So it fell to Senator Hayne of South Carolina to state Calhoun's ideas. This he did in a very able speech. To him Daniel Webster of Massachusetts replied in the most brilliant speeches ever delivered in Congress. The Constitution, Webster declared, was "the people's constitution, the people's government; made by the people and answerable to the people. The people have declared that this constitution ... shall be the supreme law." The Supreme Court of the United States alone could declare a national law to be unconstitutional; no state could do that. He ended this great speech with the memorable words, "Liberty and Union, now and forever, one and inseparable."

**306. Nullification, 1832~33.**—In 1832 Congress passed a new tariff act. The South Carolinians decided to try Calhoun's weapon of nullification. They held a convention, declared the act null and void, and forbade South Carolinians to obey the law. They probably thought that Jackson would not oppose them. But they should have had no doubts on that subject. For Jackson already had proposed his famous toast on Jefferson's birthday, "Our federal Union, it must be preserved." He now told the Carolinians that he would enforce the laws, and he set about doing it with all his old-time energy. He sent ships and soldiers to Charleston and ordered the collector of that port to collect the duties. He then asked Congress to give him greater power. And Congress passed the Force Bill, giving him the power he asked for. The South Carolinians, on their part, suspended the nullification ordinance and thus avoided an armed conflict with "Old Hickory", as his admirers called Jackson.

**307. The Compromise Tariff, 1833.** —The nullifiers really gained a part of the battle, for the tariff law of 1832 was repealed. In its place Congress passed what was called the Compromise Tariff. This compromise was the work of Henry Clay, the peacemaker. Under it the duties were to be gradually lowered until, in 1842, they would be as low as they were by the Tariff Act of 1816.

**308. The Second United States Bank.**—Nowadays any one with enough money can open a national bank under the protection of the government at Washington. At this time, however, there was one great United States Bank. Its headquarters were at Philadelphia and it had branches all over the country. Jackson, like Jefferson, had very grave doubts as to the power of the national government to establish such a bank. Its size and its prosperity alarmed him. Moreover, the stockholders and managers, for the most part, were his political opponents. The United States Bank also interfered seriously with the operations of the state banks—some of which were managed by Jackson's friends. The latter urged him on to destroy the United States Bank, and he determined to destroy it.

**309. Struggle over the Bank Charter.**—The charter of the bank would not come to an end until 1836, while the term for which Jackson had been elected in 1828 would come to an end in 1833. But in his first message to Congress Jackson gave notice that he would not give his consent to a new charter. Clay and his friends at once took up the challenge. They passed a bill rechartering the bank. Jackson vetoed the bill. The Clay men could not get enough votes to pass it over his veto. The bank question, therefore, became one of the issues of the election of 1832. Jackson was reflected by a large majority over Clay. The people were clearly on his side, and he at once set to work to destroy the bank.

**310. Removal of the Deposits.**—In those days there was no United States Treasury building at Washington, with great vaults for the storing of gold, silver, and paper money. There were no sub-treasuries in the important commercial cities. The United States Bank and its branches received the government's money on deposit and paid it out on checks signed by the proper government official. In 1833 the United States Bank had in its vaults about nine million dollars belonging to the government. Jackson directed that this money should be drawn out as required, to pay the government's expenses, and that no more government money should be deposited in the bank. In the future it should be deposited in certain state banks. The banks selected were controlled by Jackson's political friends and were called the "pet banks."

**311. Jackson's Specie Circular, 1836.**—the first result of the removal of the deposits was very different from what Jackson had expected. At this time there was active speculation in Western lands. Men who had a little spare money bought Western lands. Those who had no money in hand, borrowed money from the banks and with it bought Western lands. Now it happened that many of the "pet banks" were in the West. The government's money, deposited with them, tempted their managers to lend money more freely. This, in turn, increased the ease with which people could speculate. Jackson saw that unless something were done to restrain this speculation, disaster would surely come. So he issued a circular to the United States land officers. This circular was called the Specie Circular, because in it the President forbade the land officers to receive anything except gold and silver and certain certificates in payment for the public lands.

**312. Payment of the Debt, 1837.**—The national debt had now all been paid. The government was collecting more money than it could use for national purposes. And it was compelled to keep on collecting more money than it could use, because the Compromise Tariff made it impossible to reduce duties any faster than a certain amount each year. No one dared to disturb the Compromise Tariff, because to do so would bring on a most bitter political fight. The government had more money in the "pet banks" than was really safe. It could not deposit more with them.

**313. Distribution of the Surplus, 1837.**—A curious plan was now hit upon. It was to loan the surplus revenues to the states in proportion to their electoral votes. Three payments were made to the states. Then the Panic of 1837 came, and the government had to borrow money to pay its own necessary expenses. Before this occurred, however, Jackson was no longer President. In his place was Martin Van Buren, his Secretary of State, who had been chosen President in November,1836.

CHAPTER 30

# 1837—1844年，民主党与辉格党

## DEMOCRATS AND WHIGS, 1837~1844

314. 公元1837年大恐慌——这场恐慌的直接原因就是杰克逊干涉银行、发布《使用金属通货公告》以及分配盈余。它是这样发生的：《使用金属通货公告》一经发布，纸币持有者立即去银行兑换黄金和白银以便从政府手中购买土地。而联邦政府也从银行取钱以支付分配给各州的那份盈余。银行因此不得不卖掉它们的财产，并要求借贷者偿还贷款。那些欠银行钱的人也因此不得不卖掉财产向银行还钱。因此，每个人都想卖东西，但是几乎没有人想买。物价急剧下跌。人们都觉得自己很穷，甚至买不起新衣服。工厂和矿场纷纷倒闭，银行也纷纷宣告破产。成千上万男女工人失业。他们甚至没钱给自己和家人买食物。可怕的面包暴动发生了。一段时间之后，人们才振作起来。但是“美好时代”很久之后才再次来临。

315. 独立国库体系——该怎样处置联邦政府的钱呢？没人会想到把它存进州立银行。克莱及其支持者们认为最好建立一家新的合众国银行。但范布伦提出了反对意见。范布伦的方案简单来说就是在华盛顿和主要城市建立一些用来储存钱的地下室。主贮藏库或主国库设在华盛顿，下属贮藏库或国库分库设在其他城市。海关收税员把他们征收的钱交到国库分库。这样，联邦政府就独立于国家的普通商业事务之外。1840年，国会通过了一项法律来实施此方案。但是在这个方案开始起作用之前，范布伦就卸任总统了。

316. 民主党与辉格党——“和睦时代”只有一个政党——共和党。1824年的混乱时期，该党分裂成了几个以各自的领导人命名的派系：亚当斯派、杰克逊派、克莱派等。不久，亚当斯派和克莱派开始联合起来，并自称国家共和党。他们这样做是因为他们希望以国家开支逐渐积累国家资源。杰克逊派则自称民主共和党，因为他们支持人民的权利。不久之后，他们放弃了“共和党”这个词，简单地自称民主党。国家共和党放弃了他们的全称转而以伟大的英国自由派政党——“辉格党”的名字取而代之。他们这样做是因为他们支持改革。

317. 公元1840年大选——威廉·亨利·哈里逊将军是《独立宣言》签署者之一、来自弗吉尼亚的本杰明·哈里逊[①]（Benjamin Harrison，1726~1791）的儿子。哈里逊将军已经移民西部了。他因在蒂珀卡努和1812年战争中的表现而声名鹊起。1836年，他曾获得辉格党的提名，但是竞选失败。这时，辉格党再次提名他为总统候选人，并提名来自弗吉尼亚的约翰·泰勒（John Tyler，1790~1862）为副总统候选人。范布伦是个好总统，但他的任期与恐慌和萧条时代相伴。他是一个富人，而且举办了很多派对。显然，他不像哈里逊一样是“人民中的一员”。一个民主党演说家对哈里逊冷嘲热讽，说他只想要一个属于自己的圆木小屋和一壶苹果酒。辉格党急忙抓住了这个描述。他们在街道的角落里修建了圆木小屋，并用大马车拖着那些圆木小屋在大街上走动。他们还召

威廉·亨利·哈里逊
第九任美国总统
（1841年3月~1841年4月）

① 本杰明·哈里逊是美国开国元勋之一，曾作为弗吉尼亚代表参加第二届大陆会议，后担任弗吉尼亚州第五任州长。

开了大量的露天会议。人们在会上齐唱“蒂珀卡努和泰勒”之歌。哈里逊和泰勒几乎获得了所有的总统选举人票，于是他们分别当选为总统和副总统。

一张纪念哈里逊总统的传单

下方小字写着“一千六百万人们沉痛哀悼”

318. 公元1841年，哈里逊之死——这位人民的总统于1841年3月4日宣誓就职。这是“政党分肥制”确立以来第一次由一个新的政党控制联邦政府。数以千计的求官者涌入华盛顿。他们甚至睡在白宫偏僻的角落里。他们日复一日，从早到晚地向哈里逊提出他们的请求。一天清早，在求官者起床之前，哈里逊就出去散步了。他染上了风寒，很快就去世了——就在他就职仪式之后刚刚过了一个月的时候。约翰·泰勒继任为总统。

319.泰勒和辉格党——泰勒总统不是哈里逊和克莱那样的辉格党人，也不是杰克逊那样的民主党人。他是不喜欢杰克逊思想的民主党人。作为总统，他证明了自己并非一名辉格党人。泰勒非常高兴地签署了一项废除《独立国库法》的法案，因为那是一项他不喜欢的民主党措施；但他也拒绝签署一项建立新合众国银行的法案。既无银行又无国库，联邦政府的业务几乎不可能维持。但它却仍然以某种方式维持了下去。泰勒非常高兴地签署了一项新的关税法案。该法案于1842年获得通过。这倒是合情合理的，因为《妥协关税》在那一年到期。

约翰·泰勒
第十任美国总统（1841~1845）

320. 公元1842年，美英签订条约——泰勒政府做的最重要的事情就是1842年和英国签订了条约。自从1783年《和平条约》签订以来，就缅因东北部边界的问题，美英两国一直存在争议。如果按照《和平条约》的字面意思划定这个边界，上加拿大①的人民就几乎没法在冬季到达新布伦瑞克或新斯科舍。在每年的这个时候，圣劳伦斯河都会结冰，而标准的缅因州北部边界离圣劳伦斯河太近，以至于很难修建一条全部位于英属领地的道路。因此，英国用尽各种方式逃避解决这个问题。美英这时商定：美国拥有佛蒙特州和纽约州北部的一小块加拿大土地，但是放弃缅因州最东北部的土地。他们还商定遣返逃到对方领土内的罪犯。他们还达成了进一步的协定，即共同遏制来自非洲西海岸的奴隶贸易。

321. 电报——本杰明·富兰克林和约瑟夫·亨利（Joseph Henry，1797~1878）获得了一些有关电的伟大发现。但是，塞缪尔·F. B. 摩尔斯（Samuel Finley Breese Morse，1791~1872）才是第一个把电应用于实践的人。摩尔斯发现，如果一个人在一根导线的一端按下一个键，电流就能在同一时间在这根导线的另一端按下另一个键。另外，位于导线远端的那个键经过一番设置，可以靠一个类似钟表的机械装置

塞缪尔·芬利·布里斯·摩尔斯

① 上加拿大是五大湖北岸的英属殖民地，地处圣劳伦斯河上游，故名。英国在1774年根据《巴黎和约》从法国手上获得该地的所有权，后将其划入魁北克。魁北克在美国独立战争时接收了许多的效忠派难民，他们与当地原有的法国居民在文化、观念等方面都有冲突，故英国在1790年将魁北克一分为二，北部为上加拿大，居民为有英美血统的效忠派，使用英国制度管理；南部为下加拿大，居民为法国后裔，保留法国管理制度。

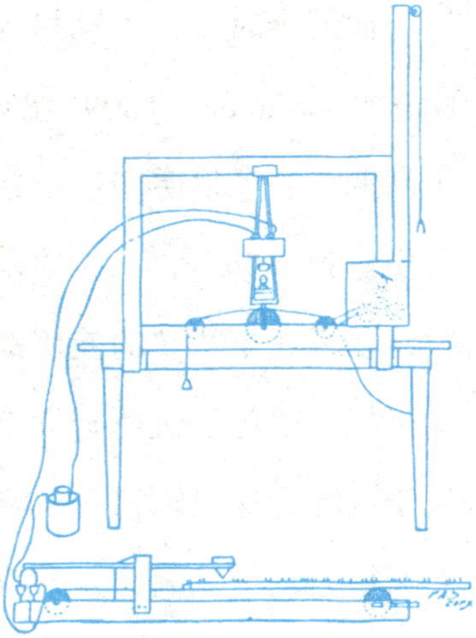

第一台发报机

在一张纸上慢慢地划出一道压痕。这时，如果这个在导线一端的人只是按一下那个键，这个压痕看起来就会像一个点。如果他按住的时间长一些，压痕看起来就像一个短破折号。摩尔斯用这些点和破折号合成了一个字母系统。如一个破折号代表了字母“t”等。有一阵子，人们仅仅是嘲笑摩尔斯。但是，国会最终拨给了他足够的钱，让他在华盛顿和巴尔的摩之间建立一条电报线。这条线于1844年开通，而且从一开始就证明了这是一个成功之举。其他线路不久也建立起来了，而且经过了大量改进的摩尔斯系统至今还在使用。电报让长途火车的运作成为可能，因为所有火车都能由一个部门负责管理，这样它们就不会相撞。它还让相距遥远的人们之间的通信成为可能，并且能在一两个小时内收到答复。由于这两个原因，电报非常重要，它和铁路一起为把全国不同地区的人民联系起来发挥了巨大的作用。

塞勒斯·霍尔·麦考密克

**322. 麦考密克收割机**——每种重要作物的产量都取决于特定工具的出现。例如，在轧棉机使得轻易分离棉籽和棉纤维成为可能之前，棉花一直不受重视。而小麦种植的成功则取决于快速收割作物的能力。小麦完全成熟之前必须保持直立生长。当小麦成熟后，人们必须迅速将其收割并储藏起来，以免被雨淋湿。每年都有几周的时间需要大量的劳动力投入麦田。而那个时候，很难找到这么多劳动力。塞勒斯·H. 麦考密克（Cyrus Hall McCormick，1809~1884）通过发明马拉收割机为小麦种植者解决了这个问题。这项发明产生于1831年，但是直到1845年这种收割机才得到普遍应用。到1855年，马拉收割机的使用每年能给全国增加五千五百万美元的财富。每一年，它的使用都把文明的边缘向西推进五十英里。要是没有收割机械，西部的快速开发将是不可能实现的。而要是没有自由白人迅速定居于西部，这个国家在1845年至1865年间的整个历史就会与它实际的样子有天壤之别了。因此，与蒸汽机车或轧棉机一样，马拉收割机也对我们的政治史产生了重大的影响[①]。

第一台马拉收割机

现代（19世纪末的）收割机

① 这句话暗示出这些重要发明是导致美国内战不可避免的部分因素，同时也影响了内战中各方势力的形成。蒸汽交通工具的使用加快了北方工业的发展，同时又和收割机一起加快了西部的发展，而轧棉机则加快了南方种植业的发展，也间接巩固了奴隶制在南方的重要地位。这些地域的经济发展因素导致了各地发展需求、生活方式、政治理念等一系列差异。

## 【Original Text】

**314. The Panic of 1837.**—The Panic was due directly to Jackson's interference with the banks, to his Specie Circular, and to the distribution of the surplus. It happened in this way. When the Specie Circular was issued, people who held paper money at once went to the banks to get gold and silver in exchange for it to pay for the lands bought of the government. The government on its part drew out money from the banks to pay the states their share of the surplus. The banks were obliged to sell their property and to demand payment of money due them. People who owed money to the banks were obliged to sell their property to pay the banks. So every one wanted to sell, and few wanted to buy. Prices of everything went down with a rush. People felt so poor that they would not even buy new clothes. The mills and mines were closed, and the banks suspended payments. Thousands of working men and women were thrown out of work. They could not even buy food for themselves or their families. Terrible bread riots took place. After a time people began to pluck up their courage. But it was a long time before "good times" came again.

**315. The Independent Treasury System.**—What should be done with the government's money? No one could think of depositing it with the state banks. Clay and his friends thought the best thing to do would be to establish a new United States Bank. But Van Buren was opposed to that. His plan, in short, was to build vaults for storing money in Washington and in the leading cities. The main storehouse or Treasury was to be in Washington, subordinate storehouses or sub-treasuries were to be established in the other cities. To these sub-treasuries the collectors of customs would pay the money collected by them. In this way the government would become independent of the general business affairs of the country. In 1840 Congress passed an act for putting this plan into effect. But before it was in working order, Van Buren was no longer President.

**316. Democrats and Whigs.**—In the Era of Good Feeling there was but one party—the Republican party. In the confused times of 1824 the several sections of the party took the names of their party leaders: the Adams men, the Jackson men, the Clay men, and so on. Soon the Adams men and the Clay men began to act together and to call themselves National Republicans. This they did because they wished to build up the nation's resources at the expense of the nation. The Jackson men called themselves Democratic Republicans, because they upheld the rights of the people. Before long they dropped the word "Republican" and called themselves simply Democrats. The National Republicans dropped the whole of their name and took that of the great English liberal party—the Whigs. This they did because they favored reform.

**317. Election of 1840.**—General William Henry Harrison was the son of Benjamin Harrison of Virginia, one of the signers of the Declaration of Independence. General Harrison had moved to the West and had won distinction at Tippecanoe, and also in the War of 1812. The Whigs nominated him in 1836, but he was beaten. They now renominated him for President, with John Tyler of Virginia as candidate for Vice-President. Van Buren had made a good President, but his term of office was associated with panic and hard times. He was a rich man and gave great parties. Plainly he was not a "man of the people, "as was Harrison. A Democratic orator sneered at Harrison, and said that all he wanted was a log cabin of his own and a jug of cider. The Whigs eagerly seized on this description. They built log cabins at the street corners and dragged through the streets log cabins on great wagons. They held immense open-air meetings at which people sang songs of "Tippecanoe and Tyler Too." Harrison and Tyler received nearly all the electoral votes and were chosen President and Vice-President.

**318. Death of Harrison, 1841.**—The people's President was inaugurated on March 4, 1841. For the first time since the establishment of the Spoils System a new party came into control of the government. Thousands of office-seekers thronged to Washington. They even slept in out-of-the-way corners of the White House. Day after day, from morning till night, they pressed their claims on Harrison. One morning early, before the office-seekers were astir, he went out for a walk. He caught cold and died suddenly, just one month after his inauguration. John Tyler at once became President.

**319. Tyler and the Whigs.**—President Tyler was not a Whig like Harrison or Clay, nor was he a Democrat like Jackson. He was a Democrat who did not like Jackson ideas. As President, he proved to be anything but a Whig. He was willing to sign a bill to repeal the Independent Treasury Act, for that was a Democratic measure he had not liked; but he refused to sign a bill to establish a new Bank of the United States. Without either a bank or a treasury, it was well-nigh impossible to carry on the business of the government. But it was carried on in one way or another. Tyler was willing to sign a new tariff act, and one was passed in 1842. This was possible, as the Compromise Tariff came to an end in that year.

**320. Treaty with Great Britain, 1842.**—Perhaps the most important event of Tyler's administration was the signing of the Treaty of 1842 with Great Britain. Ever since the Treaty of Peace of 1783, there had been a dispute over the northeastern boundary of Maine. If the boundary had been run according to the plain meaning of the Treaty of Peace, the people of Upper Canada would have found it almost impossible to reach New Brunswick or Nova Scotia in winter.

At that time of the year the St. Lawrence is frozen over, and the true northern boundary of Maine ran so near to the St. Lawrence that it was difficult to build a road which would be wholly in British territory. So the British had tried in every way to avoid settling the matter. It was now arranged that the United States should have a little piece of Canada north of Vermont and New York and should give up the extreme northeastern corner of Maine. It was also agreed that criminals escaping from one country to the other should be returned. A still further agreement was made for checking the slave trade from the coast of western Africa.

**321. The Electric Telegraph.** —Benjamin Franklin and Joseph Henry made great discoveries in electricity. But Samuel F. B. Morse was the first to use electricity in a practical way. Morse found out that if a man at one end of a line of wire pressed down a key, electricity could be made at the same moment to press down another key at the other end of the line of wire. Moreover, the key at the farther end of the line could be so arranged as to make an impression on a piece of paper that was slowly drawn under it by clockwork. Now if the man at one end of the line held his key down for only an instant, this impression would look like a dot. If he held it down longer, it would look like a short dash. Morse combined these dots and dashes into an alphabet. For instance, one dash meant the letter "t", and so on. For a time people only laughed at Morse. But at length Congress gave him enough money to build a line from Baltimore to Washington. It was opened in 1844, and proved to be a success from the beginning. Other lines were soon built, and the Morse system, greatly improved, is still in use. The telegraph made it possible to operate long lines of railroad, as all the trains could be managed from one office so that they would not run into one another. It also made it possible to communicate with people afar off and get an answer in an hour or so. For both these reasons the telegraph was very important and with the railroads did much to unite the people of the different portions of the country.

**322. The McCormick Reaper.**—Every great staple depends for its production on some particular tool. For instance, cotton was of slight importance until the invention of the cotton gin made it possible cheaply to separate the seed from the fiber. The success of wheat growing depended upon the ability quickly to harvest the crop. Wheat must be allowed to stand until it is fully ripened. Then it must be quickly reaped and stored away out of the reach of the rain and wet. For a few weeks in each year there was a great demand for labor on the wheat farms. And there was little labor to be had. Cyrus H. McCormick solved this problem for the wheat growers by inventing a horse reaper. The invention was made in 1831, but it was not until 1845 that the reaper came into general use. By 1855 the use of the horse reaper was adding every year fifty-five million dollars to the wealth of the country. Each year its use moved the fringe of civilization fifty miles farther west. Without harvesting machinery the rapid settlement of the West would have been impossible. And had not the West been rapidly settled by free whites, the whole history of the country between 1845 and 1865 would have been very different from what it has been. The influence of the horse reaper on our political history, therefore, is as important as the influence of the steam locomotive or of the cotton gin.

# QUESTIONS AND TOPICS
# 问题与论题

## CHAPTER 28

§§ 293, 294.—Compare the condition of the United States in 1830 and 1800 as to (1) extent, (2) population, (3) interests and occupation of the people. Illustrate these changes by maps, diagrams, or tables.

§§ 295, 296.—a. How had the use of steamboats increased?

b. Why had this led to the separation of the West and the East? How was it proposed to overcome this difficulty?

c. Do you think that roads should be built at national expense? Give your reasons.

d. Mark on a map the Erie Canal, and show why it was so important. Describe the effects of its use.

§§ 297, 298.—a. Do you think that railroads should be carried on by the state or by individuals? Why?

b. What influence has the railroad had upon the Union? Upon people's minds? Upon the growth of cities? (Take your own city or town and think of it without railroads anywhere.)

§§ 299, 300.—a. Explain how one discovery or invention affected other industries (as shown, for instance, in the use of anthracite coal).

b. How did these inventions make large cities possible?

c. Why is the education of our people so important?

d. What were the advantages of Webster's "Dictionary"?

## CHAPTER 29

§§ 301, 302.—a. Why is this chapter called the "Reign of Andrew Jackson"? Do you think that a President should "reign"?

b. In what respects was Jackson fitted for President?

c. What is meant by his "kitchen cabinet"?

d. What is a "party machine"? How was it connected with the "spoils system"?

e. Did the "spoils system" originate with Jackson?

§§ 303, 304.—a. Compare carefully the North and the South. Why was the North growing rich faster than the South?

b. Where have you already found the ideas expressed in Calhoun's Exposition? Why was this doctrine so dangerous? Are the states "sovereign states"?

§ 305.—a. What view did Webster take? How does his speech show the increase of the love of the Union?

b. What is the "supreme law of the land"? Whose business is it to decide on the constitutionality of a law? Is this wise?

§§ 306, 307.—a. How did South Carolina oppose the Act of 1832?

b. How did Jackson oppose the South Carolinians?

c. Would a state be likely to nullify an act of Congress now? Give your reasons.

§§ 308, 309.—a. Was the United States Bank like the national banks of the present day?

b. Why did Jackson dislike and distrust the United States Bank?

c. If a bill is vetoed by the President, how can it still be made a law?

§ 310.—a. Where did the United States government keep its money?

b. How did Jackson try to ruin the United States Bank?

§§ 311-313.—a. Why did people wish to buy Western lands? How did the favoring the "pet banks" increase speculation?

b. What was done with the surplus? What was the effect of this measure?

c. How did Jackson try to stop speculation?

## CHAPTER 30

§§ 314, 315.—a. Why did "prices go down with a rush"?

b. Describe the Independent Treasury plan. Where is the nation's money kept today?

§§ 316, 317.—a. State briefly the reasons for the split in the Republican party. Had you lived in 1840, for whom would you have voted? Why?

b. Give an account of the early life of Harrison.

c. Describe the campaign of 1840, and compare it with the last presidential campaign.

§§ 318, 319.—a. What party came into power in 1841? Under the spoils system what would naturally follow?

b. To what party did Tyler belong?

c. Why was it difficult for the government to carry on its business without a bank or a treasury?

§ 320.—a. What dispute had long existed with Great Britain?

b. Why did the British object to the boundary line laid down in the Treaty of 1783? Show on a map how the matter was finally settled.

§§ 321,322.—a. Explain carefully the application of electricity made by Morse. Of what advantage has the telegraph been to the United States?

b. How did the McCormick reaper solve the difficulty in wheat growing? What were the results of this invention?

c. Compare its influence upon our history with that of the cotton gin.

## GENERAL QUESTIONS
## 综合性问题

a. Why is the period covered by this division so important?

b. Give the principal events since the Revolution which made Western expansion possible.

c. Explain, using a chart, the changes in parties since 1789.

d. What were the good points in Jackson's administration? The mistakes?

## SUGGESTIONS TO THE TEACHER
## 给教师的建议

The personality of Andrew Jackson, representing as he does a new element in social and political life, deserves a careful study. The financial policy of his administration is too difficult for children. With brief comparisons with present-day conditions the study of this subject can be confined to what is given in the text. Jackson's action at the time of the nullification episode may well be compared with Buchanan's inaction in 1860~61. The constitutional portions of Webster's great speeches are too hard for children, but his burning words of patriotism may well be learned by the whole class. The spoils system may be lightly treated here. It can best be studied in detail later in connection with civil service reform.

# 第十一篇
PART XI

# 1844—1859年，各准州的奴隶制
SLAVERY IN THE TERRITORIES, 1844-1859

## Books for Study and Reading
## 研究和阅读用书

**References.**—Scribner's *Popular History*, IV; McMaster's *With the Fathers*, Coffin's *Building the Nation*, 314-324.

**Home Readings.**—Wright's *Stories of American Progress*; Bolton's *Famous Americans*; Brooks's *Boy Settlers*; Stowe's *Uncle Tom's Cabin*; Lodge's *Webster*.

CHAPTER 31

# 废奴运动的开端

# BEGINNING OF THE ANTISLAVERY AGITATION

323. 南方奴隶制的发展——1787年以来，宾夕法尼亚州和俄亥俄河以南的奴隶制得到了很大发展。华盛顿、杰斐逊、亨利①，以及弗吉尼亚的其他一些要人都反对奴隶制。但是，他们没有找到终结奴隶制的方法——甚至是仅限于弗吉尼亚也办不到。南卡罗来纳人和佐治亚人反对所有限制奴隶制的议案。他们甚至曾拒绝加入联邦，除非他们的奴隶至少有一部分在国会拥有代表权。而且，在根据宪法成立的第一届国会中，他们强烈反对一切限制奴隶制的议案。后来，惠特尼的轧棉机问世。这立即使奴隶劳动力在各棉花种植州变得极为有利可图，并使和平解放南部奴隶的全部希望化为泡影。

324. 废奴主义者的出现——1830年前后，一场支持黑人的新运动兴起了。北方的某些人，比如威廉·埃勒里·钱宁②（William Ellery Channing，1780~1842），提议释放奴隶，并赔偿奴隶主的损失。他们建议把出售公共土地所获得的钱用在这方面。但是，这些提议没有引起任何反响。然而，没过多久，威廉·劳埃德·加里森（William Lloyd Garrison，1805~1879）就开始在波士顿发行了名为《解放者》的报纸。他希望完全废除奴隶制，而

① 即帕特里克·亨利。

② 这位威廉·埃勒里·钱宁与本书作者的父亲姓名完全相同，后者是前者的侄子。前者是一位神学家，而后者是一位诗人。后人为区分二者，在提到他们的时候，往往将前者称为“学者钱宁”（Dr. Channing），将后者称为埃勒里·钱宁。

《解放者》报的刊头

且不给奴隶主任何赔偿。有一段时间，他几乎孤军奋战。随后，逐渐有人来援助他，于是“废奴协会”就创建起来了。

**325. 反废奴主义者**——不要以为没有人反对这些废奴主义者。他们遭到了最强烈的反对。虽然没有多少北方人想要在北方重建奴隶制，但是，许多北方人都不希望煽动反奴隶制的情绪，因为他们认为这会损害商业。有些人甚至声称反奴隶制运动会导致联邦的毁灭。这种思想中存在很多真实的成分。因为加里森越来越直言不讳了。他谴责联邦中存在奴隶主，并希望推翻宪法，因为它允许奴隶制存在。纽约州、新泽西州和新罕布什尔州都爆发了反对废奴主义者的暴动。波士顿的暴动者抓住了加里森，并拖着他在大街上游行（1835年）。

**326. 公元1831年，弗吉尼亚州的奴隶叛乱**——大约在加里森在波士顿创办《解放者》的时候，弗吉尼亚州爆发了一场奴隶叛乱。领导叛乱的是一个名叫纳特·特纳（Nat Turner，1800~1831）的奴隶，因此这场叛乱通常被称为“纳特·特纳叛乱”。这是一个小事件，很

纳特·特纳被捕

容易就被镇压下去了。但是南方人惊恐了起来，因为他们觉得北方人煽动反奴隶制肯定会导致更多的叛乱。他们呼吁政府禁止通过邮局寄送《解放者》和类似的“煽动性出版物”。

327. 请愿权——自由人最神圣的权利之一就是为纠正不平而请愿申诉的权利。在过去的殖民地时代，英国议会甚至曾拒绝听取殖民地人民提出的请愿。但是第一条宪法修正案禁止国会制定任何阻止合众国公民请愿的法律。曾经担任总统的约翰·昆西·亚当斯这时是众议员。1836年，他多次呈递请愿书，请求国会禁止哥伦比亚特区的奴隶制。而卡尔霍恩那样的南方人认为这些请愿书是对南方奴隶主的侮辱。国会不能阻止反对奴隶制的人民请愿，但是能阻止宣读呈递上来的请愿书。于是，国会用《限制言论自由的决议案》来达到这个目的。亚当斯因为这些决议案侵犯了他的选民的权利而提出抗议。但是，它们还是获得了通过。请愿书这时源源不断地涌进国会。亚当斯甚至呈递一份来自一些黑人奴隶的请愿书。

328. 北方人态度的转变——所有这些事件让北方人的态度产生了一个巨大的转变。许多不太关注黑人奴隶的人开始密切关注新闻自由和请愿权。他们当中的许多人并不同情废奴主义者，但是他们希望对奴隶制的扩张加以限制。与此同时，南方人正团结起来反对一切干涉奴隶制的尝试。他们甚至决定在合众国添加新的蓄奴准州。

## 【ORIGINAL TEXT】

**323. Growth of Slavery in the South.**—South of Pennsylvania and of the Ohio River slavery had increased greatly since 1787. Washington, Jefferson, Henry, and other great Virginians were opposed to the slave system. But they could find no way to end it, even in Virginia. The South Carolinians and Georgians fought every proposition to limit slavery. They even refused to come into the Union unless they were given representation in Congress for a portion at least of their slaves. And in the first Congress under the Constitution they opposed bitterly every proposal to limit slavery. Then came Whitney's invention of the cotton gin. That at once made slave labor vastly more profitable in the cotton states and put an end to all hopes of peaceful emancipation in the South.

**324. Rise of the Abolitionists.**—About 1830 a new movement in favor of the negroes began. Some persons in the North, as, for example, William Ellery Channing, proposed that slaves should be set free, and their owners paid for their loss. They suggested that the money received from the sale of the public lands might be used in this way. But nothing came of these suggestions. Soon, however, William Lloyd Garrison began at Boston the publication of a paper called the Liberator. He wished for complete abolition without payment. For a time he labored almost alone. Then slowly others came to his aid, and the Antislavery Society was founded.

**325. Opposition to the Abolitionists.**—It must not be thought that the abolitionists were not opposed. They were most vigorously opposed. Very few Northern men wished to have slavery reestablished in the North. But very many

Northern men objected to the antislavery agitation because they thought it would injure business. Some persons even argued that the antislavery movement would bring about the destruction of the Union. In this idea there was a good deal of truth. For Garrison grew more and more outspoken. He condemned the Union with slaveholders and wished to break down the Constitution, because it permitted slavery. There were anti-abolitionist riots in New York, New Jersey, and New Hampshire. In Boston the rioters seized Garrison and dragged him about the streets (1835).

**326. Slave Rebellion in Virginia, 1831.**—At about the time that Garrison established the Liberator at Boston, a slave rebellion broke out in Virginia. The rebels were led by a slave named Nat Turner, and the rebellion is often called "Nat Turner's Rebellion." It was a small affair and was easily put down. But the Southerners were alarmed, because they felt that the Northern antislavery agitation would surely lead to more rebellions. They called upon the government to forbid the sending of the Liberator and similar "incendiary publications" through the mails.

**327. The Right of Petition.**—One of the most sacred rights of freemen is the right to petition for redress of grievances. In the old colonial days the British Parliament had refused even to listen to petitions presented by the colonists. But the First Amendment to the Constitution forbade Congress to make any law to prevent citizens of the United States from petitioning. John Quincy Adams, once President, was now a member of the House of Representatives. In 1836 he presented petition after petition, praying Congress to forbid slavery in the District of Columbia. Southerners, like Calhoun, thought these petitions were insulting to Southern slaveholders. Congress could not prevent the antislavery people petitioning. They could prevent the petitions being read when presented. This they did by passing "gag-resolutions." Adams protested against these resolutions as an infringement on the rights of his constituents. But the resolutions were passed. Petitions now came pouring into Congress. Adams even presented one from some negro slaves.

**328. Change in Northern Sentiment.**—All these happenings brought about a great change of sentiment in the North. Many people, who cared little about negro slaves, cared a great deal about the freedom of the press and the right of petition. Many of these did not sympathize with the abolitionists, but they wished that some limit might be set to the extension of slavery. At the same time the Southerners were uniting to resist all attempts to interfere with slavery. They were even determined to add new slave territory to the United States.

CHAPTER 32

# 墨西哥战争

THE MEXICAN WAR

329. 得克萨斯共和国——1821年，墨西哥人从西班牙的统治下获得了独立，并建立了墨西哥共和国。不久，就有移民从美国来到这个新兴共和国的东北部定居。这个地区被称为得克萨斯。墨西哥政府授予了这些定居者大片的土地。在一段时间内，一切都令人满意。随后，墨西哥人和德克萨斯人之间爆发了战争。在来自田纳西州的移民塞缪尔·休斯顿（Samuel Houston，1793~1863）的带领下，得克萨斯人赢得了圣哈辛托战役，并俘虏了墨西哥共和国的总统桑塔·安纳（Antonio López de Santa Anna，1794~1876）将军。得克萨斯人随后建立了得克萨斯共和国（1836年），并申请作为合众国的一个州加入联邦。

塞缪尔·休斯顿

330. 南方人和得克萨斯——得克萨斯申请加入联邦给许多南方人带来了惊喜。作为墨西哥共和国一部分的得克萨斯一直是自由的土地。不过，得克萨斯非常能适应棉花种植的需求。如果能获准加入联邦，它肯定会成为一个或几个蓄奴州。接纳得克萨斯的问题首先出现在了杰克逊面前。杰克逊认为，接纳得克萨斯会遭到北方的强烈反对。于是，他把整个事情搁置了下来，而且不打算对其做任何处理。泰勒则采取了截然不同的行动。

在他的指示下，合众国与得克萨斯签订了一个条约。这个条约规定合众国接纳得克萨斯加入联邦。但是，参议院拒绝了批准这个条约。因此，这件事成为1844年总统选举中最重要的问题。

**331. 公元1844年大选**——泰勒总统本来一直很想连任。但是，两大主要党派都不希望他担任领袖。民主党原本很乐意提名范布伦——要是他不曾反对接纳得克萨斯的话。作为替代，他们提名了公开宣称接纳得克萨斯的田纳西人詹姆斯·K. 波尔克（James Knox Polk，1795~1849）。辉格党提名了亨利·克莱，他对得克萨斯问题没有固定的看法——他今天这样说，另一天又有另一种说法。其结果是导致反对奴隶制的人和反对接纳得克萨斯的人组成了一个新的政党。他们自称自由党，并提名了一个总统候选人。自由党没有获得多少选票。不过他们获得的票数却足以使克莱落选，于是波尔克当选为总统。

詹姆斯·诺克斯·波尔克
第十一任美国总统（1845~1849）

**332. 公元1845年，兼并德克萨斯**——泰勒这时敦促国会接纳得克萨斯。国会两院通过了一个联合决议案。该决议案规定，接纳得克萨斯，并且在得克萨斯同意的前提下，除得克萨斯州之外，再将当时得克萨斯的领土分成四个州。在实际接纳得克萨斯之前，泰勒已经不再是总统了。不过，波尔克还是贯彻实施了泰勒的政策。于是，1845年7月4日，得克萨斯成为合众国的一个州。

**333. 公元1846年，墨西哥战争爆发**——墨西哥人从未承认过得克萨斯的独立。他们这时对合众国准许它加入表示抗议。关于得克萨斯州南部边界的纠纷也出现了。由于不能就此达成共识，波尔克总统命令扎卡里·泰勒将军（Zachary Taylor, 1784~1850）进军格兰德河并占领那块有争议的领土。泰勒完成了他的指令。于是，墨西哥人向他发起了进攻。波尔克向国会汇报了这些事实，于是国会批准总统将战争进行下去，理由是“战争已经存在，并且是由墨西哥自身挑起的”。

扎卡里·泰勒

第十二任美国总统（1849-1850）

**334. 泰勒领导的战役**——墨西哥战争明显分为三个部分：（1）泰勒向前挺进渡过格兰德河；（2）斯科特[①]领导的战役，这场战役以占领墨西哥城而告终；（3）夺取加利福尼亚。泰勒的目标是坚守格兰德河战线，随后进入墨西哥，并尽可能给墨西哥军造成大的伤亡。在正式宣战之前，帕洛阿尔托战役和雷萨卡德拉帕尔马战役就已经打响了（1846年8月9日）。这些胜利让泰勒控制了格兰德河。9月，他渡过了格兰德河。到此为止，一切顺利。但是到了冬天，泰勒的许多

美墨战争中美方进军路线图

① 即曾经参加1812年对英战争的温菲尔德·斯科特将军。

士兵被调去参加斯科特的战役去了。这似乎是墨西哥人的机会。他们以四倍于泰勒的兵力向他发起了进攻。1847年2月，这场战役在布埃纳维斯塔打响了。泰勒击退了墨西哥人并给他们造成了巨大伤亡。这是泰勒战场的最后一场战役。

温菲尔德·斯科特

**335. 斯科特入侵墨西哥**——斯科特的作战计划是：在韦拉克鲁斯登陆，然后向两百英里外的墨西哥城进军，攻陷这座城市，强迫墨西哥人达成和平。一切都完全按照计划进行。在海军的帮助下，斯科特攻陷了韦拉克鲁斯。他的兵力只有墨西哥军的四分之一，但他仍在塞罗戈多消灭了墨西哥军（1847年4月）。那里有一条越过海岸山脉通往墨西哥城的道路。他们谨慎而巧妙地连续行军，最终看到了墨西哥城。墨西哥共和国的首都四面都是沼泽，一些狭窄的堤道将其与陆地连接起来，只能通过这些堤道才能到达那里。1847年8月20日，经过三场激战，斯科特打败了墨西哥军。9月14日，他率军进入了墨西哥城。这时，他只剩下六千名能够继续服役的士兵了。

**336. 夺取加利福尼亚**——加利福尼亚是墨西哥在其本土以北的太平洋沿岸殖民地的名称。当时有许多美国人定居于此，尤其是在蒙特里。得知美墨战争的爆发后，他们建立了一个自己的共和国。他们的国旗上画着一只灰熊，

加利福尼亚共和国的“熊旗”

因此他们的共和国通常被称为“熊共和国”[1]。海军准将斯托克顿（Robert Field Stockton，1795~1866）率领一小支舰队停泊于太平洋海岸。他和约翰·C. 弗里蒙特（John Charles Frémont，1813~1890）一直都在支援“熊共和国”的人民，直到卡尼上校（Stephen Watts Kearny，1794~1848）由美国经圣达菲来接应他们。

**337. 公元1848年，和平条约**——美墨战争的直接原因是墨西哥不愿意不经过斗争就放弃得克萨斯。不过，墨西哥人还曾非常不公正地对待过许多美国人，而且欠了他们很多钱。1848年，美国和墨西哥签订了一个和平条约。墨西哥同意放弃它对得克萨斯、加利福尼亚、新墨西哥、内华达、犹他、科罗拉多的所有权。美国则同意从墨西哥撤军，赔偿墨西哥1500万美元，并支付墨西哥境内的美国公民所要求的赔偿金。这笔赔偿金共计350万美元。因此，合众国最终为这块面积巨大且极富价值的新增领土支付了1850美元。到了要划定边界线的时候，美国和墨西哥的专员没能达成共识。于是，美国又支付了1000万美元，获得了格兰德河和科罗拉多河之间的狭长的土地。这就形成了合众国今天的南部边界。1853年，詹姆斯·加兹登（James Gadsden，1788~1858）代表合众国签订了这个协议，而那块买来的土地也就常被称为“加兹登购地”。

**338. 俄勒冈问题**——不仅西南部边界有争议，西北部也长期存在一个边界争端，不过它在波尔克的总统任期内得到了解决。俄勒冈是位于西属加利福尼亚、墨属加利福尼亚以及俄属阿拉斯加之间的整个地区。美国和英国都宣称自己完全拥有俄勒冈的所有权。由于不能就此达成共识，双方决定共同占有这个地区。随着时间的推移，美国定居者和传教士开始越过

① 现在多称其为“熊旗共和国”（Bear Flag Republic）。

山脉前往俄勒冈。1847年，已经有7000名美国人生活在这个西北地区。

美国通过分别与英国和墨西哥签订条约获得的西部土地

**339. 公元1846年，俄勒冈条约**——现在，是时候认真解决这个问题了。“要么整个俄勒冈，要么完全放弃”“要么54度40分[①]，要么开战”成为流行的口号。合众国提出结束共同占有俄勒冈。英国政府则建议将俄勒冈一分为二，两国各得一半。1818年，合众国与英属北美的边界就已经被划定为从伍兹湖到落基山脉的北纬49度线。这时，合众国提议把这条线延长到太平洋。然而，英国政府坚持这条线的西端必须以温哥华岛和大陆之间的海峡来划定。这是为了使该岛完全属于英国。当时，美墨战争正在进行中。要同时进行两场战争是很困难的。于是，合众国让步了。1846年，两国签订了条约。合众国没有得到“整个俄勒冈”，而是得到了其中的一半。不过，这是一块非常好的地区，不仅包括现在的俄勒冈州，还包括落基山脉以西的北纬42度和北纬49度之间的整个地区。

① 根据美英两国从1818年至1842年一系列谈判的结果，北纬54° 40′ 至北纬40° 之间的俄勒冈是两国共有地区。因此，这句口号的意思就是美国人希望能把美国西北边界划定在北纬54° 40′ 上，也就是说要完全拥有俄勒冈。

## 【ORIGINAL TEXT】

**329. The Republic of Texas.**—The Mexicans won their independence from Spain in 1821 and founded the Mexican Republic. Soon immigrants from the United States settled in the northeastern part of the new republic. This region was called Texas. The Mexican government gave these settlers large tracts of land, and for a time everything went on happily. Then war broke out between the Mexicans and the Texans. Led by Samuel Houston, a settler from Tennessee, the Texans won the battle of San Jacinto and captured General Santa Anna, the president of the Mexican Republic. The Texans then established the Republic of Texas (1836) and asked to be admitted to the Union as one of the United States.

**330. The Southerners and Texas.**—The application of Texas for admission to the Union came as a pleasant surprise to many Southerners. As a part of the Mexican Republic Texas had been free soil. But Texas was well suited to the needs of the cotton plant. If it were admitted to the Union, it would surely be a slave state or, perhaps, several slave states. The question of admitting Texas first came before Jackson. He saw that the admission of Texas would be strongly opposed in the North. So he put the whole matter to one side and would have nothing to do with it. Tyler acted very differently. Under his direction a treaty was made with Texas. This treaty provided for the admission of Texas to the Union. But the Senate refused to ratify the treaty. The matter, therefore, became the most important question in the presidential election of 1844.

**331. Election of 1844.**—President Tyler would have been glad of a second term. But neither of the great parties wanted him as a leader. The Democrats would have gladly nominated Van Buren had he not opposed the acquisition of Texas. Instead they nominated James K. Polk of Tennessee, an outspoken favorer of the admission of Texas. The Whigs nominated Henry Clay, who had no decided views on the Texas question. He said one thing one day, another thing another day. The result was that the opponents of slavery and of Texas formed a new party. They called it the Liberty party and nominated a candidate for President. The Liberty men did not gain many votes. But they gained enough votes to make Clay's election impossible and Polk was chosen President.

**332. Acquisition of Texas, 1845.**—Tyler now pressed the admission of Texas upon Congress. The two houses passed a joint resolution. This resolution provided for the admission of Texas, and for the formation from the territory included in Texas of four states, in addition to the state of Texas, and with the consent of that state. Before Texas was actually admitted Tyler had ceased to be President. But Polk carried out his policy, and on July 4, 1845, Texas became one of the United States.

**333. Beginning of the Mexican War, 1846.**—The Mexicans had never acknowledged the independence of Texas. They now protested against its admission to the United States. Disputes also arose as to the southern boundary of Texas. As no agreement could be reached on this point, President Polk ordered General Zachary Taylor to march to the Rio Grande and occupy the disputed territory. Taylor did as he was ordered, and the Mexicans attacked him. Polk reported these facts to Congress, and Congress authorized the President to push on the fighting on the ground that "war exists, and exists by the act of Mexico herself."

**334. Taylor's Campaigns.**—The Mexican War easily divides itself into three parts: (1) Taylor's forward movement across the Rio Grande; (2) Scott's campaign, which ended in the capture of the City of Mexico; and (3) the seizure of California. Taylor's object was to maintain the line of the Rio Grande, then to advance into Mexico and injure the Mexicans as much as possible. The battles of Palo Alto and Resaca de la Palma (May 8, 9, 1846) were fought before the actual declaration of war. These victories made Taylor master of the Rio Grande. In September he crossed the Rio Grande. So far all had gone well. But in the winter many of Taylor's soldiers were withdrawn to take part in Scott's campaign. This seemed to be the Mexicans' time. They attacked Taylor with four times as many men as he had in his army. This battle was fought at Buena Vista, February, 1847. Taylor beat back the Mexicans with terrible slaughter. This was the last battle of Taylor's campaign.

**335. Scott's Invasion of Mexico.**—The plan of Scott's campaign was that he should land at Vera Cruz, march to the city of Mexico,—two hundred miles away,—capture that city, and force the Mexicans to make peace. Everything fell out precisely as it was planned. With the help of the navy Scott captured Vera Cruz. He had only about one-quarter as many men as the Mexicans. But he overthrew them at Cerro Gordo, where the road to the City of Mexico crosses the coast mountains (April, 1847). With the greatest care and skill he pressed on and at length came within sight of the City of Mexico. The capital of the Mexican Republic stood in the midst of marshes, and could be reached only over narrow causeways which joined it to the solid land. August 20, 1847, Scott beat the Mexicans in three pitched battles, and on September 14 he entered the city with his army, now numbering only six thousand men fit for active service.

**336. Seizure of California.**—California was the name given to the Mexican possessions on the Pacific coast north of Mexico itself. There were now many American settlers there, especially at Monterey. Hearing of the outbreak of the

Mexican War, they Set up a republic of their own. Their flag had a figure of a grizzly bear painted on it, and hence their republic is often spoken of as the Bear Republic. Commodore Stockton with a small fleet was on the Pacific coast. He and John C. Frémont assisted the Bear Republicans until soldiers under Colonel Kearney reached them from the United States by way of Santa Fé.

**337. Treaty of Peace, 1848.**—The direct cause of the Mexican War was Mexico's unwillingness to give up Texas without a struggle. But the Mexicans had treated many Americans very unjustly and owed them large sums of money. A treaty of peace was made in 1848. Mexico agreed to abandon her claims to Texas, California, New Mexico, Nevada, Utah, and Colorado. The United States agreed to withdraw its armies from Mexico, to pay Mexico fifteen million dollars, and to pay the claims of American citizens on Mexico. These claims proved to amount to three and one-half million dollars, In the end, therefore, the United States paid eighteen and one-half million dollars for this enormous and exceedingly valuable addition to its territory. When the time came to run the boundary line, the American and Mexican commissioners could not agree. So the United States paid ten million dollars more and received an additional strip of land between the Rio Grande and the Colorado rivers. This gave the United States its present southern boundary. This agreement was made in 1853 by James Gadsden for the United States, and the land bought is usually called the Gadsden Purchase.

**338. The Oregon Question.**— It was not only in the Southwest that boundaries were disputed; in the Northwest also there was a long controversy which was settled while Polk was President. Oregon was the name given to the whole region, between Spanish and Mexican California and the Russian Alaska. The United States and Great Britain each claimed to have the best right to Oregon. As they could not agree as to their claims, they decided to occupy the region jointly. As time went on American settlers and missionaries began to go over the mountains to Oregon. In 1847 seven thousand Americans were living in the Northwest.

**339. The Oregon Treaty, 1846.**—The matter was now taken up in earnest. "All Oregon or none," "Fifty-four forty or fight," became popular cries. The United States gave notice of the ending of the joint occupation. The British government suggested that Oregon should be divided between the two nations. In 1818 the boundary between the United States and British North America had been fixed as the forty-ninth parallel from the Lake of the Woods to the Rocky Mountains. It was now proposed to continue this line to the Pacific. The British government, however, insisted that the western end of the line should follow the channel between Vancouver's Island and the mainland so as to make that island entirely British. The Mexican War was now coming on. It would hardly do to have two wars at one time. So the United States gave way and a treaty was signed in 1846. Instead of "all Oregon," the United States received about one-half. But it was a splendid region and included not merely the present state of Oregon, but all the territory west of the Rocky Mountains between the forty-second and the forty-ninth parallels of latitude.

CHAPTER 33

# 1850年的妥协

## THE COMPROMISE OF 1850

**340. 公元1846年，《威尔莫特附加条款》**——该如何处理俄勒冈和从墨西哥获得的广大领土？它们应该是自由的土地还是蓄奴的土地？为了理解这个问题所引发的争议，我们必须往前追溯一点，学习一下《威尔莫特附加条款》。甚至早在美墨战争全面爆发之前，这个问题就摆在了国会面前。所有人都承认得克萨斯必定是一个蓄奴州。大部分人都同意俄勒冈将是自由的土地。因为它太靠北，不利于黑人生存发展。但是加利福尼亚和新墨西哥又该如何处理？宾夕法尼亚州的戴维·威尔莫特（David Wilmot, 1814~1868）认为它们应该是自由的土地。他是一位众议院成员。1846年，他提议在拨款给总统购买墨西哥土地的法案上加上一项附加条款，即联邦政府购买的任何土地上都不得发展奴隶制。这项附加条款最终遭到了否决。但是，这件事引起了人民的极大关注，而这个问题也成了1848年大选中最重要的议题。

**341. 公元1848年，泰勒当选总统**——有三位候选人参加了1848年的总统竞选。第一位是来自密歇根州的刘易斯·卡斯（Lewis Cass, 1782~1866）。他是民主党候选人。他支持“占地者主权论”，即允许各准州人民自己选择该地区是否要有奴隶制[①]。辉格党候选人是布纳维斯塔战役

① 换言之，关于奴隶制的取舍，各州有权自行决定，国会无权干涉。这种思想后来被斯蒂芬·阿诺德·道格拉斯发展为“居住在该地的人有权处理该地事务”，即“人民主权论”（popular sovereignty）。

的胜利者泰勒将军。辉格党没有提出任何关于立场的声明。第三位候选人是马丁·范布伦，他已经担任过一届总统。尽管是一位民主党人，但他并不支持奴隶制的扩张。他被那些不信奉“占地者主权论”的民主党人和一个自称 “自由土地党”的新政党提名为候选人。废奴主义者（或自由党）也提名了一位候选人，但是他退出了竞选，转而支持范布伦。辉格党提名了来自纽约州的米勒德·菲尔莫尔（Millard Fillmore，1800~1874）为副总统候选人。他为辉格党吸引了许多纽约州的选票。范布伦也吸引了许多民主党的选票。这样，纽约州被泰勒和菲尔莫尔拿下了。这就决定了大选的结果，于是这两名辉格党候选人分别当选为正副总统。

**342. 加利福尼亚**——在美墨和平条约获得批准之前，甚至在这个条约签订之前，人们就已经在加利福尼亚发现了黄金。关于这个发现的各种报道很快就传到了西部海岸的各城镇。人们立即放下手头的事情，赶到山区挖掘黄金。几个月之后，关于这个发现的传闻开始传到美国东部地区。起初，人们不太关注这些传言。但是，当波尔克总统宣布发现了黄金的时候，人们就开始认为这肯定是真的了。不久，数以百计的淘金者动身前往加利福尼亚。随后，又有数以千计的人渴望去加利福尼亚。第一批到来的

1847年的旧金山

人被称为“四九年人”，因为他们大多数是在1849年到来的。到那一年年底，加利福尼亚已经有八万移民了。

**343. 加利福尼亚申请加入联邦**——加利福尼亚当时有八万白人，但是他们几乎没有任何类型的政府。因此，这些人于1849年11月召开了一次大会，起草了一部宪法，并要求作为一个州加入联邦。这部宪法的特别之处在于，它禁止加利福尼亚发展奴隶制。许多“四九年人”是南方人。可即便是他们也不想要奴隶制。其原因是：他们要在土里挖掘并获得黄金。他们不能允许奴隶主使用奴隶在他们的矿场采矿，因为自由的白人劳动力从来就不能与黑人奴隶一起工作。因此，他们不希望加利福尼亚有奴隶制。

**344. 一个分裂的国家**——加利福尼亚人民的行动立即把奴隶制问题带到人们面前。许多南方人渴望脱离联邦，去建立一个蓄奴邦联。而许多废奴主义者渴望在北方建立一个自由的共和国。许多热爱联邦的北方人则认为，奴隶制应该被限制在那些已经存在奴隶制的州当中。他们认为，在各准州中不应允许奴隶制存在，因为准州是属于合众国全体人民的。他们主张，如果各准州能够保持自由，那么，当准州的人民在制定州宪法时，就会像加利福尼亚人民之前所做的那样禁止奴隶制。他们或许是对的，但也正是由于这个原因，南方人希望在准州发展奴隶制。这些观点所包含的情绪是如此强烈，联邦看起来就要分裂了。

**345. 泰勒总统的对策**——泰勒将军如今是总统。民众日益高涨的情绪让他焦虑不安。他决定在人民变得更加激动之前立即解决这个问题。因此，他派遣了代理人到加利福尼亚和新墨西哥呼吁人民立刻申请加入联邦。当国会于1850年开会的时候，泰勒陈述了加利福尼亚作为自由州加入联邦的要求。南方人生气了，因为他们一直以为加利福尼亚肯定会成为一个蓄奴州。

**346. 克莱的妥协方案**——这时，亨利·克莱站出来提出了“心的团结”。他的方案旨在通过使各地人民互相妥协来结束南方人和北方人之间的全部争端。例如，南方人要允许加利福尼亚作为自由州加入联邦，同意废除哥伦比亚特区的奴隶贸易。作为回报，北方人则应在所有其他方面向南方人让步。他们要允许哥伦比亚特区的奴隶制存在，还要无条件地或不反对奴隶制地同意新墨西哥和犹他组建准州。得克萨斯宣称它拥有上述新墨西哥准州的一部分土地。于是，克莱提议合众国向得克萨斯购买这些土地。最后，克莱提议国会通过一项严厉的《逃亡奴隶法》。显而易见，克莱的方案整体上无疑是对南方有利的。几乎没人同意通过这整个方案。但是，当针对其中各个部分进行投票时，所有的部分又都通过了。在人们为这个妥协案欢呼雀跃之际，泰勒总统逝世了。于是，副总统米勒德·菲尔莫尔继任为总统。

米勒德·菲尔莫尔

第十三任美国总统（1850~1853）

**347. 《逃亡奴隶法》**——宪法规定，在一州服劳役的人逃到另一个州后，必须根据他为其服劳役之人的要求被遣还给后者[①]。1793年，国会已

① 详见本书附录《美利坚合众国宪法》第四条第二款，该条款后由1865年通过的第十三条宪法修正案修改，该修正案规定，除依法判罪者所受的刑罚之外，禁止美国境内所有地区存在奴隶制或强制性劳役。

经通过了一项法案来执行宪法的这条规定。但是这项法案很少得到执行，因为它的执行一直是交由各州去完成，而北方舆论又是反对遣返逃亡奴隶的。1850年的这部法律则将那项法案的执行交给联邦政府官员去负责。奴隶主的代理人们指认了许多人为逃亡奴隶，却没有几个人被遣返到南方。执行这项法律的那些尝试的重要结果是增强了北方舆论对奴隶制的对立态度，导致了北方人加倍努力地帮助逃亡奴隶通过北方各州逃往加拿大。一个这样的正规组织被建立了起来，它被称为“地下铁道”。简而言之，《1850年妥协案》不但没有带来“心的团结”，反而增加了这个国家的两地民众间的敌意。

348. 《汤姆叔叔的小屋》——就在这一时期，哈里特·比彻·斯托夫人（Harriet Elisabeth Beecher Stowe，1811~1896）创作了《汤姆叔叔的小屋》。在这个故事中，她展现了奴隶制令人愉悦的一面——黑

哈里特·伊丽莎白·比彻·斯托夫人

一张《汤姆叔叔的小屋》的宣传海报

人的无忧无虑和好心肠。不过，她也在其中展现了奴隶制令人不快的一面——鞭笞人类、贩卖人类、猎杀人类。当然，根本就不存在一名像“汤姆叔叔”这样的奴隶。这个故事只不过是一位北方杰出女性所认知的一幅奇异的奴隶制画面罢了。这本书在南方卖了成千上万册，在北方亦是如此。根据此书改编而成的各种戏剧被搬上了舞台。南方人民在阅读《汤姆叔叔的小屋》时几乎不考虑其中那些令人不快的东西：他们喜欢其中令人愉悦的东西。北方人嘲笑种植园生活的漂亮画面：他们因那些残忍的故事感动得流泪。《汤姆叔叔的小屋》和《逃亡奴隶法》让北方人坚信必须限制奴隶制的扩张。

## 【Original Text】

**340. The Wilmot Proviso, 1846.**—What should be done with Oregon and with the immense territory received from Mexico? Should it be free soil or should it be slave soil? To understand the history of the dispute which arose out of this question we must go back a bit and study the Wilmot Proviso. Even before the Mexican War was fairly begun, this question came before Congress. Every one admitted that Texas must be a slave state. Most people were agreed that Oregon would be free soil. For it was too far north for negroes to thrive. But what should be done with California and with New Mexico? David Wilmot of Pennsylvania thought that they should be free soil. He was a member of the House of Representatives. In 1846 he moved to add to a bill giving the President money to purchase land from Mexico a proviso that none of the territory to be acquired at the national expense should be open to slavery. This proviso was finally defeated. But the matter was one on which people held very strong opinions, and the question became the most important issue in the election of 1848.

**341. Taylor elected President, 1848.**—Three candidates contested the election of 1848. First there was Lewis Cass of Michigan, the Democratic candidate. He was in favor of "squatter Sovereignty," that is, allowing the people of each territory to have slavery or not as they chose. The Whig candidate was General Taylor, the victor of Buena Vista. The Whigs put forth no statement of principles. The third candidate was Martin Van Buren, already once President. Although a Democrat, he did not favor the extension of slavery. He was nominated by Democrats who did not believe in "squatter sovereignty," and by a new party which called itself the Free Soil party. The abolitionists or Liberty party also nominated a candidate, but he withdrew in favor of Van Buren. The Whigs had nominated Millard Fillmore of New York for Vice-President. He attracted to the Whig ticket a good many votes in New York. Van Buren also drew a good many votes from the Democrats. In this way New York was carried for Taylor and Fillmore. This decided the election, and the Whig candidates were chosen.

**342. California.**—Before the treaty of peace with Mexico was ratified, even before it was signed, gold was discovered in California. Reports of the discovery soon reached the towns on the western seacoast. At once men left whatever they were doing and hastened to the hills to dig for gold. Months later rumors of this discovery began to reach the eastern part of the United States. At first people paid little attention to them. But when President Polk said that gold had been found, people began to think that it must be true. Soon hundreds of gold-seekers started for California. Then thousands became eager to go. These first comers were called the Forty-Niners, because most of them came in the year 1849. By the end of that year there were eighty thousand immigrants in California.

**343. California seeks Admission to the Union.**—There were eighty thousand white people in California, and they had almost no government of any kind. So in November, 1849, they held a convention, drew up a constitution, and demanded admission the Union as a state. The peculiar thing about this constitution was that it forbade slavery in California. Many of the Forty-Niners were Southerners. But even they did not want slavery. The reason was that they wished to dig in the earth and win gold. They would not allow slave holders to work their mining claims with slave labor, for free white laborers had never been able to work alongside of negro slaves. So they did not want slavery in California.

**344. A Divided Country.**—This action of the people of California at once brought the question of slavery before the people. Many Southerners were eager to found a slave confederacy apart from the Union. Many abolitionists were eager to found a free republic in the North. Many Northerners, who loved the Union, thought that slavery should be confined to the states where it existed. They thought that slavery should not be permitted in the territories, which belonged to the people of the United States as a whole. They argued that if the territories could be kept free, the people of those territories, when they came to form state constitutions, would forbid slavery as the people of California had just done. They were probably right, and for this very reason the Southerners wished to have slavery in the territories. So strong was the feeling over these points that it seemed as if the Union would split into pieces.

**345. President Taylor's Policy.**—General Taylor was now President. He was alarmed by the growing excitement. He determined to settle the matter at once before people could get any more excited. So he sent agents to California and to New Mexico to urge the people to demand admission to the Union at once. When

Congress met in 1850, he stated that California demanded admission as a free state. The Southerners were angry. For they had thought that California would surely be a slave state.

**346. Clay's Compromise Plan.**—Henry Clay now stepped forward to bring about a "union of hearts." His plan was to end all disputes between Northerners and Southerners by having the people of each section give way to the people of the other section. For example, the Southerners were to permit the admission of California as a free state, and to consent to the abolition of the slave trade in the District of Columbia. In return, the Northerners were to give way to the Southerners on all other points. They were to allow slavery in the District of Columbia. They were to consent to the organization of New Mexico and Utah as territories without any provision for or against slavery. Texas claimed that a part of the proposed Territory of New Mexico belonged to her. So Clay suggested that the United States should pay Texas for this land. Finally Clay proposed that Congress should pass a severe Fugitive Slave Act. It is easily seen that Clay's plan as a whole was distinctly favorable to the South. Few persons favored the passage of the whole scheme. But when votes were taken on each part separately, they all passed. In the midst of the excitement over this compromise President Taylor died, and Millard Fillmore, the Vice-President, became President.

**347. The Fugitive Slave Act.**—The Constitution provides that persons held to service in one state escaping into another state shall be delivered up upon claim of the person to whom such service may be due. Congress, in 1793, had passed an act to carry out this provision of the Constitution. But this law had seldom been enforced, because its enforcement had been left to the states, and public opinion in the North was opposed to the return of fugitive slaves. The law of 1850 gave the enforcement of the act to United States officials. The agents of slave owners claimed many persons as fugitives. But few were returned to the South. The important result of these attempts to enforce the law was to strengthen Northern public opinion against slavery. It led to redoubled efforts to help runaway slaves through the Northern states to Canada. A regular system was established. This was called the "Underground Railway." In short, instead of bringing about "a union of hearts," the Compromise of 1850 increased the ill feeling between the people of the two sections of the country.

**348. "Uncle Tom's Cabin."**—It was at this time that Mrs. Harriet Beecher Stowe wrote "Uncle Tom's Cabin." In this story she set forth the pleasant side of slavery—the light-heartedness and kind-heartedness of the negroes. In it she also set forth the unpleasant side of slavery—the whipping of human beings, the selling of human beings, the hunting of human beings. Of course, there never was such a slave as Uncle Tom. The story is simply a wonderful picture of slavery as it appeared to a brilliant woman of the North. Hundreds of thousands of copies of this book were sold in the South as well as in the North. Plays founded on the book were acted on the stage. Southern people when reading "Uncle Tom" thought little of the unpleasant things in it: they liked the pleasant things in it. Northern people laughed at the pretty pictures of plantation life: they were moved to tears by the tales of cruelty. "Uncle Tom's Cabin" and the Fugitive Slave Law convinced the people of the North that bounds must be set to the extension of slavery.

CHAPTER 34

# 围绕堪萨斯展开的斗争

THE STRUGGLE FOR KANSAS

349. 公元1852年，皮尔斯当选总统——这时，新一届大选的时间到了。辉格党已经以两名老兵获得了成功，于是他们认为应该再试着推出一名军人，因而他们提名了墨西哥的征服者——温菲尔德·斯科特将军。民主党也提名了一名军人，即来自新罕布什尔州的富兰克林·皮尔斯（Franklin Pierce，1804~1869）。他曾在墨西哥北部与泰勒并肩作战。民主党和辉格党都声称他们将支持《1850年妥协案》，但是许多选民认为让一位民主党人入主白宫较为稳妥，于是就投票选择了皮尔斯。他们很快就发现自己的这个判断是大错特错了。

富兰克林·皮尔斯

第十四任美国总统（1853~1857）

350. 道格拉斯的《内布拉斯加法案》——皮尔斯总统相当平稳地开始了他的任期。然而，在1854年，伊利诺伊参议员道格拉斯（Stephen Arnold Douglas，1813~1861）提出了一个法案，以组建内布拉斯加准州。我们一定记得，1820年，密苏里作为一个蓄奴州加入了联邦。而1848年，爱荷华又作为自由州加入了联邦。爱荷华州以北是明尼苏达自由准州。密苏里州、爱荷华州和明尼苏达的西面是一片广袤的地区，还没有建立起任何类型的政府。这个地区全部位于1820年妥协线以北，而且根据该妥协案，它将永远处于自由状态。但是，道格拉斯声称《1820年妥协案》已经被《1850年妥协案》替代了。于是，他提议由内布拉斯加的居民决定这个准州是成为自由的土地还是蓄奴的土地，犹如《1820年妥协案》从未获得通过一样。刹那间，一场惊人的骚乱爆发了。

斯蒂芬•阿诺德•道格拉斯

**351. 1854年，《堪萨斯–内布拉斯加法案》**——这时，道格拉斯更改了他的法案，以便做出组建两个准州的规定。他把其中的一个准州命名为堪萨斯。除了向西延伸到落基山脉，它几乎和现在的堪萨斯州拥有相同的边界。另一个准州被命名为内布拉斯加。它拥有堪萨斯以北以及密苏里河与落基山脉之间的全部土地。北方的反奴隶制领袖猛烈地抨击了这个法案。俄亥俄州的蔡斯（Salmon Portland Chase，1808~1873）提出，这是一种背信之举。马萨诸塞州的萨姆纳（Charles Sumner，1811~1874）对这一论战感到高兴，因为他提出人民现在必须在自由和奴隶制之间做出选择。一些独立的民主党人发布了《一个呼吁》。他们呼吁同胞们打开地图看看道格拉斯提议接纳奴隶制的地区是一个多么广袤的地区。他们否认《密苏里妥协案》已被废止。尽管如此，这个法案还是被国会批准并被皮尔斯总

《堪萨斯–内布拉斯加法案》所规定的接受奴隶制的区域（阴影部分）

统签署通过了。

352. 亚伯拉罕·林肯——亚伯拉罕·林肯（Abraham Lincoln，1809~1865）生于肯塔基州。他和父母一起搬到了印第安纳，随后又搬到了伊利诺伊。林肯小时候家境贫寒，他不得不努力工作。但是，他抓住了一切机会阅读和学习。即便是在田间犁地时，他也在思考；在家中度过漫漫长夜时，他也在借着火光学习。他长大后成为一名律师，并担任过一届国会议员。《堪萨斯-内布拉斯加法案》的通过引起了他前所未有的愤慨。他认为，不论一个人是黑人还是白人，若不经过其本人的同意，任何人都没有权利去支配他。他还认为，在堪萨斯的奴隶制问题得到解决之前必然会发生流血事件，而第一滴血流下之际就是联邦开始解体之时。

林肯的书橱

林肯当土地测量员时使用过的工具和工具袋

353. 堪萨斯定居点——在关于《堪萨斯-内布拉斯加法案》的辩论中，纽约州参议员西沃德（William Henry Seward，1801~1872）对南方人说："来吧，然后……我们将参与争夺堪萨斯土地的竞争，上帝会把胜利给予人数占优势的一方，因为这一方是正确的。"西沃德说得没错。胜利最终的确属于那些反对奴隶制扩张的人。但是，胜利的到来还需要一段漫长的时间。这项法案刚获得通过，武装起来的“南方之子”① 就越过密苏里州的边界，建立了艾奇逊镇。随后，大批武装起来的定居者从北方和东方赶来。他们建立了劳伦斯和托皮卡这两个镇，然后进行选举。这时，数百人涌出了密苏里州边界，他们在堪萨斯以多数选票击败了自由派定居者，然后返回了家园。这个准州的议会就以这种方式被选了出来②，并将密苏里州的法律——奴隶法规以及所有规定——作为堪萨斯的法律。看来，堪萨斯似乎就要失去自由了。

354. 托皮卡会议——这时，自由州一派的选民在托皮卡召开了一次会议。他们起草了一部宪法，并向国会申请堪萨斯作为自由州加入联邦。自由州派和蓄奴州派各自选出了一名国会代表。这时，众议院负责处理这件事，并任命了一个调查委员会。该委员会以支持自由州派的立场提交了报告，于是众议院投票允许堪萨斯作为自由州加入联邦。但是，参议院可不会同意任何类似这样的事。堪萨斯内部的斗争仍在继续，并且每个月都变得比以前更为激烈。

355. 共和党——堪萨斯-内布拉斯加斗争所导致的最重要的结果就是共和党的形成。这一党派由来自其他政党中所有反对道格拉斯的堪萨斯-内布拉斯加政策的人组成。慢慢地，他们开始把自身看成一个政党，并且采用了杰斐逊、麦迪逊和门罗的那个旧党派的名称——共和党。

---

① 1854年由一些密苏里人建立的秘密组织，其宗旨就是要使堪萨斯成为蓄奴州。他们的活动主要是鼓动南方人向堪萨斯移民，保护堪萨斯的蓄奴州派移民，阻挠堪萨斯变成自由州。

② 这种从一个州跑到另一个州参加投票选举的行为无疑是一种舞弊，但是皮尔斯总统对其结果的合法性表示认可，甚至替换了对此提出异议的安德鲁·里德州长，因此该地区也就产生了一个支持奴隶制的议会。

詹姆斯·布坎南

第十五任美国总统（1857~1861）

**356. 公元1856年，布坎南当选总统**——辉格党和一无所知党[1]提名了米勒德·菲尔莫尔为总统候选人，却对奴隶制避而不谈。民主党提名了宾夕法尼亚州的詹姆斯·布坎南为总统候选人，提名了肯塔基州的约翰·C. 布雷肯里奇（John Cabell Breckinridge，1821~1875）为副总统候选人。他们宣布赞成《堪萨斯-内布拉斯加法案》，并支持从严格意义上去解释宪法。共和党提名了约翰·C. 弗里蒙特。他们反对奴隶制的扩张，而且提出了一个主张以国家开支进行国内改良的政策。民主党赢得了选举；但是共和党获得了四个州以外的整个北方的支持。

德雷德·斯科特

**357. 公元1857年，德雷德·斯科特案判决**——这时，联邦最高法院对德雷德·斯科特案[2]做出了判决。该判决结束了人们就奴隶制问题达成妥协的全部希望。德雷德·斯科特（Dred Scott，1799~1858）生来就是一名奴隶。多数法官[3]宣称，一个人一旦成为奴隶就永远不能成为美国公

① 该党派又被称为“美国人党”（American Party）。它产生于19世纪50年代初，最初是一个由本土主义者组成的秘密组织，当组织成员受到外人询问其组织的活动目的或纲领时，皆以“一无所知”作答，因此得名。该党派以保护新教，排斥天主教为由，主张限制外国人移民到美国，延长其归化年限，并限制其选举权。该党派只针对外国移民和天主教徒，对奴隶制问题并不关心。

② 德雷德·斯科特是一名黑人奴隶。他曾跟随其主人先后到自由州伊利诺伊和自由准州威斯康星居住，后回到蓄奴州密苏里。在其主人死后，斯科特向密苏里州地方法院提起诉讼，要求获得自由，理由是自己曾在自由州居住过。该案一直上诉到联邦最高法院。最高法院判决斯科特败诉。

③ 最高法院中审理此案的法官共有八位，其中五位来自南方，三位来自北方。所谓“多数法官”，也就是说南方法官的意见决定了最终的判决。

民，也永远不能在美国法庭上提起诉讼。他们还宣布《密苏里妥协案》是不合法的。奴隶主完全有权利把他们的财产——包括奴隶——带到各准州，国会也不能阻止他们。

**358. 公元1858年，林肯和道格拉斯的辩论**——这时，是否让道格拉斯再次当选参议员的问题摆在了伊利诺伊州人民的面前。亚伯拉罕·林肯站出来和他竞选。“一栋内部分裂的房子立不住”，林肯说，“这个政府不能维持一半蓄奴和一半自由的状态……它将变成完全是其中一种或完全是另一种情形。”他向道格拉斯发出了挑战，要在公众面前和他辩论这些问题。道格拉斯接受了这个挑战。他们在众人面前接连进行了七场辩论。林肯迫使道格拉斯为他的“人民主权论”进行辩护。为此，道格拉斯宣称各准州的议会可以制定反对奴隶制的法律。当然，这一主张与德雷德·斯科特判决是相对立的。于是，道格拉斯赢得了竞选并重返参议院。而林肯却通过这件事在全国赢得了声望。

**359. “流血的堪萨斯”**——与此同时，堪萨斯境内已经爆发了内战。蓄奴州派攻击了劳伦斯镇，杀死了一些自由州派的定居者，还放火烧了一些建筑。从纽约州移民来的约翰·布朗（John Brown，1800~1859）率领自由州派的定居者偷袭了一帮蓄奴州派的人，并杀死了其中的五人。到1857年，自由州派的选民变得非常多，已经没法靠从密苏里找人参加投票来击败他们了，而且他们还选出了一个自由州派的议会。但是，那个不合法的蓄奴州派议会已经规定在莱康普顿召开制宪会议。这次会议被蓄奴州派的人控制，并通过了一部支持奴隶制的宪法。布坎南总统把这部宪法呈递给了国会，要求允许堪萨斯作为蓄奴州加入联邦。但是，道格拉斯不忍看到堪萨斯定居者的愿望遭到违背。他强烈反对这个建议，于是它遭到了否决。直到1861年，堪萨斯才作为一个自由州加入联邦。

360. 公元1859年，约翰·布朗的突袭——在堪萨斯的时候，约翰·布朗想出了一个大胆的计划。那就是在南部的群山中占据一个险要之地，并在那里保护从主人手中逃出来的奴隶。他期望以这种方式在两年之内粉碎奴隶制。他只带着19个人就夺取了弗吉尼亚的哈珀渡口，并占据了那里的一个合众国兵工厂。但是，他和他的大多数追随者不久就被抓获。弗吉尼亚当局将他当作叛国者和杀人犯给处决了。共和党的领袖们谴责他的行动是“最严重的犯罪”。但是，这件事让南方的领袖们坚信：现在，是时候退出联邦，建立一个“南部邦联”了。

哈珀渡口

【ORIGINAL TEXT】

**349. Pierce elected President, 1852.**—It was now Campaign time for a new election. The Whigs had been successful with two old soldiers, so they thought they would try again with another soldier and nominated General Winfield Scott, the conqueror of Mexico. The Democrats also nominated a soldier, Franklin Pierce of New Hampshire, who had been in northern Mexico with Taylor. The

Democrats and Whigs both said that they would stand by the Compromise of 1850. But many voters thought that there would be less danger of excitement with a Democrat in the White House and voted for Pierce for that reason. They soon found that they were terribly mistaken in their belief.

**350. Douglas's Nebraska Bill.**—President Pierce began his term of office quietly enough. But in 1854 Senator Douglas of Illinois brought in a bill to organize the Territory of Nebraska. It will be remembered that in 1820 Missouri had been admitted to the Union as a slave state. In 1848 Iowa had been admitted as a free state. North of Iowa was the free Territory of Minnesota. Westward from Missouri, Iowa, and Minnesota was an immense region without any government of any kind. It all lay north of the compromise line of 1820, and had been forever devoted to freedom by that compromise. But Douglas said that the Compromise of 1820 had been repealed by the Compromise of 1850. So he proposed that the settlers of Nebraska should say whether that territory should be free soil or slave soil, precisely as if the Compromise of 1820 had never been passed. Instantly there was a tremendous uproar.

**351. The Kansas-Nebraska Act, 1854.**—Douglas now changed his bill so as to provide for the formation of two territories. One of these he named Kansas. It had nearly the same boundaries as the present state of Kansas, except that it extended westward to the Rocky Mountains. The other territory was named Nebraska. It included all the land north of Kansas and between the Missouri River and the Rocky Mountains. The antislavery leaders in the North attacked the bill with great fury. Chase of Ohio said that it was a violation of faith. Sumner of Massachusetts rejoiced in the fight, for he said men must now take sides for freedom or for slavery. Some independent Democrats published "An Appeal." They asked their fellow-citizens to take their maps and see what an immense region Douglas had proposed to open to slavery. They denied that the Missouri Compromise had been repealed. Nevertheless, the bill passed Congress and was signed by President Pierce.

**352. Abraham Lincoln.**—Born in Kentucky, Abraham Lincoln went with his parents to Indiana and then to Illinois. As a boy he was very poor and had to work hard. But he lost no opportunity to read and to study. At the plow or in the long evenings at home by the firelight he was ever thinking and studying. Growing to manhood he became a lawyer and served one term in Congress. The passage of the Kansas-Nebraska Act aroused his indignation as nothing had ever aroused it before. He denied that any man had the right to govern another man, be he white or be he black, without that man's consent. He thought that blood would surely be shed before the slavery question would be settled in Kansas, and the first shedding of blood would be the beginning of the end of the Union.

**353. Settlement of Kansas.**—In the debate on the Kansas-Nebraska bill Senator Seward of New York said to the Southerners: "Come on, then…We will engage in competition for the soil of Kansas, and God give the victory to the side that is strong in numbers as it is in right." Seward spoke truly. The victory came to those opposed to the extension of slavery. But it was a long time in coming. As soon as the act was passed, armed "Sons of the South" crossed the frontier of Missouri and founded the town of Atchison. Then came large bands of armed settlers from the North and the East. They founded the towns of Lawrence and Topeka. An election was held. Hundreds of men poured over the boundary of Missouri, outvoted the free-soil settlers in Kansas, and then went home. The territorial legislature, chosen in this way, adopted the laws of Missouri, slave code and all, as the laws of Kansas. It seemed as if Kansas were lost to freedom.

**354. The Topeka Convention.**—The free-state voters now held a convention at Topeka. They drew up a constitution and applied to Congress for admission to the Union as the free state of Kansas. The free-state men and the slave-state men each elected a Delegate to Congress. The House of Representatives now took the matter up and appointed a committee of investigation. The committee reported in favor of the free-state men, and the House voted to admit Kansas as a free state. But the Senate would not consent to anything of the kind. The contest in Kansas went on and became more bitter every month.

**355. The Republican Party.**—The most important result of the Kansas-Nebraska fight was the formation of the Republican party. It was made up of men from all the other parties who agreed in opposing Douglas's Kansas-Nebraska policy. Slowly they began to think of themselves as a party and to adopt the name of the old party of Jefferson, Madison, and Monroe— Republican.

**356. Buchanan elected President, 1856.**—The Whigs and the Know-Nothings nominated Millard Fillmore for President and said nothing about slavery. The Democrats nominated James Buchanan of Pennsylvania for President and John C. Breckinridge of Kentucky for Vice-President. They declared their approval of the Kansas-Nebraska Act and favored a strict construction of the Constitution. The Republicans nominated John C. Frémont. They protested against the extension of slavery and declared for a policy of internal improvements at the expense of the nation. The Democrats won; but the Republicans carried all the Northern states save four.

**357. The Dred Scott Decision, 1857.**—The Supreme Court of the United States now gave a decision in the Dred Scott case that put an end to all hope of compromise on the slavery question. Dred Scott had been born a slave. The majority of the judges declared that a person once a slave could never become a citizen of the United States and bring suit in the United States courts. They also declared that the Missouri Compromise was unlawful. Slave owners had a clear right to carry their property, including slaves, into the territories, and Congress could not stop them.

**358. The Lincoln and Douglas Debates, 1858.**—The question of the reëlection of Douglas to the Senate now came before the people of Illinois. Abraham Lincoln stepped forward to contest the election with him. "A house divided against itself cannot stand," said Lincoln. "This government cannot endure half slave and half free…It will become all one thing or all the other." He challenged Douglas to debate the issues with him before the people, and Douglas accepted the challenge. Seven joint debates were held in the presence of immense crowds. Lincoln forced Douglas to defend the doctrine of "popular sovereignty." This Douglas did by declaring that the legislatures of the territories could make laws hostile to slavery. This idea, of course, was opposed to the Dred Scott decision. Douglas won the election and was returned to the Senate. But Lincoln had made a national reputation.

**359. "Bleeding Kansas."**—Meantime civil war had broken out in Kansas, Slavery men attacked Lawrence, killed a few free-state settlers, and burned several buildings. Led by John Brown, an immigrant from New York, free-state men attacked a party of slave-state men and killed five of them. By 1857 the free-state voters had become so numerous that it was no longer possible to outvote them by bringing men from Missouri, and they chose a free-state legislature. But the fraudulent slave-state legislature had already provided for holding a constitutional convention at Lecompton. This convention was controlled by the slave-state men and adopted a constitution providing for slavery. President Buchanan sent this constitution to Congress and asked to have Kansas admitted as a slave state. But Douglas could not bear to see the wishes of the settlers of Kansas outraged. He opposed the proposition vigorously and it was defeated. It was not until 1861 that Kansas was admitted to the Union as a free state.

**360. John Brown's Raid, 1859.**—While in Kansas John Brown had conceived a bold plan. It was to seize a strong place in the mountains of the South, and there protect any slaves who should run away from their masters. In this way he expected to break slavery in pieces within two years. With only nineteen men he seized Harper's Ferry, in Virginia, and secured the United States arsenal at that place. But he and most of his men were immediately captured. He was executed by the Virginian authorities as a traitor and murderer. The Republican leaders denounced his act as "the gravest of crimes." But the Southern leaders were convinced that now the time had come to secede from the Union and to establish a Southern Confederacy.

# QUESTIONS AND TOPICS
# 问题与论题

## CHAPTER 31

§ 323.—a. Why were the people of South Carolina so opposed to any limitation of slavery? How did they show their opposition?

b. Had slavery disappeared in the North because people thought that it was wrong?

§§ 324, 325.—a. What suggestions were made by some in the North for the ending of slavery? What do you think of these suggestions?

b. For what did Garrison contend, and how did he make his views known? Why were these views opposed in the North?

§ 326.—a. Why were the Southerners so alarmed by Nat Turner's Rebellion?

b. What power had Congress over the mails? How would you have voted on this question?

§§ 327, 328.—a. Why is the right of petition so important? How is this right secured to citizens of the United States?

b. Why should these petitions be considered as insulting to slaveholders?

c. Why were the Southerners so afraid of any discussion of slavery?

## CHAPTER 32

§§ 329, 330.—a. Show by the map the extent of the Mexican Republic.

b. Why did Texas wish to join the United States? What attitude had Mexico taken on slavery?

§§ 331,332.—a. Explain carefully how the Texas question influenced the election of 1844.

b. What was the Liberty party? How did its formation make the election of Polk possible?

c. What is a "joint resolution"?

§ 333.—How did the Mexicans regard the admission of Texas? What dispute with Mexico arose? Did Mexico begin the war?

§§ 334, 335.—a. What was the plan of Taylor's campaign? Of Scott's campaign?

b. Mention the leading battles of Taylor's campaign. Of Scott's campaign.

§§ 336, 337.—a. What action did the American settlers in California take? With what result?

b. Explain by a map the Mexican cessions of 1848 and 1853.

§§ 338, 339.—a. What was the extent of Oregon in 1845?

b. How was the dispute finally settled? Explain by a map.

c. What was the extent of Oregon in 1847? Is it the same today?

d. Of what value was this region to the United States?

## CHAPTER 33

§§ 340, 341.—a. Why was there little question whether Oregon would be slave or free?

b. Explain carefully Wilmot's suggestion. What would be the arguments in

Congress for and against this "proviso"?

c. What is meant by "squatter sovereignty"? What do you think of the wisdom and justice of such a plan?

§§ 342, 343.—a. Describe the discovery of gold in California and the rush thither. What difference did one year make in the population of California?

b. What attitude did California take on the slavery question? Why?

§§ 344, 345.—a. How had the question of slavery already divided the country?

b. What extreme parties were there in the North and the South?

c. Why was the question about the territories so important?

d. What action did President Taylor take? Why? What do you think of the wisdom of this policy?

§§ 346, 347.—a. State the provisions of Clay's compromise plan. Which of these favored the North? The South?

b. What law had been made as to fugitive slaves? Why had it not been enforced? Why was the change made in 1850 so important?

c. How would you have acted had you been a United States officer called to carry out the Fugitive Slave Law?

§ 348.—a. Who was Mrs. Stowe? What view did she take of slavery?

b. Were there any good points in the slave system?

c. Why is this book so important?

## CHAPTER 34

§§ 349-351.—a. Who were the candidates in 1852? Who was chosen? Why?

b. What doctrine did Douglas apply to Kansas and Nebraska?

c. Why did Chase call this bill "a violation of faith"?

d. Was Douglas a patriot? Chase? Sumner? Pierce?

§ 352.—a. Give an account of the early life and training of Abraham Lincoln.

b. What did he think of the Kansas-Nebraska Act?

§§ 353, 354.—a. What effect did the Kansas-Nebraska Act have on the settlement of Kansas?

b. Describe the election. Do you think that laws made by a legislature so elected were binding?

c. Explain the difference in the attitude of the Senate and House on the Kansas question.

§§ 355, 356.—a. How was the Republican party formed?

b. Were its principles like or unlike those of the Republican party of Jefferson's time? Give your reasons.

§ 357.—a. What rights did the Supreme Court declare a slave could not possess? Was a slave a person or a thing?

b. What power does the Constitution give Congress over a territory? (Art. IV, Sec. 3.)

§ 358.—a. Explain carefully the quotations from Lincoln's speeches.

b. Was the doctrine of popular sovereignty necessarily favorable to slavery? Give illustrations to support your reasons.

c. Was Douglas's declaration in harmony with the decision of the Supreme Court?

§§ 359, 360.—a. Compare the attitude of Douglas and Buchanan upon the admission of Kansas.

b. Describe John Brown's raid. Was he a traitor?

## GENERAL QUESTIONS
## 综合性问题

a. Give, with dates, the important laws as to slavery since 1783.

b. What were the arguments in favor of the extension of slavery? Against it?

c. Find and learn a poem against slavery by Whittier, Lowell, or Longfellow.

d. Make a table of elections since 1788, with the leading parties, candidates, and principal issues. Underline the name of the candidate elected.

## SUGGESTIONS TO THE TEACHER
## 给教师的建议

Preparation is especially important in teaching this period. The teacher will find references to larger books in Channing's *Students' History*.

Show how the question of slavery was really at the basis of the Mexican War. Geographical conditions and the settlement of the Western country should be carefully noted. A limited use of the writings and speeches of prominent men and writers is especially valuable at this point.

Have a large map of the United States in the class room, cut out and fasten upon this map pieces of white and black paper to illustrate the effects of legislation under discussion, and also to illustrate the various elections.

The horrors of slavery should be but lightly touched. Emphasize especially the fact that slavery prevented rather than aided the development of the South, and was an evil economically as well as socially.

# 第十二篇

PART XII

# 1860—1861年，退出联邦

SECESSION, 1860~1861

## Books for Study and Reading
## 研究和阅读用书

**References.**—Scribner's *Popular History*, IV, 432~445; McMaster's *School History*, chap. xxvi (industrial progress, 1840~60).

**Home Readings.**—Page's *The Old South*.

## CHAPTER 35

# 1860年的合众国

## THE UNITED STATES IN 1860

361．国家的发展——这时，合众国的领土是杰斐逊当选总统时的三倍。它包含了超过300万平方英里的土地。这个广阔领域已有三分之一有人居住。在这个世纪的60年内，人口的增长甚至快过领土的增长。1800年，有550万人生活在合众国。1860年，有超过3100万人居住在合众国境

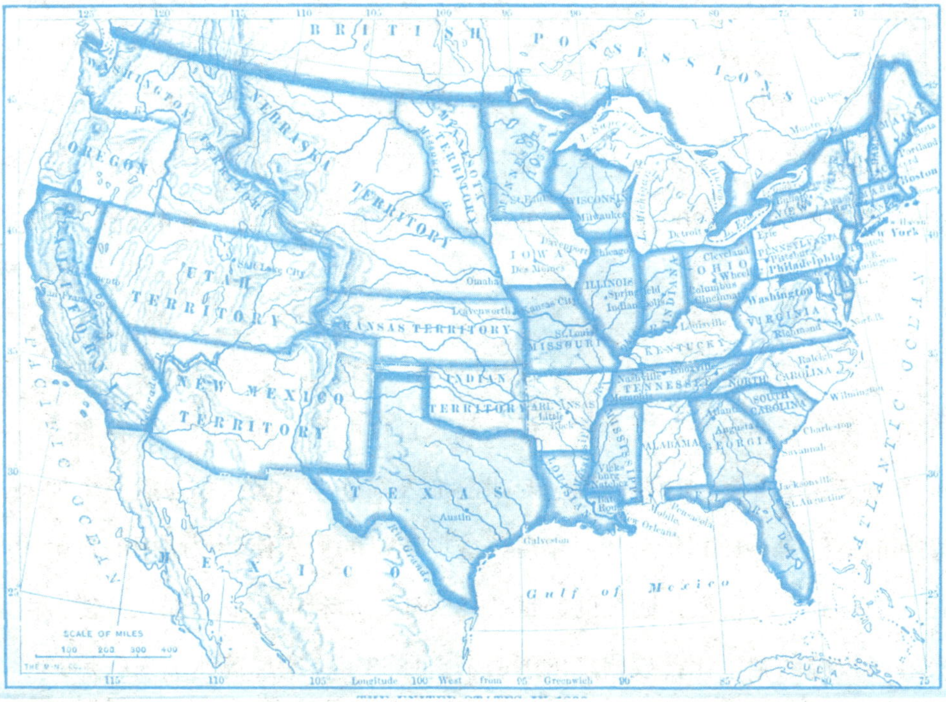


1860年的美国

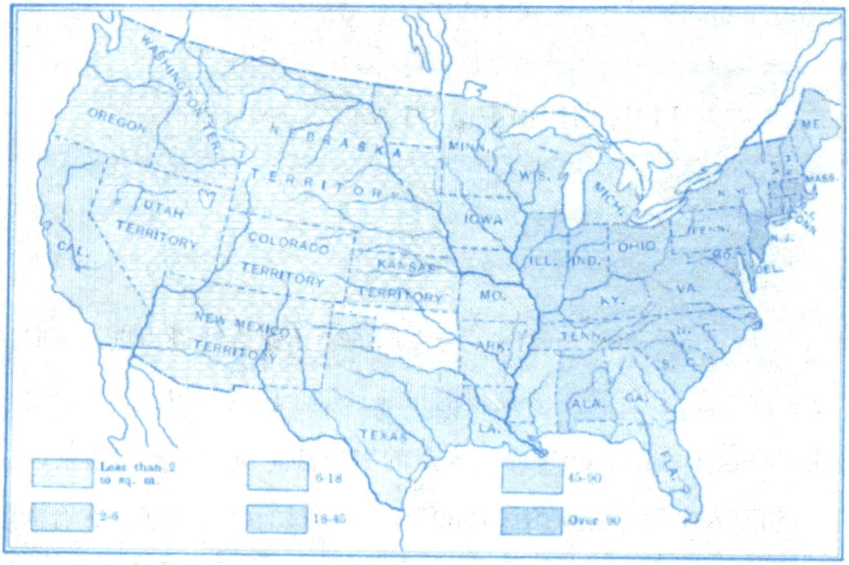


1860年的美国人口密度分布图

内。这些人当中，将近500万人是外来的白人移民。这些移民中又有半数以上是最近10年内才到来的，并且他们几乎都定居在北方的自由州。在3100万总人口中，只有1200万人生活在蓄奴州，而且这些人当中有400多万人是黑人奴隶。

362. 政治力量的变化——国会的控制权这时已经转而落在了北方自由州的手中。长期以来，大多数众议员都来自自由州。而这时，来自北方的参议员又比南方多。这要归因于新州的加入。德克萨斯州是最后一个加入联邦的蓄奴州（1845年）。两年后，威斯康星的加入使参议院中的自由州席位数达到了与蓄奴州同等的数量。1850年，加利福尼亚的加入又使自由州在参议院的席位比蓄奴州多出了两个。1858年，明尼苏达加入联邦，多出的席位增加到了四个。1859年，俄勒冈加入联邦，多出的席位又增加到了六个。至此，蓄奴州已经彻底失去了国会的控制权。

**363. 城市**——制造业、农业和商业的巨大发展带动了对外贸易的大幅增长。这进而导致了北部和西部大型城市的建立。这些城市是纽约市和芝加哥市。它们发展如此之快，是因为它们是贯通莫霍克河谷交通线的东西端点。纽约市这时有超过80万的常住居民。纽约市内的人口比整个南卡罗来纳州的人口还要多。人口增长最快的是芝加哥。1840年，这座城市只有5000人；这时，它有10.9万常住居民。辛辛那提和圣路易斯各自有16万人，它们还是西部最大的城市，而圣路易斯也是所有蓄奴州中最大的城市。几乎和圣路易斯拥有同样多人口的新奥尔良则是南方唯一的大城市。

**364. 各州**——各州的情况和城市的情况一样——北方的发展超过了南方。1790年，弗吉尼亚州的常住居民是纽约州和宾夕法尼亚州的总和。1860年，弗吉尼亚州的常住居民只有这两个州常住居民的总和的四分之一。事实上，1860年，纽约州有将近400万常住居民，这几乎和1791年整个合众国的常住居民一样多。不过西北各州的发展更引人注目。这时，俄亥俄州比弗吉尼亚州多100万人，在整个联邦位居第三。伊利诺伊州位居第四，而印第安纳州则位居第六。我们通过研究地图可以发现一些更有趣的事实，即某几个州的人口密度或者每平方英里人口数。1860年，俄亥俄州、宾夕法尼亚州、马里兰州、特拉华州、新泽西州、纽约州、康涅狄格州、罗得岛州和马萨诸塞州每平方英里看来都有超过45人的常住居民，而南方没有一个州每平方英里达到45人。这同时也向我们表明：南方州尽管在面积上比北方州大，却远不如后者那样强盛。

**365. 城市生活**——过去，大城镇和小城镇没什么不同，只不过面积大一些而已。大城镇中的生活也和小地方相差无几。然而，它们这时已经与以往截然不同了。首先，城市可以负担许多小镇负担不起的事情。其次，

一辆公共马车

城市必须拥有某些设施，否则它的人民就会死于疾病，或在大街上走路时遇害。出于这些理由，北方城市的街道上都铺了路，装了路灯，而且有警察站岗。随后，也有大型下水道带走城市的废物，巨大的铁管将淡水输送给城市里的每一个人。马拉轨道车和公共马车把居民从城市的一处带到另一处，而铁路则从周边地区给他们带来食物。

366. 交通——1849年至1858年间，美国修建了21000英里的铁路。到1860年，实际运营的铁路已经超过了30000英里。在1850年，要是不从铁路转乘蒸汽船，一个人就没法从纽约去奥尔巴尼。而到了1860年，已经有了一条从纽约市直达密西西比河的铁路。在我们看来，旅行依然是不舒服的。火车车厢是简陋的，颠簸得厉害。一辆火车只能运行一段较短的距离，随后，乘客就得下车，弄些东西吃，查看一下他们放在另一辆火车上的行李。即使有这一切不便之处，坐在最糟糕的火车车厢里旅行也比乘坐老式的驿站马车好得多。更多的蒸汽船投入了使用，尤其是在五大湖以及西部的河流上。

霍勒斯·格里利

367. 教育——最近的三十年也是知识进步的三十年。许多学院建立了起来，尤其是在西北地区。这时还没有能称得上是大学的机构，但是，越来越多的注意力被放在了科学以及对法律和医药的专业人才的教育培养上。报业也实现了现代化。1835年创刊的《纽约先驱报》是第一份真正的报纸。不过，霍勒斯·格里利（Horace Greeley，1811~1872）主编的《纽约论坛报》对美国产生的影响比其他任何报纸都要大。格里利有许多怪异之处，但是他是那个时代最能干的人之一。他呼吁制定一项分配公共土地的自由政策，而且一直在宣扬："到西部去，年轻人，到西部去。"杂志业也比从前好了很多。美国第一流的作家们正在创作他们最好的一些作品。

**368. 发明的进步**——电报这时已经得到了广泛使用。它使报纸能够以从未有过的方式告诉人们正在发生的事情。足以使生活更加舒适的发明或许要数缝纫机了。伊莱亚斯·豪（Elias Howe, Jr.，1819~1867）是第一个造出真正可用的缝纫机的人。其他发明家们在他的基础上做出了改进，使得缝纫机还能够缝制布料以外的东西，比如皮革。农业机械这时得到了广泛的应用。马拉收割机已经得到了很大改进，无数的机械被发明了出来，使农业劳动更容易、更经济。数以百计的日用品，比如摩擦火柴、胶鞋，这些年也都投入了使用。简而言之，从杰克逊就任总统到南方各州退出联邦之间的这三十年是进步巨大的年代。但是这些进步几乎完全局限在北方。在南方，1860年的生活几乎和1830年——甚至是1800年——完全一样。正如一名南方的演说家提到南方时所说的那样："现代文明的激流和漩涡与它擦肩而过。"

伊莱亚斯·豪

## 【ORIGINAL TEXT】

**361. Growth of the Country.**—The United States was now three times as large as it was at Jefferson's election. It contained over three million square miles of land. About one-third of this great area was settled. In the sixty years of the century the population had increased even faster than the area had increased. In 1800 there were five and a half million people living in the United States. In 1860 there were over thirty-one million people within its borders. Of these nearly five millions were white immigrants. More than half of these immigrants had come in the last ten years, and they had practically all of them settled in the free states of the North. Of the whole population of thirty-one millions only twelve millions lived in the slave states, and of these more than four millions were negro slaves.

**362. Change of Political Power.**—The control of Congress had now passed into the hands of the free states of the North. The majority of the Representatives had long been from the free states. Now more Senators came from the North than from the South. This was due to the admission of new states. Texas (1845) was the last slave state to be admitted to the Union. Two years later the admission of Wisconsin gave the free states as many votes in the Senate as the slave states had. In 1850 the admission of California gave the free states a majority of two votes in the Senate. This majority was increased to four by the admission of Minnesota in 1858, and to six by the admission of Oregon in 1859. The control of Congress had slipped forever from the grasp of the slave states.

**363. The Cities.**—The tremendous increase in manufacturing, in farming, and in trading brought about a great increase in foreign commerce. This in turn led to the building up of great cities in the North and the West. These were New York and Chicago; and they grew rapidly because they formed the two ends of the line of communication between the East and the West by the Mohawk Valley. New York now contained over eight hundred thousand inhabitants. It had more people within its limits than lived in the whole state of South Carolina. The most rapid growth was seen in the case of Chicago. In 1840 there were only five thousand people in that city; it now contained one hundred and nine thousand inhabitants. Cincinnati and St. Louis, each with one hundred and sixty thousand, were still the largest cities of the West, and St. Louis was the largest city in any slave state. New Orleans, with nearly as many people as St. Louis, was the only large city in the South.

**364. The States.**—As it was with the cities so it was with the states—the North had grown beyond the South. In 1790 Virginia had as many inhabitants as the states of New York and Pennsylvania put together. In 1860 Virginia had only about one-quarter as many inhabitants as these two states. Indeed, in 1860 New York had nearly four million inhabitants, or nearly as many inhabitants as the whole United States in 1791. But the growth of the states of the Northwest had been even more remarkable. Ohio now had a million more people than Virginia and stood third in population among the states of the Union. Illinois was the fourth state and Indiana the sixth. Even more interesting are the facts brought out by a study of the map showing the density of population or the number of people to the square mile in the several states. It appears that in 1860 Ohio, Pennsylvania, Maryland, Delaware, New Jersey, New York, Connecticut, Rhode Island, and Massachusetts each had over forty-five inhabitants to the square mile, while not a single Southern state had as many as forty-five inhabitants to the square mile. This shows us at once that although the Southern states were larger in extent than the Northern states, they were much less powerful.

**365. City Life.**—In the old days the large towns were just like the small towns except that they were larger. Life in them was just about the same as in the smaller places. Now, however, there was a great difference. In the first place the city could afford to have a great many things the smaller town could not pay for. In the second place it must have certain things or its people would die of disease or be killed as they walked the streets. For these reasons the streets of the Northern cities were paved and lighted and were guarded by policemen. Then, too, great sewers carried away the refuse of the city, and enormous iron pipes brought fresh water to every one within its limits. Horse-cars and omnibuses carried its inhabitants from one part of the city to another, and the railroads brought them food from the surrounding country.

**366. Transportation.**—Between 1849 and 1858 twenty-one thousand miles of railroad were built in the United States, In 1860 there were more than thirty thousand miles of railroad in actual operation. In 1850 one could not go from New York to Albany without leaving the railroad and going on board a steamboat. In 1860 one continuous line of rails ran from New York City to the Mississippi River. Traveling was still uncomfortable according to our ideas. The cars were rudely made and jolted horribly. One train ran only a comparatively short distance. Then the traveler had to alight, get something to eat, and see his baggage placed on another train. Still, with all its discomforts, traveling in the worst of cars was better than traveling in the old stagecoaches. Many more steamboats were used, especially on the Great Lakes and the Western rivers.

**367. Education.**—The last thirty years had also been years of progress in learning. Many colleges were founded, especially in the Northwest. There was still no institution which deserved the name of university. But more attention was being paid to the sciences and to the education of men for the professions of law and medicine. The newspapers also took on their modern form. The New York Herald, founded in 1835, was the first real newspaper. But the New York Tribune, edited by Horace Greeley, had more influence than any other paper in the country. Greeley was odd in many ways, but he was one of the ablest men of the time. He called for a liberal policy in the distribution of the public lands and was forever saying, "Go West, young man, go West." The magazines were now very much better than in former years, and America's foremost writers were doing some of their best work.

**368. Progress of Invention.**—The electric telegraph was now in common use. It enabled the newspapers to tell the people what was going on as they never had done before. Perhaps the invention that did as much as any one thing to make life easier was the sewing machine. Elias Howe was the first man to make a really practicable sewing machine. Other inventors improved upon it, and also made machines to sew other things than cloth, as leather. Agricultural machinery was now in common use. The horse reaper had been much improved, and countless machines had been invented to make agricultural labor more easy and economical. Hundreds of homely articles, as friction matches and rubber shoes, came into use in these years. In short, the thirty years from Jackson's inauguration to the secession of the Southern states were years of great progress. But this progress was confined almost wholly to the North. In the South, living in 1860 was about the same as it had been in 1830, or even in 1800. As a Southern orator said of the South, "The rush and whirl of modern civilization passed her by."

CHAPTER 36

# 1860—1861年，退出联邦

## SECESSION, 1860~1861

369. 公元1860年，共和党提名——关于共和党提名竞选总统的人选，有四个名字特别被提及。那就是西华德、蔡斯、卡梅伦（Simon Cameron，1799~1889）和林肯。其中，西华德的名气最大。他在关于《1850年妥协案》的辩论中曾宣称存在比宪法“更高级的法律”，也就是“人们心中的自然法”。在另一次演讲中，他把关于奴隶制斗争称为“无法抑制的冲突”。这些措辞让他得到了反对奴隶制的人的爱戴。但是，它们让许多温和派共和党人无法拥护他。俄亥俄州的参议员蔡斯也曾直言不讳地谴责奴隶制。来自宾夕法尼亚州的参议员卡梅伦是一个能干的政治领袖。但是，这些人都因“太惹人关注而不能当好一名总统候选人”。他们树敌太多了。林肯也曾有过直率的言论。但是，他在国内政坛一直都不显眼。他比任何其他候选人都更有可能吸引温和派选民。经过一场激烈的竞争，他获得了提名。共和党的党纲声明该党无意干涉各州既存的奴隶制；但是它也宣称该党反对奴隶制的扩张。这个纲领支持以国家开支来进行国内改良。它也赞成保护性制度。

威廉·亨利·西华德

370. 民主党提名——民主党在南卡罗来纳州的查尔斯顿召开了大会。

北方民主党和南方民主党的分歧很快就显露了出来。北方民主党愿意接受并执行德雷德·斯科特案的判决。可南方民主党要求党纲必须对积极保护各准州的奴隶制做出承诺。而这一点，北方民主党并不认同。于是，会议就此中断，并在巴尔的摩继续召开。不过代表们还是没能在那里达成共识。最终，他们提名了两个总统候选人。北方民主党提名道格拉斯，并在党纲中提倡“人民主权论”。南方民主党则提名了肯塔基州的约翰·C. 布雷肯里奇，并在自己的党纲中提倡州权，还提倡由联邦政府来保护各准州的奴隶制。

**371. 立宪联邦党**——除这三个候选人外，各党中谨慎而胆小的人联合起来组建了“立宪联邦党”[①]。他们提名田纳西州州长约翰·贝尔（John Bell，1796~1869）为总统候选人。他们在党纲中声明支持维护宪法与联邦，对奴隶制却避而不谈。

**372. 公元1860年，林肯当选总统**——在四名候选人参选而民主党又处于无可救药的分裂状态的前提下，林肯的当选几乎没有任何悬念。他赢得了除密苏里州和新泽西州之外的所有北方州的支持。他共获得了180张选票。布雷肯里奇赢得了除弗吉尼亚州、肯塔基州和田纳西州这三个“边界州”之外所有南方州的支持。他获得了72张选票。贝尔赢得了三个南方“边界州”的支持。道格拉斯则赢得了密苏里州和新泽西州的支持。林肯毫无悬念地当选为总统。他获得了大多数总统

亚伯拉罕·林肯
第十六任美国总统（1861~1865）

① 该党派主要由以前的辉格党和一无所知党成员组成。

选举人的选票。但是，他的竞选对手获得了更多普通选民的投票。因此，他是被少数选民选出的总统。

**373. 北方和南方**——林肯是少数人选出的总统，而且是被一个地区的人民选举出来的。美国历史上还有些总统是被少数人选举出来的。但是，林肯是第一个由一个地区的人民选出来的总统。此外，共和党没有获得众议院的多数席位，参议院也还控制在民主党手中。共和党至少两年之内[①]无法实施他们的主张。他们不能废除《堪萨斯-内布拉斯加法案》。他们不能接纳堪萨斯作为自由州加入联邦。哪怕是实施一条本党的政策，他们也做不到。他们在自己的党纲中声明他们无意干涉各州的奴隶制。林肯也曾反复声明，国会无权干预各州的奴隶制。这一切，南方的领袖们都知道。但是他们依然坚定地认为：是时候退出联邦，建立一个"南方邦联"了。所有南端的州第一次联合了起来。无论林肯以及共和党人说什么，南方奴隶主们都对奴隶制处于危险之中深信不疑。在建议退出联邦这件事上时，他们中的许多人认为，通过这个方式，他们可以迫使北方人接受他们的条件作为修复联邦的代价。但是，政治领袖们从未犯过比这更严重的错误。

**374. 公元1860年11月，退出联邦的威胁**——宪法允许各州选择它们认为合适的总统选举人。起初，这些总统选举人通常是由各州的议会挑选的。但是随着时间的推移，几乎所有州的总统选举人都变成由普通选民投票选举，只有一个州例外。这个坚持旧方式的州是南卡罗来纳州，它的总统选举人仍然由议会选出。1860年，南卡罗来纳州的议会履行了这项职责，随后继续开会以观望总统选举的走向。当林肯的当选已成定局的时

① 根据美国宪法第一条第三款，参议院每两年改选三分之一的议员。

候，南卡罗来纳州的议会就召开了一次州议会以考虑退出联邦的问题。在其他南方各州中，也有人反对退出联邦。尤其是在佐治亚州，以亚历山大·H. 斯蒂芬斯（Alexander Hamilton Stephens，1812~1883）为首的人反对退出联邦。他认为退出联邦“是最不可理喻的行动”。然而，他还是提出了一个议案，建议召开一次大会。事实上，南端的所有州纷纷效仿了佐治亚州的做法，召开了大会。

亚历山大·汉密尔顿·斯蒂芬斯

**375. 克里滕登妥协方案**——许多人希望即使这时也有可能以妥协阻止南方各州退出联邦。布坎南总统提议制定一条宪法修正案，以保证蓄奴州和蓄奴准州的奴隶制的安全。但是，共和党不太可能同意这个建议。最有希望的方案是肯塔基州的参议员克里滕登（John Jordan Crittenden，1787~1863）向国会提出的。他提议，应采纳如下各条宪法修正案：（1）执行《密苏里妥协》的政策；（2）根据各州人民的意愿规定该州为自由州或蓄奴州；（3）按照其逃亡奴隶的价值向奴隶主做出赔偿。国会谨慎地考虑了这个方案，但是最终还是拒绝了它——就在林肯就任总统的两天前。

**376. 公元1860~1861年，七个州退出联邦**——1860年12月17日，南卡罗来纳州大会在查尔斯顿的“退出联邦大厅”[①]召开。三天后，这次大会通过了一则宣言，宣布“此时存在于南卡罗来纳州和其他各州之间的在美利坚合众国名义下的联盟就此解除”。另外六个州不久也加入了南卡罗来

① 该建筑物原名为圣·安德鲁大厅（St. Andrew's Hall），是当时查尔斯顿著名的公共场所，当地上流社会人士常在此举行各种社交宴会，当地的重要政治性会议也常在此召开。

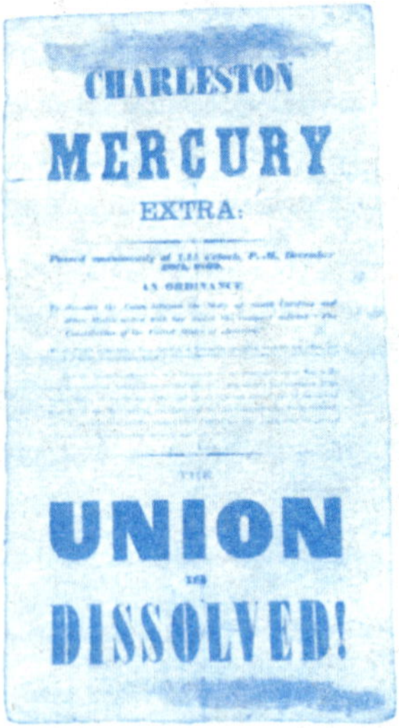
CHARLESTON
MERCURY
EXTRA:
UNION
DISSOLVED!

《南部各州脱离联邦宣言》

刊登于南卡罗来纳州的报纸《查尔斯顿信使》上

纳州的行列。它们是密西西比州、佛罗里达州、亚拉巴马州、佐治亚州、路易斯安那州和得克萨斯州。

**377. 美利坚联众国**——这些州接下来要做的事情，就是联合起来组建一个邦联。这项工作由一个议会完成，该议会的代表是由七个退出联邦的州开会选出的。这些代表在亚拉巴马的蒙哥马利集合开会。他们制定的新宪法很像合众国的宪法。但是，他们非常慎重地做出了明确的规定：该邦联的每个成员都是一个独立自主的州。他们还以更大程度的慎重做出规定：要用一切方法保护奴隶制。密西西比州的杰斐逊·戴维斯（Jefferson Davis，1808~1889）被选为临时总统。亚历山大·H. 斯蒂芬斯被选为临时副总统。

**378. 戴维斯和斯蒂芬斯的主张**——戴维斯宣称，林肯已经“向我们（南方）的制度做出了一个明确的宣战公告”。他的当选是“基于地方性的敌意”。如果“战争必然到来，它一定会在北方的土地而不是南方的土地上打响……我们将把战争带到……那些地方，在那里，剑与火炬的猎物在北方人口密集的城市里等待着我们的军队”。斯蒂芬斯则宣称，这个新政府的“基础和基石在于这一伟大真理——即：黑人不与白人平等”。

杰斐逊·戴维斯

379. 北方的犹豫——起初，当戴维斯声称北方人不愿打仗的时候，他似乎是正确的。统帅陆军的斯科特将军提议，应该允许“犯错的姐妹们”“平静地离开”。西华德似乎也持同样的看法。废奴主义者也乐于接受蓄奴州退出联邦。例如，霍勒斯·格里利写道，如果那些州选择组成一个独立的国家，“他们完全拥有这样做的道德权利”。然而布坎南总统则认为，根据宪法来看，任何州都不得退出联邦。但是，如果一个州退出联邦，他没有任何办法迫使它重返联邦。于是，他耐心地静观其变，没有采取任何行动。

## 【ORIGINAL TEXT】

**369. The Republican Nomination, 1860.**—Four names were especially mentioned in connection with the Republican nomination for President. These were Seward, Chase, Cameron, and Lincoln. Seward was the best known of them all. In the debates on the Compromise of 1850 he had declared that there was “a higher law” than the Constitution, namely, “the law of nature in men’s hearts.” In another speech he had termed the slavery contest “the irrepressible conflict.” These phrases endeared him to the anti-slavery men. But they made it impossible for many moderate Republicans to follow him. Senator Chase of Ohio had also been very outspoken in his condemnation of slavery. Senator Cameron of Pennsylvania was an able political leader. But all of these men were “too conspicuous to make a good candidate.” They had made many enemies. Lincoln had spoken freely. But he had never been prominent in national politics.

He was more likely to attract the votes of moderate men than either of the other candidates. After a fierce contest he was nominated. The Republican platform stated that there was no intention to interfere with slavery in the states where it existed; but it declared the party's opposition to the extension of slavery. The platform favored internal improvements at the national expense. It also approved the protective system.

**370. The Democratic Nominations.**—The Democratic convention met at Charleston, South Carolina. It was soon evident that the Northern Democrats and the Southern Democrats could not agree. The Northerners were willing to accept the Dred Scott decision and to carry it out. But the Southerners demanded that the platform should pledge the party actively to protect slavery in the territories. To this the Northerners would not agree. So the convention broke up to meet again at Baltimore. But there the delegates could come to no agreement. In the end two candidates were named. The Northerners nominated Douglas on a platform advocating "popular sovereignty." The Southerners nominated John C. Breckinridge of Kentucky. In their platform they advocated states' rights, and the protection of slavery in the territories by the federal government.

**371. The Constitutional Union Party.**—Besides these three candidates, cautious and timid men of all parties united to form the Constitutional Union party. They nominated Governor John Bell of Tennessee for President. In their platform they declared for the maintenance of the Constitution and the Union, regardless of slavery.

**372. Lincoln elected President, 1860.**—With four candidates in the field and the Democratic party hopelessly divided, there could be little doubt of Lincoln's election. He carried every Northern state except Missouri and New Jersey. He received one hundred and eighty electoral notes. Breckenridge carried every Southern state except the "border states" of Virginia, Kentucky, and Tennessee, and received seventy-two electoral votes. Bell carried the three "border" Southern states and Douglas carried Missouri and New Jersey. There was no doubt as to Lincoln's election. He had received a great majority of the electoral votes. But his opponents had received more popular votes than he had received. He was therefore elected by a minority of the voters.

**373. The North and the South.**—Lincoln had been elected by a minority of the people. He had been elected by the people of one section. Other Presidents had been chosen by minorities. But Lincoln was the first man to be chosen President by the people of one section. The Republicans, moreover, had not elected a majority of the members of the House of Representatives, and the Senate was still in the hands of the Democrats. For two years at least the Republicans could not carry out their ideas. They could not repeal the Kansas-Nebraska Act. They could not admit Kansas to the Union as a free state. They could not carry out one bit of their policy. In their platform they had declared that they had no intention to interfere with slavery in the states. Lincoln had said over and over again that Congress had no fight to meddle with slavery in the states. The Southern leaders knew all these things. But they made up their minds that now the time had come to secede from the Union and to establish a Southern Confederacy. For the first time all the southernmost states were united. No matter what Lincoln and the Republicans might say, the Southern slaveholders believed that slavery was in danger. In advising secession, many of them thought that by this means they could force the Northerners to accept their terms as the price of a restored Union. Never were political leaders more mistaken.

**374. Threats of Secession, November, 1860.**—The Constitution permits each state to choose presidential electors as it sees fit. At the outset these electors had generally been chosen by the state legislatures. But, in the course of time, all the states save one had come to choose them by popular vote. The one state that held to the old way was South Carolina. Its legislature still chose the state's presidential electors. In 1860 the South Carolina legislature did this duty and then remained in session to see which way the election would go. When Lincoln's election was certain, it called a state convention to consider the question of seceding from the United States. In other Southern states there was some opposition to secession. In Georgia, especially, Alexander H. Stephens led the opposition. He said that secession "was the height of madness." Nevertheless he moved a resolution for a convention. Indeed, all the southernmost states followed the example of South Carolina and summoned conventions.

**375. The Crittenden Compromise Plan.**—Many men hoped that even now secession might be stopped by some compromise. President Buchanan suggested an amendment to the Constitution, securing slavery in the states and territories. It was unlikely that the Republicans would agree to this suggestion. The most hopeful plan was brought forward in Congress by Senator Crittenden of Kentucky. He proposed that amendments to the Constitution should be adopted: (1) to carry out the principle of the Missouri Compromise; (2) to provide that states should be free or slave as their people should determine; and (3) to pay the slave owners the value of runaway slaves. This plan was carefully considered by Congress, and was finally rejected only two days before Lincoln's inauguration.

**376. Secession of Seven States, 1860~61.**—The South Carolina convention met in Secession Hall, Charleston, on December 17, 1860. Three days later it adopted a declaration "that the union now subsisting between South Carolina and other states, under the name of the United States of America, is hereby dissolved." Six other states soon joined South Carolina. These were Mississippi, Florida, Alabama, Georgia, Louisiana, and Texas.

**377. The "Confederate States of America".**—The next step was for these states to join together to form a confederation. This work was done by a convention of delegates chosen by the conventions of the seven seceding states. These delegates met at Montgomery, Alabama. Their new constitution closely resembled the Constitution of the United States. But great care was taken to make it perfectly clear that each member of the Confederacy was a sovereign state. Exceeding care was also taken that slavery should be protected in every way. Jefferson Davis of Mississippi was chosen provisional president, and Alexander H. Stephens provisional vice-president.

**378. Views of Davis and Stephens.**—Davis declared that Lincoln had "made a distinct declaration of war upon our (Southern) institutions." His election was "upon the basis of sectional hostility." If "war must come, it must be on Northern and not on Southern soil ... We will carry war ... where food for the sword and torch awaits our armies in the densely populated cities" of the North. For his part, Stephens said the new government's "foundations are laid, its cornerstone rests, upon the great truth that the negro is not equal to the white man."

**379. Hesitation in the North.**—At first it seemed as if Davis was right when he said the Northerners would not fight. General Scott, commanding the army, suggested that the "erring sisters" should be allowed to "depart in peace," and Seward seemed to think the same way. The Abolitionists welcomed the secession of the slave states. Horace Greeley, for instance, Wrote that if those states chose to form an independent nation, "they had a clear moral right so to do." For his part, President Buchanan thought that no state could constitutionally secede. But if a state should secede, he saw no way to compel it to come back to the Union. So he sat patiently by and did nothing.

# QUESTIONS AND TOPICS
# 问题与论题

## CHAPTER 35

§§ 361, 362.—a. Compare the area and population of the United States in 1800 and in 1860.

b. Compare the white population of the North and the South. Were all the Southern whites slave owners?

c. Why had the control of the House passed to the free states? Did a white man in the North and in the South have proportionally the same representation in the House? Why?

d. What change in the control of the Senate had taken place? Why? Why was this change so important?

§§ 363, 364.—a. What had caused the growth of the Northern cities? Why were there so few large cities in the slave states?

b. How had the population of the states changed since 1790? What had caused the growth of the Northwest?

c. Where was there the greatest density of population? Why?

§§ 365, 366.—a. Describe the change of life in the cities. What arrangements were made for the comfort and health of the people?

b. How had railroads increased, and what improvements had been made?

§§ 367, 368.—a. Of what use are newspapers? How do they influence the opinions of the people? What policy did Horace Greeley uphold? Why?

b. Who were some of the important writers? Mention two works of each.

c. What influence did the telegraph have? Was this important?

d. Describe some of the other inventions.

e. Why had this progress been confined mainly to the North?

## CHAPTER 36

§ 369.—a. Who were the leading Republican candidates?

b. Why was Lincoln nominated? What is the meaning of the phrase "too conspicuous"?

c. What did Seward mean by saying that there was a "higher law" than the Constitution? Why was the slavery contest "irrepressible"?

d. What declaration was made by the Republican party as to slavery? Compare this policy with the Wilmot Proviso.

§§ 370, 371.—a. What divisions took place in the Democratic party? Why?

b. What candidates were named? What policy did each uphold?

c. How had the demands of the Southerners concerning slavery increased?

d. What third party was formed? By whom? What does the name show?

§§ 372, 373.—a. What was the result of the election?

b. What was there peculiar in Lincoln's election?

c. Were the Southern states in any particular danger?

d. Why should the Southerners have felt so strongly about this election? What was their hope in threatening secession?

§§ 374, 375.—a. Give arguments for and against secession. In what other question similar to this had South Carolina led?

b. Were the people of the South generally in favor of secession?

c. What compromise did Buchanan suggest? What do you think of the wisdom of the plan?

d. Explain carefully the points in Crittenden's plan. Discuss its value.

§§ 376, 377.—a. Could one state dissolve the Union?

b. What other states followed South Carolina?

c. What government was formed by them? What two points were especially emphasized in their constitution? Why these?

§§ 378, 379.—a. What statement did Davis make as to Lincoln? Was it true or false? Give your reasons.

b. Why did Davis advocate war on Northern soil?

c. Why was there such hesitation in the North? State the opinions of Scott, Greeley, and Buchanan.

d. What would Jackson probably have done had he been President?

## GENERAL QUESTIONS
## 综合性问题

a. Was the South justified in thinking that the North would yield? Give illustrations to support your view.

b. Were the years 1857~61 more or less "critical" than the years 1783~87? Why?

c. How was the South dependent upon the North?

# SUGGESTIONS TO THE TEACHER
# 给教师的建议

The first chapter of this part should be taught very slowly, and at each point the contrast between the North and the South should be pointed out. In Chapter 36 the changed attitude of the Southern politicians should be noted and their demands clearly set forth. The fact that the slave owners while a minority in the South dominated public opinion should be pointed out.

In considering the question of secession it will be well to review the Kentucky and Virginia Resolutions, the Hartford Convention, and the Nullification episode. The weakness of Pierce and Buchanan may be contrasted with the strength of Jackson, and will serve as an introduction to the study of Lincoln's character.

# 第十三篇
# PART XIII

## 1861—1865年，统一战争

## THE WAR FOR THE UNION, 1861-1865

## Books for Study and Reading
## 研究和阅读用书

**References.**—Dodge's *Bird's–Eye View*; Scribner's *Popular History*, IV and V; McMaster's *School History*. chap, xxix (the cost of the war); Lincoln's *Inaugurals and Gettysburg Address*.

**Home Readings.**—*Battles and Leaders of the Civil War* (composed largely of articles that had previously appeared in the *Century Magazine*; Whittier's *Barbara Frietchie*; Coffin's *Winning his Way and other stories*; Soley's *Sailor Boys of '61*; Trowbridge's *Drummer Boy and other stories*; Read's *Sheridan 's Ride*; Champlin's *Young Folks ' History of the War for the Union*).

CHAPTER 37

# 1861年，民众的奋起

## THE RISING OF THE PEOPLES, 1861

380. 林肯的就职——1861年3月4日，林肯总统发表了第一届就职演说。他在演说中宣布："联邦比宪法存在的时间要长得多……任何州都不得按照自己的意愿合法地脱离联邦……按照宪法和法律，联邦是不可分裂的……我将负责使联邦法律在所有的州都得到忠实的执行。"关于奴隶制，他"无意……干涉各州既存的奴隶制"。他甚至不反对制定一条宪法修正案以禁止联邦政府干涉各州的奴隶制。但是，林肯决定维持、保护并捍卫合众国宪法。

381. 公元1861年4月，萨姆特堡沦陷——林肯的决心的坚定程度不久就受到了考验。当南卡罗来纳州退出联邦时，统帅合众国驻查尔斯顿陆军的安德森少校（Robert Anderson，1805~1871）从陆上要塞撤到了建立在港口的一个浅滩上的萨姆特堡。他手下只有八十名作战人员，而且严重缺乏食物和弹药。布坎南派遣了一艘蒸汽船——"西部之星号"——向查尔斯顿输送士兵和给养。但是，南部邦联军队向它开了火，它没有卸下士兵和给养就逃走了。林肯等了一个月，希望那些退出联邦的州能主动返回联邦。

罗伯特·安德森

随后，他决定向安德森少校派送给养，并向南卡罗来纳州州长告知他的决定。紧接着，南部邦联就向萨姆特堡开了火（4月12日）。4月14日，安德森少校投降。次日，林肯总统发布公告，召集了七万五千名志愿军。

382. 北方的奋起——这已经不再是一个让“犯错的姐妹们”平静离开的问题了。南方人已经向“昔日荣耀”[①]开火了。这已经不再是一个关于奴隶制扩张问题的争论了。此时的问题是联邦的存亡。道格拉斯立即声明支持联邦，前总统布坎南与富兰克林·皮尔斯也做了同样的声明。在密西西比河流域，成百上千的人要么同情奴隶主，要么对关于奴隶制的纷争毫不关心。但是在南部邦联攻击联邦的那一刻，他们就都奋起捍卫他们的国家和国旗了。

内战时期使用的“昔日荣耀”

383. 更多州退出联邦——南方人纷纷投到南部邦联的旗下，又有四个州加入了退出联邦的行列。它们是阿肯色州、田纳西州、北卡罗来纳州和弗吉尼亚州。弗吉尼亚人民在退出联邦问题上有巨大的分歧。最终，弗吉尼亚州退出了联邦，但是弗吉尼亚州西部也同时从弗吉尼亚州分离出去，并于两年后作为西弗吉尼亚州加入了联邦。上述四个“边界州”退出了联邦；但是另外四个“边界州”仍然留在联邦之内。它们是特拉华州、马里兰州、肯塔基州和密苏里州。

384. 边界州——马里兰州和肯塔基州的人民在退出联邦这个问题上

① “昔日荣耀”（Old Glory）是美国人对星条旗的爱称。

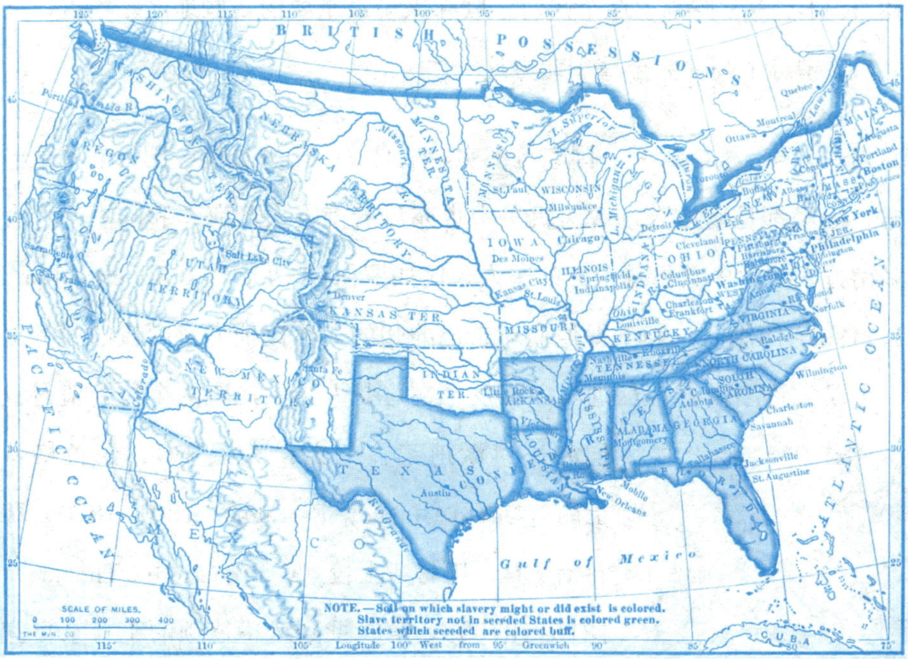


蓄奴州和退出联邦的州

分成了势均力敌的两派。他们甚至试图自立为中立州。但是他们的中立对于退出联邦的州会非常有利，因而这是不能允许的。林肯始终如一的温和态度和肯塔基州许多明智的领袖的爱国之心使这个州留在了联邦。不过，马里兰州对保卫华盛顿非常重要，因此必须采取更为积极的措施。在密苏里州，一个势力庞大而激进的政党希望加入邦联，但是，南部联邦的两名支持者——弗兰克·P. 布莱尔（Francis Preston Blair, Jr.，1821~1875）和纳撒尼尔·莱昂（Nathaniel Lyon,

弗兰克·P. 布莱尔

纳撒尼尔·莱昂

1818~1861）——控制了这个州对于联邦来说最重要的一些地区。不过，一年之后，密苏里州才完全属于北方这一边。

385. 保卫华盛顿——国家首都实际上是一个南方城镇，因为它的大多数常住居民都是南方人，政府机关中也充斥着南方人。海军和陆军里也有很多南方人。大多数出身南方的军人，比如罗伯特·E. 李（Robert Edward Lee，1807~1870），都觉得他们对自己的州的义务比他们对国旗的义务更大。但是，许多南方官员则与之相反。在这些人当中，有两个特别值得我们心怀感激地记住的人：大卫·G. 法拉格特上尉（David Glasgow Farragut，1801~1870）和乔治·H. 托马斯上校（George Henry Thomas，1816~1870）。第一批到达华盛顿的士兵来自宾夕法尼亚州；但是，他们来的时候没有装备武器。不久，马萨诸塞州第六军团也赶来了。在穿过巴尔的摩时，这个军团遭到了袭击。几名士兵丧生，其他人也受伤了。这一天是1861年4月19日——列克星敦之役和康科德之役的纪念日。这是这场战争中的第一个流血事件。

罗伯特·爱德华·李

## 【Original Text】

**380. Lincoln's Inauguration.**—On March 4, 1861, President Lincoln made his first inaugural address. In it he declared: "The Union is much older than the Constitution ... No state upon its own motion can lawfully get out of the Union ... In view of the Constitution and the laws the Union is unbroken ... I shall take care that the laws of the Union be faithfully executed in all the states." As to slavery, he had "no purpose ... to interfere with the institution of slavery in the states where it exists." He even saw no objection to adopt an amendment of the Constitution to prohibit the Federal government from interfering with slavery in the states. But he was resolved to preserve, protect, and defend the Constitution of the United States.

**381. Fall of Fort Sumter, April, 1861.**—The strength of Lincoln's resolve was soon tested. When South Carolina seceded, Major Anderson, commanding the United States forces at Charleston, withdrew from the land forts to Fort Sumter, built on a shoal in the harbor. He had with him only eighty fighting men and was sorely in need of food and ammunition. Buchanan sent a steamer, the *Star of the West*, to Charleston with supplies and soldiers. But the Confederates fired on her, and she steamed away without landing the soldiers or the supplies. Lincoln waited a month, hoping that the secessionists would come back to the Union of their own accord. Then he decided to send supplies to Major Anderson and told the governor of South Carolina of his decision. Immediately (April 12) the Confederates opened fire on Fort Sumter. On April 14 Anderson surrendered. The next day President Lincoln issued a proclamation calling for seventy-five thousand volunteers.

**382. Rising of the North.** —There was no longer a question of letting the "erring sisters" depart in peace. The Southerners had fired on "Old Glory. "There was no longer a dispute over the extension of slavery. The question was now whether the Union should perish or should live. Douglas at once came out for the Union and so did the former Presidents, Buchanan and Franklin Pierce. In the Mississippi Valley hundreds of thousands of men either sympathized with the slaveholders or cared nothing about the slavery dispute. But the moment the Confederates attacked the Union, they rose in defense of their country and their flag.

**383. More Seceders.**—The Southerners flocked to the standards of the Confederacy, and four more states joined the ranks of secession. These were Arkansas, Tennessee, North Carolina, and Virginia. In Virginia the people were sharply divided on the question of secession. Finally Virginia seceded, but the western Virginians, in their turn, seceded from Virginia and two years later were admitted to the Union as the state of West Virginia. Four "border states" had seceded; but four other "border states" were still within the Union. These were Delaware, Maryland, Kentucky, and Missouri.

**384. The Border States.**—The people of Maryland and of Kentucky were evenly divided on the question of secession. They even tried to set up as neutral states. But their neutrality would have been so greatly to the advantage of the seceders that this could not be allowed. Lincoln's firm moderation and the patriotism of many wise leaders in Kentucky saved that state to the Union. But Maryland was so important to the defense of Washington that more energetic means had to be used. In Missouri, a large and active party wished to join the Confederacy. But two Union men, Frank P. Blair and Nathaniel Lyon, held the most important portions of the state for the Union. It was not until a year later, however, that Missouri was safe on the Northern side.

**385. To the Defense of Washington.**—The national capital was really a Southern town, for most of the permanent residents were Southerners, and the offices were filled with Southern men. In the army and navy, too, were very many Southerners. Most of them, as Robert E. Lee, felt that their duty to their state was greater than their duty to their flag. But many Southern officers felt differently. Among these were two men whose names should be held in grateful remembrance, Captain David G. Farragut and Colonel George H. Thomas. The first soldiers to arrive in Washington were from Pennsylvania; but they came unarmed. Soon they were followed by the Sixth Massachusetts. In passing through Baltimore this regiment was attacked. Several men were killed, others were wounded. This was on April 19, 1861,—the anniversary of the battles of Lexington and Concord. It was the first bloodshed of the war.

## CHAPTER 38

# 1861~1862年，从布尔溪到默夫里斯伯勒

## BULL RUN TO MURFREESBORO’, 1861~1862

386. 战斗的自然条件——事实证明，打倒加入南部邦联的各州是非常困难的。阿勒格尼山脉把南方分成了两个大战场。深且急的河流从阿勒格尼山脉流入大西洋或密西西比河。这些河流中的任意一条都是一道天然屏障。第一道屏障是波托马克河与俄亥俄河。当南部邦联从这道屏障被击退后，他们很快就能找到另一道稍微靠南一些的同样优良的屏障。而且，南方只有部分地区被开发过。好走的路不多，而糟糕的路却不少。地图上只标出了好路。按照这些地图，北方的士兵们不得不长途跋涉，而南方军队经常从北方人不知道的小路行军，因此他们只要行进较短的距离就可以往返两个战场或两个重要据点。

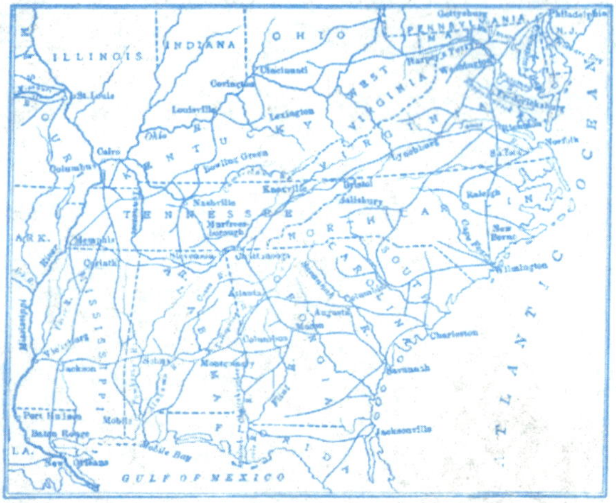

南方的道路与河流

387. 公元1861年7月，布尔溪战役——北方士兵渡过波托马克河到达弗吉尼亚州，发现南部邦联军驻守在了马纳萨斯路口附近的布尔溪。另一支北方军队从哈珀渡口向谢南多厄河谷挺进。他们同样发现一支南部邦联

约瑟夫·埃格尔斯顿·约翰斯顿

军队挡住了他们的去路。联邦当时的作战计划非常明确：麦克道威尔将军（Irvin McDowell, 1818~1885）在布尔溪攻打南部邦联军，与此同时，帕特森将军（Robert Patterson, 1792~1881）在谢南多厄河谷攻打南部邦联军，并使这支南部邦联军疲于应战而不能去支援他们在布尔溪的同伴。结果，事情的进展与设想的截然不同，因为帕特森将军撤退了。这让谢南多厄河谷的南部邦联将军约翰斯顿（Joseph Eggleston Johnston, 1807~1891）得以抽身去支援在布尔溪节节败退的南部邦联军。麦克道威尔猛烈地进攻，攻破了邦联军的防线；但是，他无法坚守住他的阵地。联南部邦军起初是缓慢地撤退。随后，他们开始惊慌失措，仓皇逃回了华盛顿。第一场战役以联邦的惨败而告终。

乔治·B. 麦克莱伦

**388. 波托马克军**——布尔溪战役在弗吉尼亚东部展开的同时，联邦军队在西弗吉尼亚打了一些胜仗。这些胜仗是乔治·B. 麦克莱伦将军（George Brinton McClellan, 1826~1885）指挥的。他当时来到了华盛顿，接管守卫首都前线的军队。在秋季、冬季和春季期间，他极其细心且富于技巧地训练了他的士兵。1862年3月，这支波托马克军作为一支训练有素的部队离开了他们的营地。

**389. 北弗吉尼亚军**——与此同时，南部邦联政府已经召集了大量

托马斯·乔纳森·杰克逊

士兵。南方达到参战年龄的白人远远少于北方。但是在南方，达到参战年龄的白人都能够被配置在前线，因为黑人奴隶能生产军队需要的食物，也能完成修筑要塞的繁重劳动。南部邦联的首都这时定在了弗吉尼亚州詹姆斯河畔的里士满。负责保卫这个首都的军队被称为“北弗吉尼亚军”。约瑟夫·E．约翰斯顿是这支军队的指挥官；但是罗伯特·E．李和托马斯·J．杰克逊（Thomas Jonathan Jackson，1824~1863）（“石墙”杰克逊[①]）才是这支军队中最有才干的军官。

390. 半岛作战方案——波托马克河与詹姆斯河之间的地区河网密布，有拉帕汉诺克河、马塔伯尼河，以及帕门基河，而且该地区的一部分是荒野。麦克莱伦计划率军经水路到达詹姆斯河、约克河与帕门基河之间的半岛。随后他就能踏上一条通向里士满的畅通无阻的道路。这条路上没有任何需要与敌军争夺的河。而约翰斯顿将不得不离开他位于布尔溪的营地并向南进军以保卫里士满。这个方案的重大缺陷是：约翰斯顿有可能不去迎战麦克莱伦，反而去攻打华盛顿。杰克逊将军也驻扎在谢南多厄河谷。他也有可能沿着该河谷下行，渡过波托马克河，占领华盛顿。于是，政府留下了七万五千名麦克莱伦军的士兵以保卫联邦首都。

391. “莫尼特号”和“梅里马克号”——3月8日，一艘外形怪异

① 杰克逊在之前的布尔溪战役中给己方军队提供了有力的支援，被支援的将军为了激励士兵们，说道：“看，杰克逊像一面石墙一样屹立在那里。（Look, there stands Jackson like a stone wall.）”从此，杰克逊就获得了“石墙”的绰号，他的部队也被称为“石墙旅”。

的船驶出了弗吉尼亚州的诺福克港，向停泊在门罗要塞附近的联邦舰队发起了进攻。它摧毁了“坎伯兰号”和“国会号”这两艘木制护卫舰，并开始摧毁“明尼苏达号”。它随后驶回了诺福克港。这艘强大的军舰是原来的“梅里马克号”护卫舰①。南部邦联军在它的甲板上面建了一间铁屋。联邦护卫舰的炮弹对这些铁壁无法造成损害，只能滚落。但是那天夜里，一艘外形更奇怪的船出现在了门罗要塞。这就是“莫尼特号”，一座漂浮的堡垒，由钢铁打造而成。它是由瑞典移民约翰·埃里克森（John Ericsson，1803~1889）设计出来的。当“梅里马克号”回来准备彻底摧毁“明尼苏达号”的时候，“莫尼特号”径直向它驶去。两艘装甲舰鏖战了很久。最后，“梅里马克号”逃走了，并且再也没有回来继续战斗。

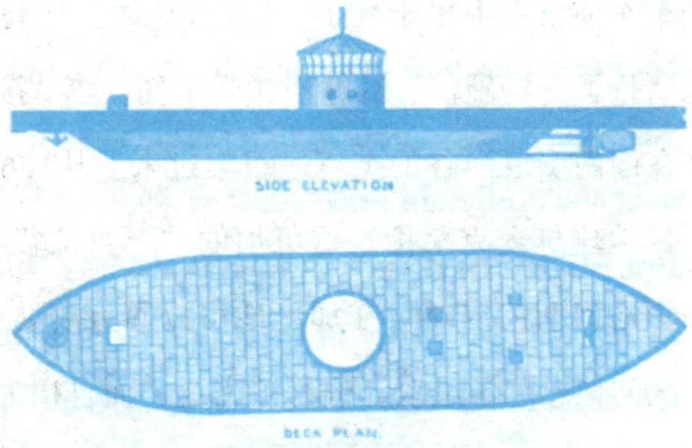

早期装甲舰的侧面图和俯视图

392. 公元1862年，半岛战役——到5月底，麦克莱伦已经占领了一个距里士满不到10英里的据点。与此同时，杰克逊在谢南多厄河谷的攻势十分猛烈，因此华盛顿政府拒绝向麦克莱伦输送更多士兵，尽管约翰斯顿已

① 这里所说的“原来的”，意思是这艘战舰已经改换了名称。美国内战初期，南方基本上没有海军，更没有战舰。然而，在弗吉尼亚州退出联邦之后，当时美国最大的造船厂——位于弗吉尼亚州诺福克附近的哥斯波特海军造船厂就落到了南部邦联军手中。联邦在撤出弗吉尼亚之前，凿沉了当时该厂正在建造的大型炮舰“梅里马克号”，但是后来南部邦联军又把它打捞上来，并改装成装甲舰，并改名为“弗吉尼亚号”——这是人类军事史上第一艘投入战斗的装甲舰。而“莫尼特号”与“梅里马克号”在汉普顿锚地的这场海战，也结束了木质军舰的时代，开启了装甲舰的时代。

经率军前去保卫里士满了。5月31日，波托马克军和北弗吉尼亚军在费尔奥克斯打了一场硬仗。约翰斯顿受了伤，李[①]接任了他的总司令一职。李把驻守在谢南多厄河谷的杰克逊召集过来。从1862年6月26日到7月2日，他日复一日地攻打麦克莱伦。这可怕的“七日战役”迫使麦克莱伦把根据地转移到了詹姆斯河河畔，在那里他可以靠近舰队。在莫尔文高地，李和杰克逊再次向他发起了进攻，但是被击退，而且损失惨重。

约翰·波普

**393. 第二次布尔溪战役**——波托马克军仍然驻扎在对里士满造成威胁的地方。李想到，如果他向驻华盛顿前线的军队发动一次猛攻，林肯就会召回麦克莱伦。于是，杰克逊军没有任何预兆地突然出现在了马纳萨斯路口。麦克莱伦立刻接到命令，要把他的部队经水路转移到波托马克河，并接受指挥华盛顿前线军队的约翰·波普将军（John Pope，1822~1892）的领导。麦克莱伦奉命完成了任务。但是，李比他的行动还要快。在波普完全掌控波托马克军之前，李就在布尔溪附近向联邦军队发起了攻击。他打败了他们，把他们赶出了战场，并迫使他们撤回到保卫华盛顿的各个要塞当中（1862年8月）。

安布罗斯·埃弗雷特·伯恩赛德

**394. 公元1862年，安蒂特姆战役**——这时，李已经率兵渡过波托马克河来到了马里兰州。但是，他遇到了比预想中更多的阻力。麦克莱伦再次被任命为总司令。他把军队紧密地集结到一

① 即罗伯特·E. 李。

起，驻防在李的军队和华盛顿之间，并对李和弗吉尼亚州之间的联系造成威胁。南部邦联军撤退了。麦克莱伦发现他们坚守在安蒂特姆附近，于是袭击了他们。联邦军队作战英勇，但是军旅作家们认为麦克莱伦没有很好地规划他的进攻。无论如何，波托马克军的损失超过了一万两千人，而邦联军的损失还不到一万人，而且李也成功地撤回了弗吉尼亚州。于是麦克莱伦被撤销了指挥权。安布罗斯·E. 伯恩赛德（Ambrose Everett Burnside，1824~1881）成了波托马克军的司令。

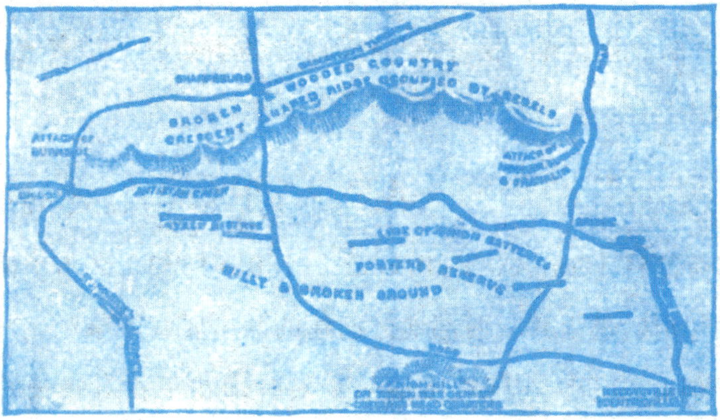

安蒂特姆战役地图（绘制于战时）

395. 公元1862年12月，弗雷德里克斯堡——伯恩赛德发现李坚守在玛丽高地。玛丽高地突出地耸立在拉帕汉诺克河南岸的小镇弗雷德里克斯堡后面。伯恩赛德发起了正面进攻。他的士兵不得不渡过河流，冒着致命的炮火向高地发起猛攻——结果却徒然无功。他损失了一万三千人，而南部邦联军只损失了四千人。“好战的乔”胡克（Joseph Hooker，1814~1879）这时接替伯恩赛

约瑟夫·胡克

德担任了波托马克军的司令。现在，我们要把注意力转向西部，看看那里在1861年至1862年间发生了什么事。

396. 格兰特与托马斯——伊利诺伊州出现了一位训练有素的军人。他拥有旺盛的精力和不屈的意志，他就是尤利塞斯·辛普森·格兰特（Ulysses Simpson Grant，1822~1885）。他毕业于西点军校，参加过美墨战争。1861年9月，他占领了位于俄亥俄河与密西西比河交汇处的凯罗市。1862年1月，乔治·H. 托马斯将军在坎伯兰河上游流域的密尔斯普林斯打败了一支南部邦联军队。就这样，格兰特与托马斯为联邦保住了俄亥俄州与东肯塔基的防线。

397. 公元1862年2月，亨利堡与多纳尔森堡——1862年2月，格兰特将军和富特准将（Andrew Hull Foote，1806~1863）袭击了南部邦联军为阻止联邦炮舰进入邦联西部地区而建的两个要塞。亨利堡几乎立刻就投降了，但联邦军队在围攻多纳尔森堡时却花了相对较长的时间。不久，南部邦联守军开始失去战意，巴克纳将军（Simon Bolivar Buckner，1823~1914）要求投降的条件。"无条件投降"，格兰特答复道，于是巴克纳投降了。这时，田纳西河下游与坎伯兰河下游都掌控在了联邦军队手中。

398. 新奥尔良的重要性——新奥尔良与密西西比河下游地区对双方都很重要，因为南方人要是占据了这个地区，就可以进入得克萨斯州，然后经过得克萨斯州到达墨西哥。联邦舰队正在封锁南方的每一处重要港口。但是，只要和墨西哥的陆上贸易得以维持，南方就能坚持下去。密西西比河也有许多入海口，因此也很难阻止军舰出入。出于这些原因，联邦政府

一个战时使用的信封（上面画的人是法拉格特将军）

决定夺取新奥尔良与密西西比河下游。这次远征的司令是在路易斯安那州长大的法拉格特。政府给了他一支当时所能提供的最好的舰队，还给了他一支军队以供调遣。

**399. 公元1862年4月，攻陷新奥尔良**——法拉格特率领舰队进入了密西西比河，却发现他向上游航行的线路被河岸上的两个要塞所阻。要塞南面的河上设置了一条横跨河流的大铁链，还有一支内河炮艇舰队——其中有一两艘装甲舰——在要塞前待命。然而，铁链、要塞和炮艇在法拉格特坚强的意志面前都要让道。夜里，他在猛烈的炮击中率舰队穿过了要塞。一旦到达这两个要塞的上游，新奥

一艘内河炮艇

尔良就任由他摆布了。新奥尔良沦陷了，而那两个要塞不久也被联邦军队攻陷。至此，南部邦联失去了密西西比河下游地区的控制权。

**400. 公元1862年4月、5月，夏伊洛与科林斯湾**——这时，哈勒克将军（Henry Wager Halleck，1815~1872）负责指挥联邦军队在西部的军事行动。他命令格兰特率军沿着田纳西河向上游航行，直达匹兹堡登陆地，然后在那里等候比尔（Don Carlos Buell，1818~1898），后者将率大军从纳什维尔经陆路而来。格兰特将他的部队驻守在夏伊洛教堂与匹兹堡登陆地之间的田纳西河西岸。南部邦联的西部司令艾伯特·西德尼·约翰斯顿（Albert Sidney Johnston，1803~1862）突然向他发起了猛攻。很快，联邦军就被赶到了河里。在这种情况下，许多指挥官可能都会选择撤退，但是格兰特以惊人的勇气坚持了下来。那天下午，比尔的先头部队到达了河的另一边。当天夜里，他们渡过了这条河。格兰特的外围部队也赶到了战场前线。第二天早上，格兰特发动了反攻，他步步为营，迫使南部邦联军退出了战场。随后，哈勒克统合了格兰特、比尔和波普的军队，然后夺取了科林斯湾。

亨利·韦杰·哈勒克

**401. 布拉格在田纳西州与肯塔基州**——这时，布拉克斯顿·布拉格将军（Braxton Bragg，1817~1876）率领着一支部队前往查塔努加，这支军队是夏伊洛与科林斯湾战役中南部邦联军的主力部队。随后，他迅速穿

布拉克斯顿·布拉格　唐·卡洛斯·比尔

过田纳西州与肯塔基州，到达俄亥俄河畔的路易斯维尔附近。比尔奉命追击他。两军在佩里维尔进行了一场非决定性的战役。随后，布拉格撤到了查塔努加。没过几个月，他再次踏上了征程。这时，罗斯克兰斯（William Starke Rosecrans，1819~1898）接替了比尔的职务。他在默夫里斯伯勒攻击了布拉格。在很长一段时间内，双方一直势均力敌。然而最后，南部邦联军战败并退出了战场。

## 【Original Text】

**386. Nature of the Conflict.**—The overthrow of the Confederate states proved to be very difficult. The Alleghany Mountains cut the South into two great fields of war. Deep and rapid rivers flowed from the mountains into the Atlantic or into the Mississippi. Each of these rivers was a natural line of defense. The first line was the Potomac and the Ohio. But when the Confederates were driven from this line, they soon found another equally good a little farther south. Then again the South was only partly settled. Good roads were rare, but there were many poor roads. The maps gave only the good roads. By these the Northern soldiers had to march while the Southern armies were often guided through paths unknown to the Northerners, and thus were able to march shorter distances between two battlefields or between two important points.

**387. The Bull Run Campaign, July, 1861.**—Northern soldiers crossed the Potomac into Virginia and found the Confederates posted at Bull Run near Manassas Junction. Other Northern soldiers pressed into the Shenandoah

Valley from Harper's Ferry. They, too, found a Confederate army in front of them. The plan of the Union campaign is now clear: General McDowell was to attack the Confederates at Bull Run, while General Patterson attacked the Confederates in the Valley, and kept them so busy that they could not go to the help of their comrades at Bull Run. It fell out otherwise, for Patterson retreated and left the Confederate general, Johnston, free to go to the aid of the sorely pressed Confederates at Bull Run. McDowell attacked vigorously and broke the Confederate line; but he could not maintain his position. The Union troops at first retreated slowly. Then they became frightened and fled, in all haste, back to Washington. The first campaign ended in disaster.

**388. The Army of the Potomac.**—While the Bull Run campaign was going on in eastern Virginia, Union soldiers had been winning victories in western Virginia. These were led by General George B. McClellan. He now came to Washington and took command of the troops operating in front of the capital. During the autumn, winter, and spring he drilled his men with great skill and care. In March, 1862, the Army of the Potomac left its camps a splendidly drilled body of soldiers.

**389. The Army of Northern Virginia.**—Meantime the government of the Confederacy had gathered great masses of soldiers. There were not nearly as many white men of fighting age in the South as there were in the North. But what men there were could be placed in the fighting line, because the negro slaves could produce the food needed by the armies and do the hard labor of making forts. The capital of the Confederacy was now established at Richmond, on the James River, in Virginia. The army defending this capital was called the Army of Northern Virginia. It was commanded by Joseph E. Johnston; but its ablest officers were Robert E. Lee and Thomas J. Jackson (Stonewall Jackson).

**390. Plan of the Peninsular Campaign.**—The country between the Potomac and the James was cut up by rivers, as the Rappahannock, the Mattapony, and Pamunkey, and part of it was a wilderness. McClellan planned to carry his troops by water to the peninsula between the James and the York and Pamunkey rivers. He would then have a clear road to Richmond, with no great rivers to dispute with the enemy. Johnston would be obliged to leave his camp at Bull Run and march southward to the defense of Richmond. The great objection to the plan was that Johnston might attack Washington instead of going to face McClellan. General Jackson also was in the Shenandoah Valley. He might march down the Valley, cross the Potomac, and seize Washington. So the government kept seventy-five thousand of McClellan's men for the defense of the Federal capital.

**391. The *Monitor* and the *Merrimac*.**—On March 8 a queer-looking craft steamed out from Norfolk, Virginia, and attacked the Union fleet at anchor near Fortress Monroe. She destroyed two wooden frigates, the *Cumberland* and the *Congress*, and began the destruction of the *Minnesota*. She then steamed back to Norfolk. This formidable vessel was the old frigate *Merrimac*. Upon her decks the Confederates had built an iron house. From these iron sides the balls of the Union frigates rolled harmlessly away. But that night an even stranger-looking ship appeared at Fortress Monroe. This was the *Monitor*, a floating fort, built of iron. She was designed by John Ericsson, a Swedish immigrant. When the *Merrimac* came back to finish the destruction of the *Minnesota*, the *Monitor* steamed directly to her. These two ironclads fought and fought. At last the *Merrimac* steamed away and never renewed the fight.

**392. The Peninsular Campaign, 1862.**—By the end of May McClellan had gained a position within ten miles of Richmond. Meantime, Jackson fought so vigorously in the Shenandoah Valley that the Washington government refused to send more men to McClellan, although Johnston had gone with his army to the defense of Richmond. On May 31 the Army of the Potomac and the Army of Northern Virginia fought a hard battle at Fair Oaks. Johnston was wounded, and Lee took the chief command. He summoned Jackson from the Valley and attacked McClellan day after day, June 26 to July 2, 1862. These terrible battles of the Seven Days forced McClellan to change his base to the James, where he would be near the fleet. At Malvern Hill Lee and Jackson once more attacked him and were beaten off with fearful loss.

**393. Second Bull Run Campaign.**—The Army of the Potomac was still uncomfortably near Richmond. It occurred to Lee that if he should strike a hard blow at the army in front of Washington, Lincoln would recall McClellan. Suddenly, without any warning, Jackson appeared at Manassas Junction. McClellan was at once ordered to transport his army by water to the Potomac, and place it under the orders of General John Pope, commanding the forces in front of Washington. McClellan did as he was ordered. But Lee moved faster than he could move. Before the Army of the Potomac was thoroughly in Pope's grasp, Lee attacked the Union forces near Bull Run. He defeated them, drove them off the field and back into the forts defending Washington (August, 1862).

**394. The Antietam Campaign, 1862.**—Lee now crossed the Potomac into Maryland. But he found more resistance than he had looked for. McClellan was again given chief command. Gathering his forces firmly together, he kept between Lee and Washington, and threatened Lee's communications with Virginia. The Confederates drew back. McClellan found them strongly posted near the Antietam and attacked them. The Union soldiers fought splendidly. But military writers say that McClellan's attacks were not well planned. At all events, the Army of the Potomac lost more than twelve thousand men to less than ten thousand on the Confederate side, and Lee made good his retreat to Virginia. McClellan was now removed from command, and Ambrose E. Burnside became chief of the Army of the Potomac.

**395. Fredericksburg, December, 1862.**—Burnside found Lee strongly posted on Marye's Heights, which rise sharply behind the little town of Fredericksburg on the southern bank of the Rappahannock River. Burnside attacked in front. His soldiers had to cross the river and assault the hill in face of a murderous fire—and in vain. He lost thirteen thousand men to only four thousand of the Confederates. "Fighting Joe" Hooker now succeeded Burnside as commander of the Army of the Potomac. We must now turn to the West, and see what had been doing there in 1861~1862.

**396. Grant and Thomas.**—In Illinois there appeared a trained soldier of fierce energy and invincible will, Ulysses Simpson Grant. He had been educated at West Point and had served in the Mexican War. In September, 1861, he seized Cairo at the junction of the Ohio and the Mississippi. In January, 1862, General George H. Thomas defeated a Confederate force at Mill Springs, in the upper valley of the Cumberland River. In this way Grant and Thomas secured the line of the Ohio and eastern Kentucky for the Union.

**397. Forts Henry and Donelson, February, 1862.**—In February, 1862, General Grant and Commodore Foote attacked two forts which the Confederates had built to keep the Federal gunboats from penetrating the western part of the Confederacy. Fort Henry yielded almost at once, but the Union forces besieged Fort Donelson for a longer time. Soon the Confederate defense became hopeless, and General Buckner asked for the terms of surrender. "Unconditional surrender," replied Grant, and Buckner surrendered. The lower Tennessee and the lower Cumberland were now open to the Union forces.

**398. Importance of New Orleans.**—New Orleans and the lower Mississippi were of great importance to both sides, for the possession of this region gave the Southerners access to Texas, and through Texas to Mexico. Union fleets were blockading every important Southern port. But as long as commerce overland with Mexico could be maintained, the South could struggle on. The Mississippi, too, has so many mouths that it was difficult to keep vessels from running in and out. For these reasons the Federal government determined to seize New Orleans and the lower Mississippi. The command of the expedition was given to Farragut, who had passed his boyhood in Louisiana. He was given as good a fleet as could be provided, and a force of soldiers was sent to help him.

**399. New Orleans captured, April, 1862.**—Farragut carried his fleet into the Mississippi, but found his way upstream barred by two forts on the river's bank. A great chain stretched across the river below the forts, and a fleet of river gunboats with an ironclad or two was in waiting above the forts. Chain, forts, and gunboats all gave way before Farragut's forceful will. At night he passed the forts amid a terrific cannonade. Once above them New Orleans was at his mercy. It surrendered, and with the forts was soon occupied by the Union army. The lower Mississippi was lost to the Confederacy.

**400. Shiloh and Corinth, April, May, 1862.**—General Halleck now directed the operations of the Union armies in the West. He ordered Grant to take his men up the Tennessee to Pittsburg Landing and there await the arrival of Buell with a strong force overland from Nashville. Grant encamped with his troops on the western bank of the Tennessee between Shiloh Church and Pittsburg Landing. Albert Sidney Johnston, the Confederate commander in the West, attacked him suddenly and with great fury. Soon the Union army was pushed back to the river. In his place many a leader would have withdrawn. But Grant, with amazing courage, held on. In the afternoon Buell's leading regiments reached the other side of the river. In the night they were ferried across, and Grant's outlying commands were brought to the front. The next morning Grant attacked in his turn and slowly but surely pushed the Confederates off the field. Halleck then united Grant's, Buell's, and Pope's armies and captured Corinth.

**401. Bragg in Tennessee and Kentucky.**—General Braxton Bragg now took a large part of the Confederate army, which had fought at Shiloh and Corinth, to Chattanooga. He then marched rapidly across Tennessee and Kentucky to the neighborhood of Louisville on the Ohio River. Buell was sent after him, and the two armies fought an indecisive battle at Perryville. Then Bragg retreated to Chattanooga. In a few months he was again on the march. Rosecrans had now succeeded Buell. He attacked Bragg at Murfreesboro. For a long time the contest was equal. In the end, however, the Confederates were beaten and retired from the field.

CHAPTER 39

# 《解放宣言》

# THE EMANCIPATION PROCLAMATION

402. 封锁——萨姆特堡失陷之后，林肯总统下令封锁了南部邦联的海港。南方几乎没有制造业。棉花和烟草是主要的出口产品。如果港口遭到封锁，南方既不能从欧洲引进武器和军事援助，也不能把棉花和烟草卖到欧洲。因此，它对抗联邦军队的力量就会大大削弱。联邦政府买来了各种各样的船舶，甚至是港口的渡船，并把这些船只武装起来，配置在被封锁港口的附近。在短得令人难以置信的时间里，封锁线就建立起来了。联邦军队还开始占据南部海岸，这样一来，需要封锁的地区就稳步减少。

403. 封锁的效果——随着时间的推移，封锁变得越来越严密，南方人民经受的困难也越来越大。因为不能把产品运往欧洲以换取物资，所以他们不得不用金银购买突破封锁者带来的东西。不久，南部邦联就已经没有了金银。于是，他们就发行纸币。随后，工业制品——如衣服和纸，以及南方不出产的东西——如咖啡和盐，这些东西的贮备都耗尽了。战争快要结束的时候，南方士兵已经完全没有药品可用；枪械也极度缺乏，因此甚至有人提议用矛来武装一个军团。封锁在瓦解南部的抵抗中所发挥的作用是无与伦比的。

404. 南部邦联、大不列颠与法兰西——战争刚刚打响的时候，南部邦联的领导人相信英国人和法国人会给他们提供援助。“棉花就是王。”

他们说道。要是没有定期的棉花供应，英国和法国的作坊就必然要停工。数以千计的作坊工人——男人、女人和儿童——就会挨饿。所以，法国和英国的政府会来解除封锁。他们甚至可能会强迫合众国承认南部邦联各州的独立。这种看法中存在很多真实的成分。因为英国和法国的政府害怕美国共和政体的日益强大，他们很高兴看到它分裂。可是事情的进展完全出乎南部邦联领导人的预料。在美国棉花的贮备用尽之前，英国就找到了印度和埃及的新的棉花供应点。1862年初，联邦军队占领了棉花产区，于是美国的棉花再次得以出口。而且不管怎样，英国作坊的工人生活再艰苦也不会请求他们的政府干涉这场战争。他们十分清楚北方在为自由劳动力而战。不过，有时看起来大不列颠与法兰西似乎也会干涉这场战争。

一艘航行在密西西比河上的运棉蒸汽船

**405. 公元1861年，特伦特事件**——封锁刚形成的时候，英国和法国政府就给予了南部邦联与合众国同等的港口使用权。南方人随后派了两名代理人——梅森（James Murray Mason，1798~1871）和斯莱德尔（John Slidell，1793~1871）——前往欧洲请求外国政府承认南部邦联各州的独

查尔斯·威尔克斯

立。合众国的“圣哈辛托号”的威尔克斯船长（Charles Wilkes，1798~1877）从英国轮船“特伦特号”上带走了这两名代理人。但是，林肯立即宣布：威尔克斯对英国人所做的事，与当年英国人对我们做的事如出一辙——我们就是为了阻止这种事才进行了1812年战争。“我们必须恪守美国人的原则，”总统说道，“而且必须归还俘虏。”于是梅森和斯莱德尔获得了释放。但是英国政府没等林肯有所行动，就开始积极备战。这看起来可太不友善了，所以，合众国人民被大大地激怒了。

**406. 林肯与奴隶制**——我们应当记得，共和党曾反复强调他们无意干涉各州的奴隶制。只要和平延续下去，联邦政府就不能干涉各州的奴隶制。但是战争爆发后，总统作为总司令，可以做任何事情来打击并削弱敌人。如果解放退出联邦州的奴隶能对那些分裂分子造成伤害，他就完全有权利这样做。但是林肯明白，北方的舆论将不会赞成这个举动。在这件事上，他要遵从北方人的观点，而不能把自己的看法强加给民众。

本杰明·富兰克林·巴特勒

**407. 战争禁运品**——几乎在战争开始之前，奴隶们就纷纷逃往联邦的阵地。一天，一名南部邦联军官来到门罗要塞，要求按照《逃亡奴隶法》带走他的逃亡奴隶。巴特勒将军（Benjamin Franklin Butler，1818~1893）以奴隶是“战争禁运品”为由拒绝把他们交出去。他使用这个措辞的意思是：归还这些奴隶是不合法的，因为他们的服务对敌人有帮助。林肯总统赞成巴特勒将军的这种解决办法，于是没过多久逃亡奴隶就被人们称为“禁运品”。

408. 公元1862年，通往解放的第一步——林肯与共和党认为，国会不能干涉各州的奴隶制。然而，它可以购买奴隶，进而解放他们，或者帮助各州做这件事。于是，国会通过了一项向任何将废除本州境内的奴隶制的州提供帮助的法律。国会自身则用补偿奴隶主的方式废除了哥伦比亚特区的奴隶制。国会还在没有提供任何补偿的前提下废除了各准州的奴隶制。林肯很乐于帮助制定这些法律。此外，到1862年8月，林肯已经坚定了他的想法，认为解放退出联邦各州的奴隶将有助于“拯救联邦”，因而也将是一个正确的“战争手段”。因为每减少一个被迫劳动的黑人都会削弱南方的生产力，征服南方就会更为容易。

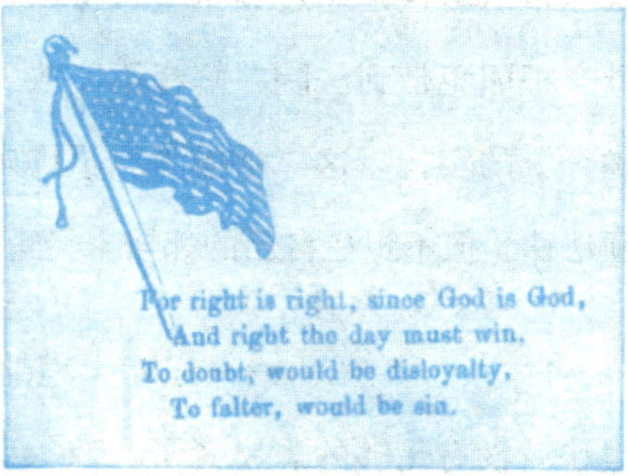


一个战时的信封

409. 公元1863年，《解放宣言》——1862年9月23日，林肯发布了一个宣言①。他在这个宣言中声明：他将在新年的第一天宣布解放合众国那时还处于叛乱状态的任何地区的奴隶。1863年1月1日，林肯发布了《解放宣言》。这个宣言只能在被联邦军队占领的那些退出联邦的州执行。它没有解放效忠州的奴隶，也没有废除任何地方的奴隶制。西弗吉尼亚州、密苏里州和马里兰州在1862年至1864年之间废除了奴隶制。最终，1865年通过

① 这个宣言又被称为《初步解放宣言》，而次年1月1日的宣言——即《解放宣言》——又被称为《最后解放宣言》。这两则宣言的重要差别在于后者进一步规定了允许黑人参加军事活动。

的第十三条宪法修正案废除了整个合众国的奴隶制。

410. 北方人的反战情绪——许多北方人认为，南方人完全有权按照他们的意愿退出联邦。这些人当中的某些人非常同情南方人，他们甚至为南方人送去了重要的情报并尽其所能地阻止联邦军队获胜。很难找到证据来指控这些南方的同情者，但是放任他们肆意妄为是危险的。于是，林肯下令逮捕并关押了他们当中的许多人。这时的宪法规定每个公民都必须接受快速审讯。这是通过颁布《人身保护令》来实施的。《人身保护令》强迫狱卒把囚犯带到法院并解释不能放人的原因。这时，林肯推迟了《人身保护令》的实行。这一举措激怒了许多人。他们很乐意让南方人被迫遵守这项法律，但不想让自己的邻居未经审判就被逮捕并囚禁起来。

411. 征兵骚乱——起初，南北双方军队都是由志愿者组成的；但是很快就没有足够的志愿者了。双方政府随后征募士兵入伍；换言之，他们通过抽签挑出某些男子，然后强制他们当兵。这种征兵遭到了北方一些地区——尤其是纽约市——的强烈反对。

抽签征兵

## 【ORIGINAL TEXT】

**402. The Blockade.**—On the fall of Fort Sumter President Lincoln ordered a blockade of the Confederate seaports. There were few manufacturing industries in the South. Cotton and tobacco were the great staples of export. If her ports were blockaded the South could neither bring in arms and military supplies from Europe, nor send cotton and tobacco to Europe to be sold for money. So her power of resisting the Union armies would be greatly lessened. The Union government bought all kinds of vessels, even harbor ferryboats, armed them, and stationed them off the blockaded harbors. In a surprisingly short time the blockade was established. The Union forces also began to occupy the Southern seacoast, and thus the region that had to be blockaded steadily grew less.

**403. Effects of the Blockade.**—As months and years went by, and the blockade became stricter and stricter, the sufferings of the Southern people became ever greater. As they could not send their products to Europe to exchange for goods, they had to pay gold and silver for whatever the blockade runners brought in. Soon there was no more gold and silver in the Confederacy, and paper money took its place. Then the supplies of manufactured goods, as clothing and paper, of things not produced in the South, as coffee and salt, gave out. Toward the end of the war there were absolutely no medicines for the Southern soldiers, and guns were so scarce that it was proposed to arm one regiment with pikes. Nothing did more to break down Southern resistance than the blockade.

**404. The Confederacy, Great Britain, and France.**—From the beginning of the contest the Confederate leaders believed that the British and the French would interfere to aid them. "Cotton is king," they said. Unless there were a regular supply of cotton, the mills of England and of France must stop. Thousands of mill hands—men, women, and children—would soon be starving. The French and the British governments would raise the blockade. Perhaps they would even force the United States to acknowledge the independence of the Confederate states. There was a good deal of truth in this belief. For the British and French governments dreaded the growing power of the American republic and would gladly have seen it broken to pieces. But events fell out far otherwise than the Southern leaders had calculated. Before the supply of American cotton in England was used up, new supplies began to come in from India and from Egypt. The Union armies occupied portions of the cotton belt early in 1862, and American cotton was again exported. But more than all else, the English mill operatives, in all their hardships, would not ask their government to interfere. They saw clearly enough that the North was fighting for the rights of free labor. At times it seemed, however, as if Great Britain or France would interfere.

**405. The Trent Affair, 1861.**—As soon as the blockade was established, the British and French governments gave the Confederates the same rights in their ports as the United States had. The Southerners then sent two agents, Mason and Slidell, to Europe to ask the foreign governments to recognize the independence of the Confederate states. Captain Wilkes of the United States ship San Jacinto took these agents from the British steamer Trent. But Lincoln at once said that Wilkes had done to the British the very thing which we had fought the War of 1812 to prevent the British doing to us. "We must stick to American principles," said the President, "and restore the prisoners." They were given up. But the British government, without waiting to see what Lincoln would do, had gone actively to work to prepare for war. This seemed so little friendly that the people of the United States were greatly irritated.

**406. Lincoln and Slavery.**—It will be remembered that the Republican party had denied again and again that it had any intention to interfere with slavery in the states. As long as peace lasted the Federal government could not interfere with slavery in the states. But when war broke out, the President, as commander-in-chief, could do anything to distress and weaken the enemy. If freeing the slaves in the seceded states would injure the secessionists, he had a perfect right to do it. But Lincoln knew that public opinion in the North would not approve this action. He would follow Northern sentiment in this matter, and not force it.

**407. Contrabands of War.**—The war had scarcely begun before slaves escaped into the Union lines. One day a Confederate officer came to Fortress Monroe and demanded his runaway slaves under the Fugitive Slave Act. General Butler refused to give them up on the ground that they were "contraband of war." By that phrase he meant that their restoration would be illegal as their services would be useful to the enemy. President Lincoln approved this decision of General Butler, and escaping slaves soon came to be called "Contrabands."

**408. First Steps toward Emancipation, 1862.**—Lincoln and the Republican party thought that Congress could not interfere with slavery in the states. It might, however, buy slaves and set them free or help the states to do this. So Congress passed a law offering aid to any state which should abolish slavery within its borders. Congress itself abolished slavery in the District of Columbia with compensation to the owners. It abolished slavery in the territories without compensation. Lincoln had gladly helped to make these laws. Moreover, by August, 1862, he had made up his mind that to free the slaves in the seceded states would help "to save the Union" and would therefore be right as a "war measure." For every negro taken away from forced labor would weaken the producing power of the South and so make the conquest of the South easier.

**409. The Emancipation Proclamation, 1863.**—On September 23, 1862, Lincoln issued a proclamation stating that on the first day of the new year he would declare free all slaves in any portion of the United States then in rebellion. On January 1, 1863, he issued the Emancipation Proclamation. This proclamation could be enforced only in those portions of the seceded states which were held by the Union armies. It did not free slaves in loyal states and did not abolish the institution of slavery anywhere. Slavery was abolished by the states of West Virginia, Missouri, and Maryland between 1862 and 1864. Finally, in 1865, it was abolished throughout the United States by the adoption of the Thirteenth Amendment.

**410. Northern Opposition to the War.**—Many persons in the North thought that the Southerners had a perfect right to secede if they wished. Some of these persons sympathized so strongly with the Southerners that they gave them important information and did all they could to prevent the success of the Union forces. It was hard to prove anything against these Southern sympathizers, but it was dangerous to leave them at liberty. So Lincoln ordered many of them to be arrested and locked up. Now the Constitution provides that every citizen shall have a speedy trial. This is brought about by the issuing a writ of habeas corpus, compelling the jailer to bring his prisoner into court and show cause why he should not be set at liberty. Lincoln now suspended the operation of the writ of habeas corpus. This action angered many persons who were quite willing that the Southerners should be compelled to obey the law, but did not like to have their neighbors arrested and locked up without trial.

**411. The Draft Riots.**—At the outset both armies were made up of volunteers; soon there were not enough volunteers. Both governments then drafted men for their armies; that is, they picked out by lot certain men and compelled them to become soldiers. The draft was bitterly resisted in some parts of the North, especially in New York City.

# CHAPTER 40
# 1863年
## THE YEAR 1863

**412. 公元1863年1月，军情**——这时，波托马克军在胡克的率领下正与北弗吉尼亚军对峙于拉帕汉诺克河畔的弗雷德里克斯堡。在西部，罗斯克兰斯驻守在默夫里斯伯勒，而布拉格正在返回查塔努加的途中。在密西西比河流域，格兰特和谢尔曼（William Tecumseh Sherman，1820~1891）已经发动了维克斯堡战役，但是到目前为止，他们还没有取得胜利。

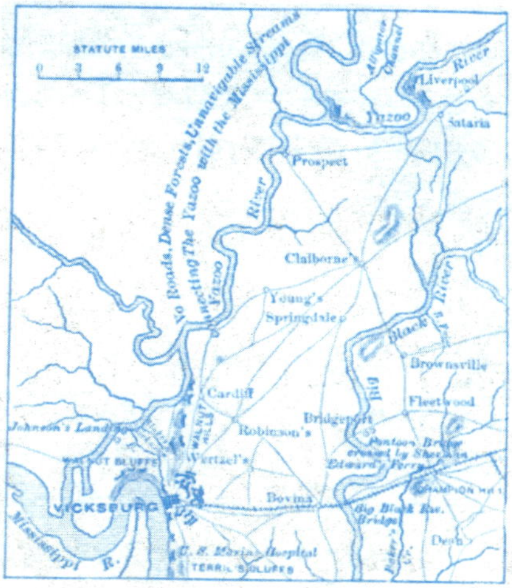


维克斯堡战役地图

**413. 维克斯堡战役初期**——维克斯堡屹立于邻河的一处高耸的悬崖上。城镇的北端竖立着排炮，它们朝着正对着悬崖的河面。攻击这个易守难攻的地方的最好方法是：从科林斯湾由陆路进军。格兰特试图这样做。但是，南部邦联军把他击退了。

**414. 公元1863年7月4日，攻陷维克斯堡**——格兰特这时率领全军沿着密西西比河顺流而下。几个月以来，他尝试了一个又一个的方案，但是每次都以失败而告终。最终，他率军沿着密西西比河西岸南下，至维克斯

大卫·迪克逊·波特

堡南面渡河，从南面和东面接近这个要塞。在这次行动中，他得到了波特（David Dixon Porter，1813~1891）率领的联邦舰队的大力支持，在渡河过程中得到了舰队的掩护。南部邦联指挥官彭伯顿（John Clifford Pemberton，1814~1881）立即率军冲出了维克斯堡。但是，格兰特击退了他，并开始从陆地的一面包围这个城镇。南部邦联军打了一场英勇的保卫战。但是，随着时间的推移，他们必定会因饥荒而屈服。1863年7月4日，彭伯顿率领三万七千名士兵举城投降了。

**415. 打通密西西比河**——这时，位于维克斯堡和新奥尔良之间的哈德逊堡是南部邦联军在密西西比河畔唯一的重要据点。7月8日，哈德逊堡投降了。几天之后，从圣路易斯驶来的“帝国号”货船驶达抵新奥尔良。密西西比河终于“不受干扰地流入了大海”。至此，南部邦联被截成了两部分。

**416. 公元1863年，李的第二次入侵**——这时，“好战的乔·胡克”负责指挥波托马克军。为了让李上当，他设法到达了南部邦联军阵线后方的玛丽高地。但是，李在钱瑟勒斯维尔向他发起了猛攻，迫使他撤到了拉帕汉诺克河对岸。随后，李再次渡过波托马克河入侵北方。这一次，他长驱直入到了宾夕法尼亚州的中央地带。胡克和他平行前进，一直保持在李和华盛顿市之间。最后，在这场战役打到一半的时候，胡克被免

乔治·戈登·米德

职，乔治·G. 米德（George Gordon Meade，1815~1872）成为波托马克军的第五任也是最后一任总司令。

417. 公元1863年7月1日，葛底斯堡——这时，米德率领联邦军向李和弗吉尼亚州之间的交通线进军。李立即后撤。双方军队都向通往南方道路的汇合之地——葛底斯堡进军。就这样，这两支军队在1863年7月1日相遇了。南方人当时的兵力相对强大一些，他们把联邦军从葛底斯堡赶到了一个名为“墓地山脊”的高地。这是一个非常有利的阵地，阵线的一端是寇普岭，另一端是圆顶山①。米德决定在这个地方开战，于是急忙调来了他所有的军队。

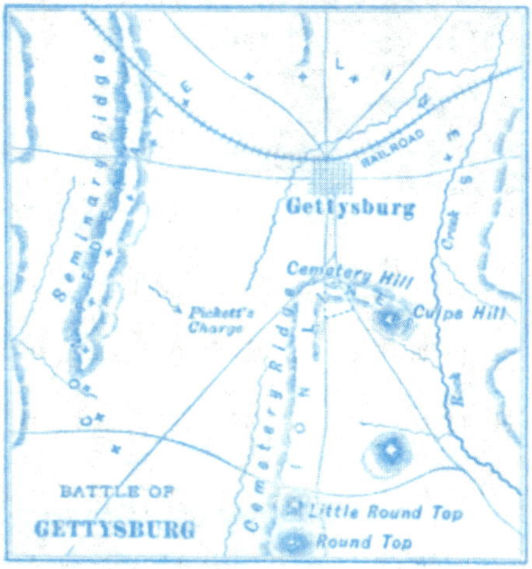


葛底斯堡之战地图

418. 公元1863年7月2日，葛底斯堡——起初，情况似乎对联邦军不利。联邦军的左翼一直从“小圆顶”延伸到“墓地山脊”山脚的原野。南部邦联军击退了这部分阵线的联邦军。但是，他们没能夺取“小圆顶”。这一天，南部邦联军也在寇普岭取得了一个据点。

从“小圆顶”山南望葛底斯堡战场

① 圆顶山（The Round Tops）是两座相邻的岩石山，高的叫大圆顶（Big Round Top），矮的叫小圆顶（Little Round Top）。

**419. 公元1863年7月3日，葛底斯堡**——这天清晨，联邦军把南部邦联军赶出了寇普岭，进而占领了整个山脊。这时，就像在莫尔文高地时那样，李再次与波托马克军战至胶着状态。但是，他可不允许失败。在弗吉尼亚人皮克特（George Edward Pickett，1825~1875）的率领下，一万三千名士兵穿过两军之间的河谷，向联邦军的中心位置发起了冲锋。他们当中的一些人甚至冲破了联邦军的战线。但是，这支冲锋队在那里停了下来。慢慢地，它开始动摇了。随后，南部邦联军撤退了——全部都逃走了。南部联邦军获得葛底斯堡战役的胜利。后来另一天，李再次遇上波托马克军，随后便撤退了。在这场可怕的战役中，南部邦联军伤亡两万两千五百人，还有五千人被北方人俘虏——参战的八万名士兵总共损失了两万八千人。联邦军共有九万三千人参战，伤亡两万三千人。维克斯堡战役和葛底斯堡战役让南方损失了六万五千名士兵——一个无法弥补

乔治·爱德华·皮克特

皮克特冲锋

的损失。我们现在该回头看看田纳西州东部了。

**420. 公元1863年9月，奇克莫加**——默夫里斯伯勒战役之后的六个月，罗斯克兰斯和布拉格一直留在他们的驻地。1863年夏，罗斯克兰斯通过一系列的巧妙行军迫使布拉格放弃了查塔努加。但是，布拉格这时得到了来自密西西比河的军队和朗斯特里特（James Longstreet，1821~1904）分队的强力增援，后者隶属于李的弗吉尼亚军。他在奇克莫加河反击了罗斯克兰斯。联邦军的右翼被赶出战场。但是，“查塔努加的岩石”托马斯[①]与他的部队仍然坚守不退。布拉格反复向他发起进攻，但是每次都以失败而告终，尽管他有两倍于托马斯的兵力。罗斯克兰斯认为己方会输掉这场战役，于是策马撤向查塔努加，但是谢里丹（Philip Henry Sheridan，1831~1888）竭尽全力援助了托马斯。第三天，托马斯和布拉格都守着各自的阵地，但是随后联邦军在未受追击的情况下撤到了查塔努加。这时，查塔努加所有联邦军队的指挥权都交给了托马斯。格兰特也受命指挥联邦所有的西部军队。

詹姆斯·朗斯特里特

**421. 公元1863年11月，查塔努加**——查塔努加的联邦军处境非常危险。因为南部邦联军完全包围了他们，而他们也无法取得食物。但是，援军很快就来了。胡克率领一万五千名波托马克军的士兵赶来，他们打开了一条道路，让粮食能够运达查塔努加。随后，格兰特也率领谢尔曼的军团

① 即乔治·亨利·托马斯。他在奇克莫加以及查塔努加战场上坚守阵地、反复击退敌军的表现让他赢得了“岩石”的绰号。

乔治·亨利·托马斯

从维克斯堡赶来。他立即派谢尔曼攻打布拉格的右翼，同时令胡克攻打布拉格的左翼。谢尔曼率军前进，但是被一条峡谷挡住了去路并停了下来。在战线的另一端，胡克一直攻到卢考特山的山腰，战斗甚至打到了云端之上①。战场中路是托马斯的部队。怀着一报查塔努加惨败之仇的渴望，他们冲破了南部邦联军的第一道防线。然后，在没有接到任何命令的情况下，他们又冲上了半山腰，突破了南部邦联军内部的重重防线。他们把南方人打得弃枪而逃，并夺取了后者的防御工事。布拉格竭尽全力地撤退了。朗斯特里特此时正在围攻诺克斯维尔。于是布拉格翻山越岭逃向李在弗吉尼亚的军队。

## 【Original Text】

**412. Position of the Armies, January, 1863.**—The Army of the Potomac, now under Hooker, and the Army of Northern Virginia were face to face at Fredericksburg on the Rappahannock. In the West Rosecrans was at Murfreesboro, and Bragg on the way back to Chattanooga. In the Mississippi Valley Grant and Sherman had already begun the Vicksburg campaign. But as yet they had had no success.

① 卢考特山常年云雾缭绕，战役发生的这一天也是如此。因为联邦军于1863年11月24日这一天在雾中击败了卢考特山的南部邦联军，所以这场战斗又被称为“云端之战”（the Battle above the Clouds）。

**413. Beginnings of the Vicksburg Campaign.**—Vicksburg stood on the top of a high bluff directly on the river. Batteries erected at the northern end of the town commanded the river, which at that point ran directly toward the bluff. The best way to attack this formidable place was to proceed overland from Corinth. This Grant tried to do. But the Confederates forced him back.

**414. Fall of Vicksburg, July 4, 1863.**—Grant now carried his whole army down the Mississippi. For months he tried plan after plan, and every time he failed. Finally he marched his army down on the western side of the river, crossed the river below Vicksburg, and approached the fortress from the south and east. In this movement he was greatly aided by the Union fleet under Porter, which protected the army while crossing the fiver. Pemberton, the Confederate commander, at once came out from Vicksburg. But Grant drove him back and began the siege of the town from the land side. The Confederates made a gallant defense. But slowly and surely they were starved into submission. On July 4, 1863, Pemberton surrendered the fortress and thirty-seven thousand men.

**415. Opening of the Mississippi.**—Port Hudson, between Vicksburg and New Orleans, was now the only important Confederate position on the Mississippi. On July 8 it surrendered. A few days later the freight steamer Imperial from St. Louis reached New Orleans. The Mississippi at last "flowed unvexed to the sea." The Confederacy was cut in twain.

**416. Lee's Second Invasion, 1863.**—"Fighting Joe Hooker" was now in command of the Army of the Potomac. Outwitting Lee, he gained the rear of the Confederate lines on Marye's Heights. But Lee fiercely attacked him at Chancellorsville and drove him back across the Rappahannock. Then Lee again crossed the Potomac and invaded the North. This time he penetrated to the heart of Pennsylvania. Hooker moved on parallel lines, always keeping between Lee and the city of Washington. At length, in the midst of the campaign, Hooker asked to be relieved, and George G. Meade became the fifth and last chief of the Army of the Potomac.

**417. Gettysburg, July 1, 1863.**—Meade now moved the Union army toward Lee's line of communication with Virginia. Lee at once drew back. Both armies moved toward Gettysburg, where the roads leading southward came together. In this way the two armies came into contact on July 1, 1863. The Southerners were in stronger force at the moment and drove the Union soldiers back through the town to the high land called Cemetery Ridge. This was a remarkably strong position, with Culp's Hill at one end of the line and the Round Tops at the other end. Meade determined to fight the battle at that spot and hurried up all his forces.

**418. Gettysburg, July 2, 1863.**—At first matters seemed to go badly with the Union army. Its left flank extended forward from Little Round Top into the fields at the foot of the ridge. The Confederates drove back this part of the Union line. But they could not seize Little Round Top. On this day also the Confederates gained a foothold on Culp's Hill.

**419. Gettysburg, July 3, 1863.**—Early on this morning the Union soldiers drove the Confederates away from Culp's Hill and held the whole ridge. Now again, as at Malvern Hill, Lee had fought the Army of the Potomac to a standstill. But he would not admit failure. Led by Pickett of Virginia, thirteen thousand men charged across the valley between the two armies directly at the Union center. Some of them even penetrated the Union lines. But there the line stopped. Slowly it began to waver. Then back the Confederates went—all who escaped. The battle of Gettysburg was won. Lee faced the Army of the Potomac for another day and then retreated. In this tremendous conflict the Confederates lost twenty-two thousand five hundred men killed and wounded and five thousand taken prisoners by the Northerners—a total loss of twenty-eight thousand out of eighty thousand in the battle. The Union army numbered ninety-three thousand men and lost twenty-three thousand, killed and wounded. Vicksburg and Gettysburg cost the South sixty-five thousand fighting men—a loss that could not be made good. We must now turn to eastern Tennessee.

**420. Chickamauga, September, 1863.**—For six months after Murfreesboro Rosecrans and Bragg remained in their camps. In the summer of 1863 Rosecrans, by a series of skillful marchings, forced Bragg to abandon Chattanooga. But Bragg was now greatly strengthened by soldiers from the Mississippi and by Longstreet's division from Lee's army in Virginia. He turned on Rosecrans, and attacked him at Chickamauga Creek. The right wing of the Union army was driven from the field. But Thomas, "the Rock of Chickamauga," with his men stood fast. Bragg attacked him again and again, and failed every time, although he had double Thomas's numbers. Rosecrans, believing the battle to be lost, had ridden off to Chattanooga, but Sheridan aided Thomas as well as he could. The third day Thomas and Bragg kept their positions, and then the Union soldiers retired unpursued to Chattanooga. The command of the whole army at Chattanooga was now given to Thomas, and Grant was placed in control of all the Western armies.

**421. Chattanooga, November, 1863.**—The Union soldiers at Chattanooga were in great danger. For the Confederates were all about them and they could get no food. But help was at hand. Hooker, with fifteen thousand men from the Army of the Potomac, arrived and opened a road by which food could reach Chattanooga. Then Grant came with Sherman's corps from Vicksburg. He at once sent Sherman to assail Bragg's right flank and ordered Hooker to attack his left flank. Sherman and his men advanced until he was stopped by a deep ravine. At the other end of the line Hooker fought right up the side of Lookout Mountain, until the battle raged above the clouds. In the center were Thomas's men. Eager to avenge the slaughter of Chickamauga, they carried the first Confederate line of defenses. Then, without orders, they rushed up the hillside over the inner lines. They drove the Southerners from their guns and seized their works. Bragg retreated as well as he could. Longstreet was besieging Knoxville. He escaped through the mountains to Lee's army in Virginia.

CHAPTER 41

# 1864—1865年，战争结束

## THE END OF THE WAR, 1864~1865

威廉·特库姆塞·谢尔曼

**422. 格兰特担任陆军总司令**——维克斯堡战役和查塔努加战役使格兰特注定要成为总司令。到此时为止，联邦军的行动一直都缺乏周密的计划。这时（1864年3月），格兰特被任命为中将，负责指挥合众国所有的陆军。格兰特决定亲自在弗吉尼亚州指挥战斗。他把西部的军事行动委托给了谢尔曼，并让托马斯负责指挥坎伯兰军。谢里丹和格兰特一起前往弗吉尼亚州，他负责指挥波托马克军的骑兵。我们将首先来看看谢尔曼、托马斯和西部军队的情况。

**423. 公元1864年，亚特兰大战役**——谢尔曼手下有十万名经验丰富的士兵，他们由托马斯、麦克弗森（James Birdseye McPherson, 1828~1864）和斯科菲尔德（John McAllister Schofield, 1831~1906）负责指挥。约瑟夫·E. 约翰斯顿接替布拉格统帅南部邦联军，他的兵力相对较少，但他占据了建有牢固工事的据点。然而，谢尔曼一周又一周地迫使他后退，直到经过两个月连续不断的战斗之后，约翰斯顿才发现自己已经退到了亚特兰大附近。这是南方最重要的制造业中心。南部邦联军必须竭尽全力保住亚特兰大。约翰斯顿显然挡不住谢尔曼。于是，胡德（John Bell

Hood，1831~1879）奉命接替了约翰斯顿的职务。南部邦联政府指望他可以一战。胡德的确尽了全力去作战。他一次次地向谢尔曼发动进攻，结果却次次被击退，而且损失惨重。于是，他放弃了亚特兰大以保存兵力。从5月到9月，谢尔曼损失了两万两千人，而南部邦联军损失了三万五千人，还失去了亚特兰大。

**424. 作战计划**——这时，胡德率军向北前往田纳西。但是谢尔曼自己没有追击他，只是派托马斯与斯科菲尔德前去追击。谢尔曼明白，南部邦联如今只是一个空壳。它的核心已经被摧毁了。要是让大部队穿过佐治亚州到达沿海地区，然后北上穿越南北卡罗来纳州并前往弗吉尼亚州——这样一个大进军将导致怎样的结果呢？这场没有对手的进军，不就是向北方、南方和欧洲的民众证明进一步的抵抗是无效的吗？谢尔曼认为答案是肯定的，而且一旦进入弗吉尼亚，他就可以帮助格兰特打垮李了。格兰特赞同谢尔曼的看法并让他实施他的计划。但是，我们先得看看托马斯与胡德那边的状况。

**425. 公元1864年，托马斯与胡德**——胡德从来不曾幻想过谢尔曼会不追击，因此他快速地向北进军，直到穿越了田纳西。随后，他花了三周的时间让他疲惫的士兵休息，同时搜集补给品。这一延误也给了托马斯时间去征兵。最后，胡德于1864年11月30日在富兰克林向斯科菲尔德发动了进攻。斯科菲尔德撤退到了纳什维尔，托马斯的主力军驻守于此。胡德紧随其后而来。托马斯花了充足的时间做好战备。格兰特对他的拖延感到焦虑，命令他出

约翰·贝尔·胡德

战。但是，托马斯不愿在做好准备之前出战。终于，他在12月15日发动了猛攻，并经过不到两天的作战就消灭了胡德的整支军队。这是西部的最后一场重大战役。

**426. 纵贯佐治亚州的远征**——摧毁亚特兰大的作坊和工厂之后，谢尔曼开始向沿海地区进军。他有六万名士兵。他们都是经验丰富的老兵，他们的行军就像在进行一次度假旅行。这支队伍绵延了六十英里。他们搜集了能得到的所有能吃的东西，还不时地停下来毁坏铁路。他们掀起铁轨，把铁轨放在用枕木生的火上加热，然后把它们绕在最近的树上。以这种方式，他们在处于半饥饿状态的北弗吉尼亚军和佐治亚南部仓库之间的铁路交通线上切开了一个六十英里长的缺口。1864年12月10日，谢尔曼到达海边。十天之后，他占领了萨凡纳，把它作为一份圣诞礼物献给了合众国。谢尔曼和托马斯联手给了南部邦联一次沉重的打击。那么，格兰特的进展又如何呢?

**427. 公元1864年，在弗吉尼亚州的格兰特**——在弗吉尼亚州，格兰特统领着米德手下的波托马克军、伯恩赛德手下的第九军团以及谢里丹手下的一支强大的骑兵部队。此外，巴特勒将军还以三万兵力驻守在詹姆斯河畔。李直属的兵力约为格兰特的一半。但是，他在其他所有方面都占优势。格兰特的作战计划是让他的左翼部队从拉帕汉诺克河向东南进军。他期望迫使李向南撤退并消灭其军队。巴特勒则向詹姆斯河上游进军。

尤利塞斯·辛普森·格兰特

第十八任美国总统（1869~1877）
“强壮、单纯、沉默……这就是那位在我们需要帮助时挺身而出的人。”——洛威尔按照这个计划，格兰特能一直处于通航水域附近，这样他就能够让他的军队容易获得食物和军需物资的补给。这个入侵方案有个重大的缺陷：它缩短了李通往所有重要据点的行军路线。这一事实以及对该地区的熟悉使南部邦联军获得了一个优势，它大大弥补了他们因人数不足造成的不利。

428. 公元1864年5月，荒野——5月4日和5日，联邦军渡过了拉皮丹河，穿过荒野向南进军。他们不久就发现自己离那场损失惨重的钱塞勒斯维尔之役的发生地已经非常接近了。那里树林茂密，并且到处都是灌木丛。那里基本没有空地，路更是稀少。正是在这种环境下，李袭击了联邦军。一切都对那位袭击者更有利，因为联邦军既无法预知他的袭击，也无法让人迅速前往受到威胁的位置。虽然如此，格兰特还是奋战了四天。随后，他巧妙地转移了军队，并从左路向斯波特斯凡尼亚县城进军。

429. 公元1864年5月，斯波特斯凡尼亚——李最先到达斯波特斯凡尼亚，并在他的战地上建了防御工事。可怕的战斗持续了数天。南部邦联军战线中有一个名为“突出部”的据点，双方曾反复攻下此处。联邦军伤亡惨重，而且格兰特无法将李击退。于是，他于5月20日再次由左侧进军，并命令他的军队前往北安娜河。但是，李再次赶到了他的前面，并占据了一个优势位置，使得对他的攻击都变得无效了。

430. 公元1864年6月，进军詹姆斯河——格兰特再次撤退，继续他南下的进军。但是，当他到达冷港的时候，李又已经在那里建立了强大的工事。两军这时正位于过去半岛战役的战场。在两周之中，格兰特一次又一次地发动进攻。随后，他于6月11日开始了最后一次进军。6月15日，联邦军到达了阿波马托克斯路口以南的詹姆斯河岸。但是，他们由于某些误解未能夺取彼得斯堡。于是，李在彼得斯堡安顿下来，而这场战役便形成了一种围攻的态势。在从拉皮丹河到詹姆斯河的这些战役中，格兰特损失了六万人。这些人有的战死了，有的负伤了，有的失踪了。李的损失要少得多——究竟少多少则不得而知。

**431. 公元1864年7~9月，彼得斯堡**——彼得斯堡守卫着里士满通往南方的道路。它事实上是里士满的一部分屏障。因为如果南部邦联军失去了对这些道路的控制，南部邦联就将不得不放弃其首都。所以，对于李来说，一定要守住彼得斯堡。而从另一方面来讲，格兰特希望控制彼得斯堡以南的道路，于是，他拉长了战线。但是每次当他延长战线的时候，南部邦联军也相应延长其战线。这个过程不可能永远持续下去。南部邦联军的兵力就要耗尽。李再也得不到任何援军了。他的防线迟早会削弱到格兰特可以冲破的地步。到那时，南部邦联就必然会放弃彼得斯堡和里士满。两年前，当里士满受到麦克莱伦威胁的时候，李曾通过突然进军华盛顿来迫使波托马克军转移。于是这时，他也分给朱巴尔·厄尔利（Jubal Anderson Early，1816~1894）一队精兵，派他穿过谢南多厄河谷向华盛顿进军。

一个位于彼得斯堡的防弹工事，如今它的上面已经绿树成荫。

**432. 公元1864年，谢里丹的河谷战役**——这时的形势和1862年的形势已经截然不同了。此时担任联邦军总司令的既不是麦克莱伦也不是波

菲利普·亨利·谢里丹

普，而是格兰特。他掌控着所有的军事行动，不受来自华盛顿的干涉，而且他的兵力也远远多过李。在不放松对彼得斯堡的攻势的同时，格兰特派出两个陆军兵团经水路赶往华盛顿。厄尔利是一个能干且作战积极的军人，但是他却推迟了对华盛顿的进攻[①]，直到联邦军从詹姆斯河赶来。随后他撤退到了谢南多厄河谷。这时，格兰特派给谢里丹四万名步兵和一万五千名骑兵，命他前往谢南多厄河谷击退厄尔利并销毁河谷中的所有给养，以免它们被其他南部邦联军部队利用。谢里丹出色地完成了任务。有一次，当谢里丹不在阵地的时候，南部邦联军偷袭了联邦军。但是，听到战斗的喧响后，谢里丹迅速策马赶赴前线。当他骑马赶来的时候，逃跑的联邦士兵又回来了。这次轮到南部邦联军被偷袭了，他们被扫荡出战场，在混乱中仓皇向河谷上游逃去（1864年10月19日）。随后，谢里丹毁掉了所有可供其他入侵军队利用的东西，然后在彼得斯堡重新加入了格兰特的大军。在这次军事行动取得了赫赫战果之后的11月，林肯再次当选为总统。

**433. 公元1863—1864年，封锁与巡洋舰**——封锁这时变得比以往任何时候都更严密。因为在1864年8月之前，法拉格特就已经率舰队进入莫比尔海湾，停止了那里的一切商业活动。谢尔曼也已经拿下了萨凡纳。1864年初，南部邦联军弃守查尔斯顿，因为它已经处于任由谢尔曼军摆布的境地，而特里（Alfred Howe Terry，1827~1890）也攻克了威明顿。南方

① 事实上，在到达华盛顿之前，厄尔利就在马里兰高地遇到了联邦的弗朗茨·西格尔军，后又在莫诺卡西与巴尔的摩指挥官卢·华莱士打了一仗。虽然厄尔利在这些战斗中取得了胜利，但已经耽误了数日行程，当他到达华盛顿附近时，已经有部分格兰特的援军赶到了华盛顿。

这时只能完全依赖自身的物资，而它们的耗尽也已经不远了。在公海上，有几艘英国援助船挂着南部邦联的旗帜。这些船中，最有名的当属“亚拉巴马号”。它在英国建造，配备着英国军火，船员也主要是英国人。1864年6月19日，合众国的“奇尔沙治号”在法国的瑟堡击沉了“亚拉巴马号”。英国人还在为南部邦联建造两艘装甲战舰。但是美国驻伦敦公使查尔斯·弗朗西斯·亚当斯先生（Charles Francis Adams, Sr.，1807~1886）提出，如果英国允许它们下水，那就意味着“战争”。于是英国政府立即买下了这两艘军舰。

大卫·格拉斯哥·法拉格特

434. 公元1865年，谢尔曼穿越卡罗来纳的行军——1865年初，谢尔曼开始了他的大进军中最艰难的那部分行军。这时，他命令军队由萨凡纳往北向弗吉尼亚州进军。南部邦联军准备要迎击他。但是，谢尔曼出发的时间比他们料想的更早，因此他也就为自己行程的第一部分赢得了一条畅通无阻的道路。约瑟夫·E. 约翰斯顿这时指挥军队迎击谢尔曼，并竭尽全力阻止他前进。有一阵子，他看起来有可能成功。在其他军队赶来救援联邦军之前，他差不多全歼了谢尔曼的先锋队。但是，谢尔曼的军队都是经验丰富的老兵，没有那么容易被打败。他们首先击退了前方的敌军，当后方出现另一支军队时，他们立即赶到防御工事的另一边，也击败了那支军队。随后，夜晚暂时中止了战斗，而在黎明到来之前，联邦军就已经强大到不可战胜了。谢尔曼继续向前挺进，到达了北卡罗来纳州的戈尔兹伯勒。在那里，从威明顿赶来的特里和从田纳西赶来的斯科菲尔德加入了他的大军。谢尔曼这时强大到足以击败任何一支南部邦联军了。他向罗利市进军并彻底切断了李与南卡罗来纳州和佐治亚州的联系（1865年4月）。

**435. 公元1865年4月，阿波马托克斯**——南部邦联的终结此时已是显而易见。李的军队正在挨饿。他们中经常有逃兵——这些逃兵不是去救助他们饱受战乱之苦的家人，就是去联邦军那里夺取食物。道路刚一变得适合行军，格兰特就率领他的十二万大军再次开始行动。他的目标是赶到李军的后方，迫使他放弃彼得斯堡。一场最后的、对联邦中心的无望的进攻只能增加格兰特的斗志。4月1日，谢里丹率领他的骑兵和一个步兵军团夺取了彼得特斯堡后方的五岔口，而且南部邦联军无法将他击退。于是，南部邦联军放弃了里士满和彼得斯堡。李曾试图逃往山区。但此时联邦军的行军速度比那些饥饿的南方人要快得多。谢里丹赶在了南方人的前面，并派兵在阿波马托克斯截断了他们的去路。他们已经无计可施，只能投降。1865年4月9日，北弗吉尼亚军的士兵——这时只剩下三万七千人——放下了他们武器。不久，约翰斯顿也投降了。剩下的小股单独的南部邦联军也被追到并俘获。

李在阿波马托克斯向格兰特投降

**436. 公元1865年4月15日，林肯遇刺**——国家的军队获得了胜利。在这胜利的时刻，林肯总统以无比的崇高和明智，独自挡在了南方人民与宣扬复仇的北方极端主义者之间。4月14日夜晚，他被一个奴隶制与退出联邦的支持者谋杀了。凡是当时年纪到了足以能记住1865年4月15日早晨的人，都永远不会忘记这个邪恶的凶手在北方引发的震惊。起初，林肯只是一个政党领袖。最后，他那纯粹的伟大秉性使他在美国人民心中赢得了一个其他人从未有过的地位。他的确是最伟大的，因为他是最典型的美国人。副总统安德鲁·约翰逊（Andrew Johnson，1808~1875）——一个来自田纳西州的主战派民主党人——成了总统。那些战败的脱离论者很快就会尝到失败的苦果。

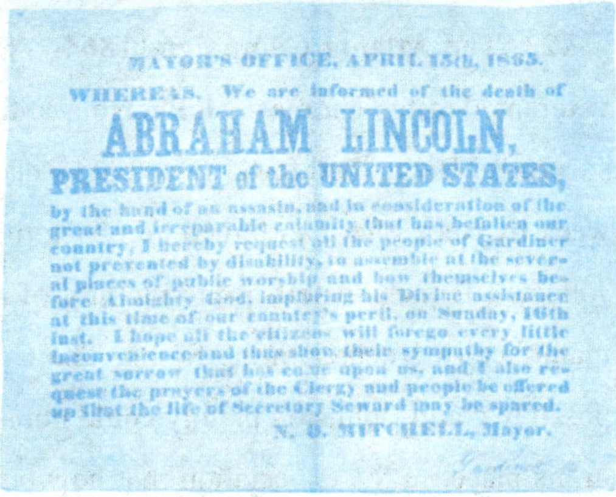
MAYOR'S OFFICE, APRIL 15th, 1865.

WHEREAS, We are informed of the death of

ABRAHAM LINCOLN,

PRESIDENT of the UNITED STATES,

by the hand of an assasin, and in consideration of the great and irreparable calamity that has befallen our country, I hereby request all the people of Gardiner not prevented by disability, to assemble at the several places of public worship and bow themselves before Almighty God, imploring his Divine assistance at this time of our country's peril, on Sunday, 16th inst. I hope all the citizens will forego every little inconvenience and thus show their sympathy for the great sorrow that has come upon us, and I also request the prayers of the Clergy and people be offered up that the life of Secretary Seward may be spared.

N. B. MITCHELL, Mayor.

华盛顿市长办公室于1865年4月15日发布的关于林肯遇害的公告

## 【ORIGINAL TEXT】

**422. Grant in Command of all the Armies.**—The Vicksburg and Chattanooga campaigns marked out Grant for the chief command. Hitherto the Union forces had acted on no well-thought-out plan. Now Grant was appointed Lieutenant

General and placed in command of all the armies of the United States (March, 1864). He decided to carry on the war in Virginia in person. Western operations he intrusted to Sherman, with Thomas in command of the Army of the Cumberland. Sheridan came with Grant to Virginia and led the cavalry of the Army of the Potomac. We will first follow Sherman and Thomas and the Western armies.

**423. The Atlanta Campaign, 1864.**—Sherman had one hundred thousand veterans, led by Thomas, McPherson, and Schofield. Joseph E. Johnston, who succeeded Bragg, had fewer men, but he occupied strongly fortified positions. Yet week by week Sherman forced him back till, after two months of steady fighting, Johnston found himself in the vicinity of Atlanta. This was the most important manufacturing center in the South. The Confederates must keep Atlanta if they possibly could. Johnston plainly could not stop Sherman. So Hood was appointed in his place, in the expectation that he would fight. Hood fought his best. Again and again he attacked Sherman only to be beaten off with heavy loss. He then abandoned Atlanta to save his army. From May to September Sherman lost twenty-two thousand men, but the Confederates lost thirty-five thousand men and Atlanta too.

**424. Plans of Campaign.**—Hood now led his army northward to Tennessee. But Sherman, instead of following him, sent only Thomas and Schofield. Sherman knew that the Confederacy was a mere shell. Its heart had been destroyed. What would be the result of a grand march through Georgia to the seacoast, and then northward through the Carolinas to Virginia? Would not this unopposed march show the people of the North, of the South, and of Europe that further resistance was useless? Sherman thought that it would, and that once in Virginia he could help Grant crush Lee. Grant agreed with Sherman and told him to carry out his plans. But first we must see what happened to Thomas and Hood.

**425. Thomas and Hood, 1864.**—Never dreaming that Sherman was not in pursuit, Hood marched rapidly northward until he had crossed the Tennessee. He then spent three weeks in resting his tired soldiers and in gathering supplies. This delay gave Thomas time to draw in recruits. At last Hood attacked Schofield at Franklin on November 30, 1864. Schofield retreated to Nashville, where Thomas was with the bulk of his army, and Hood followed. Thomas took all the time he needed to complete his preparations. Grant felt anxious at his delay and ordered him to fight. But Thomas would not fight until he was ready. At length, on December 15, he struck the blow, and in two days of fighting destroyed Hood's whole army. This was the last great battle in the West.

**426. Marching through Georgia.**—Destroying the mills and factories of Atlanta, Sherman set out for the seashore. He had sixty thousand men with him. They were all veterans and marched along as if on a holiday excursion. Spreading out over a line of sixty miles, they gathered everything eatable within reach. Every now and then they would stop and destroy a railroad. This they did by taking up the rails, heating them in the middle on fires of burning sleepers, and then twisting them around the nearest trees. In this way they cut a gap sixty miles long in the railroad communication between the half-starved army of northern Virginia and the storehouses of southern Georgia. On December 10, 1864, Sherman reached the sea. Ten days later he captured Savannah and presented it to the nation as a Christmas gift. Sherman and Thomas between them had struck a fearful blow at the Confederacy. How had it fared with Grant?

**427. Grant in Virginia, 1864.**—Grant had with him in Virginia the Army of the Potomac under Meade, the Ninth Corps under Burnside, and a great cavalry force under Sheridan. In addition General Butler was on the James River with some thirty thousand men. Lee had under his orders about one-half as many soldiers as had Grant. In every other respect the advantage was on his side. Grant's plan of campaign was to move by his left from the Rappahannock southeastwardly. He expected to push Lee southward and hoped to destroy his army. Butler, on his part, was to move up the James. By this plan Grant could always be near navigable water and could in this way easily supply his army with food and military stores. The great objection to this scheme of invasion was that it gave Lee shorter lines of march to all important points. This fact and their superior knowledge of the country gave the Confederates an advantage which largely made up for their lack in numbers.

**428. The Wilderness, May, 1864.**—On May 4 and 5 the Union army crossed the Rapidan and marched southward through the Wilderness. It soon found itself very near the scene of the disastrous battle of Chancellorsville. The woods were thick and full of underbrush. Clearings were few, and the roads were fewer still. On ground like this Lee attacked the Union army. Everything was in favor of the attacker, for it was impossible to foresee his blows, or to get men quickly to any threatened spot. Nevertheless Grant fought four days. Then he skillfully removed the army and marched by his left to Spotsylvania Court House.

**429. Spotsylvania, May, 1864.**—Lee reached Spotsylvania first and fortified his position. For days fearful combats went on. One point in the Confederate line, called the Salient, was taken and retaken over and over again. The loss of life was awful, and Grant could not push Lee back. So on May 20 he again set out on his march by the left and directed his army to the North Anna. But Lee was again before him and held such a strong position that it was useless to attack him.

**430. To the James, June, 1864.**—Grant again withdrew his army and resumed his southward march. But when he reached Cold Harbor, Lee was again strongly fortified. Both armies were now on the ground of the Peninsular Campaign.

For two weeks Grant attacked again and again. Then on June 11 he took up his march for the last time. On June 15 the Union soldiers reached the banks of the James River below the junction of the Appomattox. But, owing to some misunderstanding, Petersburg had not been seized. So Lee established himself there, and the campaign took on the form of a siege. In these campaigns from the Rapidan to the James, Grant lost in killed, wounded, and missing sixty thousand men. Lee's loss was much less—how much less is not known.

**431. Petersburg, June ~ December, 1864.**—Petersburg guarded the roads leading from Richmond to the South. It was in reality a part of the defenses of Richmond. For if these roads passed out of Confederate control, the Confederate capital would have to be abandoned. It was necessary for Lee to keep Petersburg. Grant, on the other hand, wished to gain the roads south of Petersburg. He lengthened his line; but each extension was met by a similar extension of the Confederate line. This process could not go on forever. The Confederacy was getting worn out. No more men could be sent to Lee. Sooner or later his line would become so weak that Grant could break through. Then Petersburg and Richmond must be abandoned. Two years before, when Richmond was threatened by McClellan, Lee had secured the removal of the Army of the Potomac by a sudden movement toward Washington. He now detached Jubal Early with a formidable force and sent him through the Shenandoah Valley to Washington.

**432. Sheridan's Valley Campaigns, 1864.**—The conditions now were very unlike the conditions of 1862. Now, Grant was in command instead of McClellan or Pope. He controlled the movements of all the armies without interference from Washington, and he had many more men than Lee. Without letting go his hold on Petersburg, Grant sent two army corps by water to Washington. Early was an able and active soldier, but he delayed his attack on Washington until soldiers came from the James. He then withdrew to the Shenandoah Valley. Grant now gave Sheridan forty thousand infantry and fifteen thousand cavalry, and sent him to the Valley with orders to drive Early out and to destroy all supplies in the Valley which could be used by another Southern army. Splendidly Sheridan did his work. At one time, when he was away, the Confederates surprised the Union army. But, hearing the roar of the battle, Sheridan rode rapidly to the front. As he rode along, the fugitives turned back. The Confederates, surprised in their turn, were swept from the field and sent whirling up the Valley in wild confusion (October 19, 1864). Then Sheridan destroyed everything that could be of service to another invading army and rejoined Grant at Petersburg. In the November following this great feat of arms, Lincoln was reelected President.

**433. The Blockade and the Cruisers, 1863~64.**—The blockade had now become stricter than ever. For by August, 1864, Farragut had carried his fleet into Mobile Bay and had closed it to commerce. Sherman had taken Savannah. Early in 1865 Charleston was abandoned, for Sherman had it at his mercy, and Terry captured Wilmington. The South was now absolutely dependent on its own resources, and the end could not be far off. On the open sea, with England's aid a few vessels flew the Confederate flag. The best known of these vessels was the *Alabama*. She was built in England, armed with English guns, and largely manned by Englishmen. On June 19, 1864, the United States ship *Kearsarge* sank her off Cherbourg, France. Englishmen were also building two ironclad battleships for the Confederates. But the American minister at London, Mr. Charles Francis Adams, said that if they were allowed to sail, it would be "war." The English government thereupon bought the vessels.

**434. Sherman's March through the Carolinas, 1865.**—Early in 1865 Sherman set out on the worst part of his great march. He now directed his steps northward from Savannah toward Virginia. The Confederates prepared to meet him. But Sherman set out before they expected him, and thus gained a clear path for the first part of his journey. Joseph E. Johnston now took command of the forces opposed to Sherman and did everything he could to stop him. At one moment it seemed as if he might succeed. He almost crushed the forward end of Sherman's army before the rest of the soldiers could be brought to its rescue. But Sherman's veterans were too old soldiers to be easily defeated. They first beat back the enemy in front, and when another force appeared in the rear they jumped to the other side of their field breastworks and defeated that force also. Night then put an end to the combat, and by morning the Union force was too strong to be attacked. Pressing on, Sherman reached Goldsboro' in North Carolina. There he was joined by Terry from Wilmington and by Schofield from Tennessee. Sherman now was strong enough to beat any Confederate army. He moved to Raleigh and completely cut Lee's communications with South Carolina and Georgia, April, 1865.

**435. Appomattox, April, 1865.**—The end of the Confederacy was now plainly in sight. Lee's men were starving. They were constantly deserting either to go to the aid of their perishing families or to obtain food from the Union army. As soon as the roads were fit for marching, Grant set his one hundred and twenty thousand men once more in motion. His object was to gain the rear of Lee's army and to force him to abandon Petersburg. A last despairing attack on the Union center only increased Grant's vigor. On April 1 Sheridan with his cavalry and an infantry corps seized Five Forks in the rear of Petersburg and could not be driven away. Petersburg and Richmond were abandoned. Lee tried to escape to the mountains. But now the Union soldiers marched faster than the starving Southerners. Sheridan, outstripping them, placed his men across their path at Appomattox Court House. There was nothing left save surrender. The soldiers of the Army of Northern Virginia, now only thirty-seven thousand strong, laid down their arms,

April 9, 1865. Soon Johnston surrendered, and the remaining small isolated bands of Confederates were run down and captured.

**436. Lincoln murdered, April 14, 1865.**—The national armies were victorious. President Lincoln, never grander or wiser than in the moment of victory, alone stood between the Southern people and the Northern extremists clamoring for vengeance. On the night of April 14 he was murdered by a sympathizer with slavery and secession. No one old enough to remember the morning of April 15, 1865, will ever forget the horror aroused in the North by this unholy murder. In the beginning Lincoln had been a party leader. In the end the simple grandeur of his nature had won for him a place in the hearts of the American people that no other man has ever gained. He was indeed the greatest because the most typical of Americans. Vice-President Andrew Johnson, a war Democrat from Tennessee, became President. The vanquished secessionists were soon to taste the bitter dregs of the cup of defeat.

# QUESTIONS AND TOPICS
# 问题与论题

[Use maps constantly while studying this period. The maps provided in Dodge's Bird's-Eye View are admirably adapted to this purpose.]

## CHAPTER 37

§ 380.—a. What did Lincoln say about the Union? What did he say about slavery? What oath did Lincoln take?

b. Was his inaugural conciliatory to the South?

§§ 381, 382.—a. What was the result of Buchanan's attempt to send supplies to Fort Sumter?

b. Why did Lincoln inform the governor of South Carolina of his determination to succor Fort Sumter?

c. What was the effect on Northern opinion of the attack on Fort Sumter?

d. Could the Southerners have done otherwise than fire on the flag?

§§ 383-385.—a. Why were the Virginians so divided? What resulted from this division?

b. What were the "border states"? Could these states have been neutral?

c. Describe the especial importance of Maryland.

d. What oath had the officers of the United States army and navy taken? Did Lee and other officers who resigned necessarily believe in the right of secession? Give your reasons.

## CHAPTER 38

§§ 386, 387.—a. State the advantages of the Southerners from the geographical point of view.

b. Explain how rivers were lines of defense.

c. Describe carefully the plan of the Bull Run campaign.

d. Why was the Shenandoah Valley so important?

§§ 388-390.—a. Why was McClellan placed in command of the Army of the Potomac?

b. Of what advantage to the South were the negroes?

c. Describe the plan of the Peninsular Campaign. What was the great objection to it?

§ 391.—a. Describe the Merrimac, the Monitor. Compare them with the Congress.

b. What effect did the Monitor-Merrimac fight have on McClellan's campaign?

§§ 392, 393.—a Describe the Peninsular Campaign. Why were not more soldiers sent to McClellan?

b. What is meant by the phrase "change of base"?

c. How did Lee secure the removal of McClellan's army from the James?

§§ 394, 395.—a Why did Lee invade Maryland?

b. Describe the battle of Antietam, of Fredericksburg. What was the result of each of these battles?

§§ 396, 397.—a. Give an account of the early life and training of Grant and of Thomas.

b. Why were the seizures of Cairo and Paducah and the battle of Mill Springs important?

c. What is meant by the phrase "unconditional surrender"?

§§ 398, 399.—a. Explain carefully the importance to the South of New Orleans and the lower Mississippi.

b. Give an account of Farragut's early life. How did it fit him for this work?

c. Describe the operations against New Orleans.

§ 400.—a. Explain carefully the plan of the campaign to Corinth Why was Corinth important?

b. What quality in Grant was conspicuous at Shiloh?

§ 401.—a. What was Bragg's object in invading Kentucky? How far did he succeed? Why was Chattanooga important?

## CHAPTER 39

§§ 402, 403.—a. What is a blockade? What was the effect of the blockade on the South?

b. Had sea power been in Southern hands, could the Union have been saved?

c. Why was Charleston so difficult to capture? (Compare with the Revolutionary War.)

§§ 405,406.—a. What help did the Southerners hope to obtain from Great Britain and France? Why? How were their hopes disappointed?

b. What do you think of the action of the English mill operatives?

c. Describe the Trent Affair. What do you think of Lincoln's action? Did the British government act wisely?

§§ 406, 407.—a. What had the Republican party declared about slavery in the states? What had Lincoln said in his inaugural?

b. How had the war altered Lincoln's power as President?

c. Why was it necessary for Lincoln to follow Northern sentiment?

d. What is contraband of war? How were the slaves contraband?

§§ 408, 409.—a. What steps had already been taken by Congress toward freeing the slaves?

b. How was the Emancipation Proclamation justified? Upon what would its enforcement depend?

c. What slave states were not affected by this proclamation?

d. How was slavery as an institution abolished throughout the United States?

§§ 410, 411.—a. Why was not the North united upon this war?

b. What is the force of the writ of habeas corpus? Why is it so important?

c. What was the "draft", and why was it necessary?

## CHAPTER 40

§§ 412-415.—a. Explain the position of the armies at the beginning of 1863.

b. Why was the conquest of Vicksburg so difficult? How was it finally captured?

c. What effect did the control of the Mississippi have upon the Confederacy?

§ 416.—a. What was Lee's object in invading Pennsylvania?

b. What position did the Union army keep as regards the Confederates?

§§ 417-419.—a. Describe the battle-field of Gettysburg. Why was the battle so important?

b. Describe in detail the principal events of each day of the battle.

c. Learn Lincoln's "Gettysburg Address." How was this ground hallowed? What was the great task before the people?

§§ 420, 421.—a. Describe the battle of Chickamauga. Review Thomas's services up to this time.

b. Describe the three parts of the battle of Chattanooga.

## CHAPTER 41

§§ 422, 423. —a. How had Grant shown his fitness for high command? Was it wise to have one man in command of all the armies? Why?

b. Review Sherman's career up to this time. Why did Grant impose trust in him?

c. What was the result of Hood's attacks?

§§ 424-426.—a. What was the real object of Sherman's march to the sea?

b. Describe the destruction of Hood's army. What does it show as to Thomas's ability?

c. What did Sherman's army accomplish on its way to the sea?

§§ 427-430.—a. Compare the conditions of the two armies in Virginia. Explain the advantages of the Confederates.

b. Describe the battle of the Wilderness, noting the conditions favorable to the Confederates.

c. Describe the movement to the James. What advantages had Grant not possessed by McClellan?

§§ 431,432.—a. Why was Petersburg important?

b. How did Lee try to compel the withdrawal of Grant? Why did he not succeed?

c. Describe Sheridan's work in the Shenandoah Valley. Read a short account of Sheridan's career to 1865, and state his services to the Union cause.

§ 433.—a. How had Sherman's victories affected the blockade?

b. What aid had Great Britain given to the Confederates? Why did she not give more assistance?

§§ 434, 435. —a. How did Sherman's occupation of Raleigh affect Lee?

b. Describe the condition of Lee's army. How was its capture accomplished?

§ 436.—a. Why was Lincoln's death a terrible loss to the South?

b. Why is he the greatest of all Americans?

## GENERAL QUESTIONS
## 综合性问题

a. Review the steps which led to the war for the Union.

b. What were Lincoln's personal views as to slavery? Why could he not carry them out?

c. What were Lincoln's leading characteristics? Give illustrations to support your view.

d. Study Grant's military career and try to find out why he succeeded where others failed.

e. Arrange a table of the leading campaigns, giving dates, leaders, end to be attained, important battles, and result.

f. Give the two most important battles of the war. Why do you select these?

## SUGGESTIONS TO TEACHER
## 给教师的建议

A few days spent upon a study of the field of war will save a great deal of time. Channing's *Students' History* will enable the teacher to indicate the most important strategic points. Maps have been sparingly provided in this book, as the simple plans in Dodge's Bird's-eye View can easily be reproduced on the blackboard. In general, campaigns should be studied rather than battles.

Pictures relating to this period are easily obtainable and may be freely used. It is an excellent plan to ask some veteran to describe his experiences, and the local post of the Grand Army of the Republic will often lend material aid in making the war real to the pupils. Grant's career should be especially studied, and the reasons for his successes carefully noted.

Indeed, the study of this period may well center around Lincoln and Grant. Lincoln's inaugurals are too difficult to be studied thoroughly. But the teacher can easily select portions, as the last paragraph of the second inaugural. Lincoln's Gettysburg Address should be learned by every pupil, and his letter to Greeley will throw a flood of light on Lincoln's character. In studying this period, as well as other periods, it is better to dwell on the patriotism and heroism of our soldiers, sailors, and statesmen than to point out their mistakes and personal faults.

Literature is so rich in reference to this time that nothing more than the mention of the works of Lowell, Whittier, Holmes, and Longfellow is needed.

# 第十四篇

# PART XIV

## 1865—1888年，重建与再统一

## RECONSTRUCTION AND REUNION, 1865~1888

## Books for Study and Reading

## 研究和阅读用书

**References.**—Scribner's *Popular History*, V; McMaster's *School History*, chs. xxx-xxxiii; Andrews's *Last Quarter-Century*.

**Home Readings.**—Hale's *Mr. Merriam's Scholars*.

CHAPTER 42

# 1861—1869年，约翰逊总统与重建

# PRESIDENT JOHNSON AND RECONSTRUCTION, 1861~1869

437. 林肯的重建政策——此时，这个国家面对的最大的问题是如何对待南方各州及其人民，以及如何对待那些获得自由的人。人们不能就这些问题达成共识。一些人认为，南方各州是“不可摧毁的”，它们不能退出或脱离联邦。另一些人则认为，南方各州既然已经被征服，那就应该被视为国家领土的一部分[①]。林肯认为，探究这些问题毫无用处。南方各州脱离了“和联邦的正当的实际关系”。这是显而易见的，因此要做的就是尽可能快速且平稳地恢复“正当的实际关系”[②]。早在1863年12月，林肯就已提议赦免除少数人之外的所有人——只要他们宣誓效忠于合众国，并承诺拥护宪法和《解放宣言》。林肯还曾做出承诺：只要任何一个加入南部邦联的州中有十分之一的选民做这些事情，并建立一个共和体制的政府，他就承认这个政府为这个州的政府。但是，这样一个重建的州进入国会的参议员和众议员的许可要由国会来决定。有几个州按照这个方案进行了重建。但是，舆论反对退出联邦的州以这种和缓的方式进行重建。尽管如此，民众是信任林肯的，要是林肯还活着，他或许已经劝导他们接受了他的方案。

---

① 这两种看法决定了南方各州是否还能享有“州”的权利。民主党和过去的分离主义者持前一种观点，认为应该让南部各州回到战前状态；共和党中的激进派和国家主义者持后一种观点，认为应该把南部各州视为被征服的领土，不赋予其作为州的权利。

② 这个观点是林肯在1865年4月11日的讲话中提出的，这是他生前的最后一次重要讲话。

438. 约翰逊总统的重建方案——约翰逊是一个能干的人，还是一个爱国者。但是，他完全没有林肯那种明智的耐心。与人打交道时，他也完全没有林肯那种得体与幽默。相反，在遭到反对时，他总是大发脾气。尽管他是一个南方人，但是他憎恨奴隶制和奴隶主。另一方面，他又有一种南方人对黑人的蔑视。他实际上采纳了林肯的重建政策，并试图通过发挥总统的作用来实现退出州的重建。

439. 公元1865年，第十三条宪法修正案——林肯总统颁布的《解放宣言》已经解放了南部退出州和反叛联邦政府的北部州的部分地区的奴隶。但是它没有解放效忠州的奴隶，也没有消灭作为一种制度的奴隶制本身。所以，任何一个州都能随时选择重建奴隶制。只能通过一条宪法修正案才能废除奴隶制。于是，第十三条宪法修正案于1865年12月获得通过。这条修正案宣称“在合众国境内受合众国管辖的任何地方，奴隶制和强制劳役都不得存在，但作为对依法判罪者罪行的惩罚除外”。整个合众国的奴隶制就以这种方式终结了。

440. 公元1865—1866年，国会与总统——不幸的是，许多原来的蓄奴州已经通过了强迫黑人劳动的各项法律。他们采用了一种和奴隶制差不多的强制劳动制度。1865年12月，新一届国会召开会议。共和党人占据了多数席位。他们拒绝接纳来自重建的南方州的参议员和众议员，并立即着手通过保护黑人的各项法律。1865年3月的时候，战争仍在继续，林肯也还活着，那时候国会就已经建立了自由民局以关注黑人的权益。这时（1866年2月），国会通过了一个法案以维持这个机构并赋予了它更大的权力。约翰逊立即否决了这个法案。同年7月，国会通过了另一个维持自由民局的法案。这个法案赋予该局官员非常大的权力，同时要求给黑人提供教育，并规定可以动用军队来强制人们服从这项法律。约翰逊也否决了这个法案。

441. 第十四条宪法修正案——在关于自由民局的斗争持续的时候，国会通过了《民权法案》以保护获得自由的人。该法案规定，与获得自由的人的公民权利相关的案件须在联邦法院而非各州法院进行审理。约翰逊认为，国会无权这样做。他否决了这个法案，但是国会不顾他的否决，仍然通过了这个法案。国会随后起草了第十四条宪法修正案。该修正案禁止各州剥夺公民的权利，不论他是白人还是黑人。它进一步规定，无论何时，如果一个州拒不承认一个人——除了参与叛乱的人——的公民权，就必须减少该州在国会中的代表席位。最后，该修正案对合众国的债务做出了保证，并宣布所有因支持叛乱举借的债务都无效。除田纳西州外，南方的每一个州都拒绝接受这条修正案。

442. 公元1867年，《重建法》——1866年11月底举行的国会选举对共和党非常有利。国会中的共和党成员觉得这证明了北方支持他们的重建政策。国会于1866年12月召开会议，并立即着手执行这项政策。首先，它通过了《官职任期法》以阻止约翰逊解除共和党人的职务。随后，它通过了《重建法》。约翰逊否决了这两个议案，而国会不顾他的否决，仍然通过了它们。《重建法》后来得到修改和强化。这里最好描述一下重建过程的最终形式。首先，除田纳西州外，所有退出联邦的州被划成几个军事区。每个军事区都由一个军官来管理，他手下配有士兵以执行其命令。田纳西州没有包括在这个安排之内，因为它已经接受了第十四条宪法修正案。但是所有其他由林肯或约翰逊重建的州将被再次重建。所有男性都拥有选举权，不论是黑人还是白人，只要在任何一个州中生活一年以上即可——罪犯和参与叛乱的人除外。这个例外的条件剥夺了南方原来的管制者的选举权。而这些新的选民可以制定一部州宪法并选出一个议会，该议会应认可第十四条宪法修正案。在所有这一切完成之后，来自重建州的参议员和众议员才能获准进入国会。

443. 公元1868年，弹劾约翰逊——约翰逊总统否决了所有这些法案。他称这个国会是一部分州的国会，因为国会没有按照他的想法去接纳重建州的代表。公正地讲，他对他的反对者所使用的措辞可以称得上粗鄙，而且与一个伟大国家的首脑不相称。更出格的是他拒绝受《官职任期法》的束缚。自从联邦政府形成以来，总统们总是在自认为适当的情况下撤换官员。《官职任期法》要求撤职和任命官员都必须经过参议院的同意。林肯内阁的成员中仍然在职的是埃德温·M. 斯坦顿（Edwin McMasters Stanton，1814~1869）。约翰逊撤销了他的职务，这便引发了一场风波。众议院投票宣布弹劾总统。在联邦最高法院首席大法官蔡斯主持下，参议院审理了这个弹劾案。宪法规定，三分之二的参议员投票赞成才能定罪。七名共和党参议员和所有的民主党参议员反对定罪，于是总统因一票之差被判无罪。

安德鲁·约翰逊

第十七任美国总统（1865~1869）

444. 墨西哥的法国人——法国皇帝拿破仑三世（Louis-Napoléon Bonaparte，1808~1873）趁美国内战之际，无视门罗宣言，重新在美洲建立了一个法国的殖民帝国。事实上，他一度似乎要干涉美国内战，强迫联邦政府从南部邦联各州撤军。后来，他想了一个主意。他觉得或许得克萨斯州会退出南部邦联，然后在法国的保护之下独立。这个计划失败后，他开始在墨西哥建立一个帝国，让奥地利亲王马克西米利安（Ferdinand Maximilian Joseph，1832~1867）当皇帝。内战的结束使美国得以干涉这件事。格兰特和谢里丹很乐意进军墨西哥并赶走法国人，但是西华德认为，法国人要不了多久就会不得不离开。为了加快他们的离开，他告知法国政府，他们离开得越早越好。于是法国人于1868年撤走了。马克西米利安坚持留了下来。他被墨西哥人俘获并枪决了。随后，墨西哥共和国重新建立了起来。

拿破仑三世

费迪南德·马克西米利安·约瑟夫

445. 公元1867年，购买阿拉斯加——1867年，约翰逊总统向参议院递交咨文，要求批准购买俄国在美洲的殖民地的条约。这些殖民地被称为“阿拉斯加”，包括最西北的一大片土地。需要支付的价格是七百万美元。这块购买地的历史至今仍鲜为人知。参议院大感意外，但是它批准了这个条约。直到最近几年，阿拉斯加唯一重要的物产一直都只是毛皮海豹[①]的皮。为了保护这些海豹群体，使之免于灭绝，合众国做出规定，限制每年

① 毛皮海豹，学名为海狗，又称突耳海豹，其实并不属于海豹科，而属于海狮科。

捕杀海豹的数量。但加拿大人不受这些规定的约束，而海豹群体也几乎灭亡了。最近几年，人们在阿拉斯加及与其接壤的加拿大地区发现了大量的金矿。但是，如果不先穿过阿拉斯加的话，就很难开采加拿大的金矿。这一事实让合众国与大不列颠就阿拉斯加与加拿大之间边界问题达成共识变得更加困难。

**446. 公元1868年，格兰特当选总统**——关于重建的骚乱以及国会中的共和党人与总统之间尖锐的斗争在政坛中引发了巨大的混乱。民主党提名了F．P．布莱尔（Francis Preston Blair, Jr.，1821~1875）——一位英勇的军人——为副总统候选人。对于总统候选人，他们提名了纽约州的霍雷肖·西摩（Horatio Seymour，1810~1886）。这是一个和平派民主党人 。作为纽约州州长，他在内战期间拒绝支持联邦政府。共和党提名了格兰特将军。他比西摩多获得了三十万张普通选民票。在总数为294张的总统选举人票中，格兰特获得了215张选票。

## 【Original Text】

**437. Lincoln's Reconstruction Policy.**—The great question now before the country was what should be done with the Southern states and people. And what should be done with the freedmen? On these questions people were not agreed. Some people thought that the states were "indestructible"; that they could not secede or get out of the Union. Others thought that the Southern states had been conquered and should be treated as a part of the national domain. Lincoln thought that it was useless to go into these questions. The Southern states were out of the "proper practical relations with the Union." That was clear enough. The thing to do, therefore, was to restore "proper practical relations" as quickly and as quietly as possible. In December, 1863, Lincoln had offered a pardon to all persons, with some exceptions, who should take the oath of allegiance to the United States, and should promise to support the Constitution and the Emancipation Proclamation. Whenever one-tenth of the voters in any of the Confederate states should do these things, and should set up a republican form of government, Lincoln promised to recognize that government as the state government. But the admission to Congress of Senators and Representatives from such a reconstructed state would rest with Congress. Several states were reconstructed on this plan. But public opinion was opposed to this quiet reorganization of the seceded states. The people trusted Lincoln, however, and had he lived he might have induced them to accept his plan.

**438. President Johnson's Reconstruction Plan.**—Johnson was an able man and a patriot. But he had none of Lincoln's wise patience. He had none of Lincoln's tact and humor in dealing with men. On the contrary, he always lost his temper when opposed. Although he was a Southerner, he hated slavery and slave owners. On the other hand, he had a Southerner's contempt for the negroes. He practically adopted Lincoln's reconstruction policy and tried to bring about the reorganization of the seceded states by presidential action.

**439. The Thirteenth Amendment, 1865.**—President Lincoln's Emancipation Proclamation had freed the slaves in those states and parts of states which were in rebellion against the national government. It had not freed the slaves in the loyal states. It had not destroyed slavery as an institution. Any state could reestablish slavery whenever it chose. Slavery could be prohibited only by an amendment of the Constitution. So the Thirteenth Amendment was adopted, December, 1865. This amendment declares that "neither slavery nor involuntary servitude, except as a punishment for crime shall exist within the United States, or any place subject to their jurisdiction." In this way slavery came to an end throughout the United States.

**440. Congress and the President, 1865~1866.**—Unhappily many of the old slave states had passed laws to compel the negroes to work. They had introduced a system of forced labor which was about the same thing as slavery. In December, 1865, the new Congress met. The Republicans were in the majority. They refused to admit the Senators and Representatives from the reorganized Southern states and at once set to work to pass laws for the protection of the negroes. In March, 1865, while the war was still going on, and while Lincoln was alive, Congress had established the Freedmen's Bureau to look after the interests of the negroes. Congress now (February, 1866) passed a bill to continue the Bureau and to give it much more power. Johnson promptly vetoed the bill. In the following July Congress passed another bill to continue the Freedmen's Bureau. In this bill the officers of the Bureau were given greatly enlarged powers, the education of the blacks was provided for, and the army might be used to compel obedience to the law. Johnson vetoed this bill also.

**441. The Fourteenth Amendment.**—While this contest over the Freedmen's Bureau was going on, Congress passed the Civil Rights Bill to protect the freedmen. This bill provided that cases concerning the civil rights of the freedmen should be heard in the United States courts instead of in the state courts. Johnson thought that Congress had no power to do this. He vetoed the bill, and Congress passed it over his veto. Congress then drew up the Fourteenth Amendment. This forbade the states to abridge the rights of the citizens, white or black. It further provided that the representation of any state in Congress should be diminished whenever it denied the franchise to any one except for taking part in rebellion. Finally it guaranteed the debt of the United States, and declared all debts incurred in support of rebellion null and void. Every Southern state except Tennessee refused to accept this amendment.

**442. The Reconstruction Acts, 1867.**—The Congressional elections of November, 1866, were greatly in favor of the Republicans. The Republican members of Congress felt that this showed that the North was with them in their policy as to reconstruction. Congress met in December, 1866, and at once set to work to carry out this policy. First of all it passed the Tenure of Office Act to prevent Johnson dismissing Republicans from office. Then it passed the Reconstruction Act. Johnson vetoed both of these measures, and Congress passed them both over his veto. The Reconstruction Act was later amended and strengthened. It will be well to describe here the process of reconstruction in its final form. First of all the seceded states, with the exception of Tennessee, were formed into military districts. Each district was ruled by a military officer who had soldiers to carry out his directions. Tennessee was not included in this arrangement, because it had accepted the Fourteenth Amendment. But all the other states, which had been reconstructed by Lincoln or by Johnson, were to be reconstructed over again. The franchise was given to all men, white or black, who had lived in any state for one year—excepting criminals and persons who had taken part in rebellion. This exception took the franchise away from the old rulers of the South. These new voters could form a state constitution and elect a legislature which should ratify the Fourteenth Amendment. When all this had been done, Senators and Representatives from the reconstructed state might be admitted to Congress.

**443. Impeachment of Johnson, 1868.**—President Johnson had vetoed all these bills. He had declared that the Congress was a Congress of only a part of the states, because Representatives from the states reconstructed according to his ideas were not admitted. He had used language toward his opponents that was fairly described as indecent and unbecoming the chief officer of a great nation. Especially he had refused to be bound by the Tenure of Office Act. Ever since the formation of the government the Presidents had removed officers when they saw fit. The Tenure of Office Act required the consent of the Senate to removals as well as to appointments. Among the members of Lincoln's cabinet who were still in office was Edwin M. Stanton. Johnson removed him, and this brought on the crisis. The House impeached the President. The Senate, presided over by Chief Justice Chase, heard the impeachment. The Constitution requires the votes of two-thirds of the Senators to convict. Seven Republicans voted with the Democrats against conviction, and the President was acquitted by one vote.

**444. The French in Mexico.**—Napoleon III, Emperor of the French, seized the occasion of the Civil War to set the Monroe Doctrine at defiance and to refound a French colonial empire in America. At one time, indeed, he seemed to be on the point of interfering, to compel the Union government to withdraw its armies from the Confederate states. Then Napoleon had an idea that perhaps Texas might secede from the Confederacy and set up for itself under French protection. This failing, he began the establishment of an empire in Mexico with the Austrian prince, Maximilian, as Emperor. The ending of the Civil War made it possible for the United States to interfere. Grant and Sheridan would gladly have marched troops into Mexico and turned out the French, but Seward said that the French would have to leave before long anyway. He hastened their going by telling the French government that the sooner they left the better. They were withdrawn in 1868. Maximilian insisted on staying. He was captured by the Mexicans and shot.

The Mexican Republic was reestablished.

**445. The Purchase of Alaska, 1867.**—In 1867 President Johnson sent to the Senate, for ratification, a treaty with Russia for the purchase of Russia's American possessions. These were called Alaska, and included an immense tract of land in the extreme Northwest. The price to be paid was seven million dollars. The history of this purchase is still little known. The Senate was completely taken by surprise, but it ratified the treaty. Until recent years the only important product of Alaska has been the skins of the fur seals. To preserve the seal herds from extinction, the United States made rules limiting the number of seals to be killed in any one year. The Canadians were not bound by these rules, and the herds have been nearly destroyed. In recent years large deposits of gold have been found in Alaska and in neighboring portions of Canada. But the Canadian deposits are hard to reach without first going through Alaska. This fact has made it more difficult to agree with Great Britain as to the boundary between Alaska and Canada.

**446. Grant elected President, 1868.**—The excitement over reconstruction and the bitter contest between the Republicans in Congress and the President had brought about great confusion in politics. The Democrats nominated General F. P. Blair, a gallant soldier, for Vice-President. For President they nominated Horatio Seymour of New York. He was a Peace Democrat. As governor of New York during the war he had refused to support the national government. The Republicans nominated General Grant. He received three hundred thousand more votes than Seymour. Of the two hundred and ninety-four electoral votes, Grant received two hundred and fifteen.

CHAPTER 43

# 1869—1889年，从格兰特到克利夫兰

## FROM GRANT TO CLEVELAND, 1869~1889

447. 第十五条宪法修正案——1869年2月，就在格兰特宣誓就职之前，国会又提出了一条宪法修正案。该修正案规定：合众国公民的选举权不得因种族、肤色和过去的奴隶身份而被合众国或任何州否认或剥夺。国会有权制定适当法律实施本条规定。各州议会迅速接受了这条修正案。这条修正案于1870年3月宣布生效。

448. 重建结束——只有三个州仍未完成重建。它们是弗吉尼亚州、得克萨斯州和密西西比州。1869年，国会在接纳它们重回联邦的条件中加了一条——接受第十五宪法修正案。1870年初，它们都达到了那些条件的要求，重新加入了联邦。联邦这时又完整了。1860年以来，又有四个州加入联邦。它们是堪萨斯州、西弗吉尼亚州、内华达州和内布拉斯加州。联邦这时总共有37个州。

449. 南方人和黑人——国会重建方案的第一个结果是把南方各州的控制权交给了那些获得自由的人和他们的白人盟友。在这些自由民的白人朋友中，有一些很有个性和才能的人，但他们中的大多数是从北方来的投机商人。他们被称为“提包客”，因为他们常常把他们的行李箱提在手上。少数把黑人当朋友的南方白人被他们的白人邻居称为“无赖”（scalawag）[①]。

① 这个词最初指农场里因年老或有病而无用的牲畜，后引申为无赖、流氓等义。

各种秘密社团也出现了。最著名的是“三K党”。这些秘密社团的目标是恐吓获得自由的人和他们的白人朋友并阻止他们参加选举。这导致了《强制法》的通过。这部法律规定对恐吓罪予以严惩，还规定此类案件应由联邦法院来审理；可以让驻扎在南方的联邦军人强制人们遵守这部法律。

**450. 亚拉巴马索赔案**——内战期间，由英国船厂建造，或在英国港口修整和补充煤的船只曾掠夺过美国的商船。合众国向大不列颠提出了对这些船只造成的损失的索赔要求，因为在这些船中，最著名的就是“亚拉巴马号”，所以这件事被称为“亚拉巴马索赔案”。合众国与大不列颠之间还存在关于渔场以及俄勒冈西部边界的争端。1871年，合众国与大不列颠达成一个名为《华盛顿条约》的协定。根据该条约，所有这些争端都要通过仲裁解决。关于俄勒冈边界的判决有利于合众国，但是关于渔场的判决有利于英国。亚拉巴马索赔案由驻瑞士日内瓦的五名仲裁员进行裁决。他们判定大不列颠没有以“应有的审慎”来阻止自己的港口被南部邦联滥用。他们因此裁定它向合众国赔偿1550万美元的赔偿金。

**451. 公元1871年，芝加哥火灾**——1871年10月的一个清晨，一名芝加哥妇女去牲口棚给奶牛挤奶。她提了一盏点燃的煤油灯，因为当时天还没亮。奶牛踢翻了灯。牲口棚很快就着火了。一阵狂风把火星从一间房子吹

1832年的芝加哥

1871年芝加哥大火

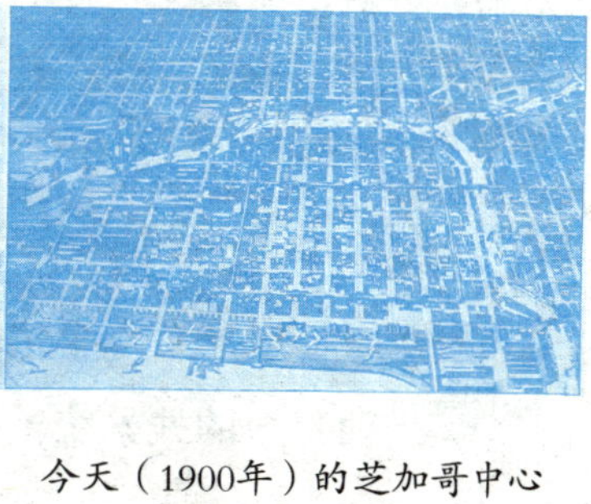
今天（1900年）的芝加哥中心

到另一间房子。就这样，从那天白天到晚上以及第二天一整天，这场大火一直在不断蔓延。价值将近两亿美元的财产被烧毁。将近十万人的家被烧光。在短得令人吃惊的时间里，烧毁的地区得以重建，芝加哥的发展也比过去更快了。

452. 政治腐败——纽约市没有发生损失两亿美元的火灾。但是，一个由城市官员组成的“圈子”窃取了该城一亿五千多万美元的资金。其他城市也有非常严重的腐败现象。没有哪个州的政府不存在受贿和贪污。人们认为许多联邦政府官员与蓄意欺诈人民有牵连。事情的真相是，内战留下了肆意花钱的风气。民众都为一夜暴富的欲望所支配。没有人仔细探究他们的钱究竟是从哪里来的。

453. 公元1872年大选——事实上，公职部门的这种情况让许多人怀疑重选格兰特担任总统是否明智。对格兰特个人的正直，人们没有丝毫的怀疑；但是人们严重怀疑他在任命官员上的判断力。重建看起来也没能让南方恢复和平与繁荣。由于这些原因，许多选民离开了共和党的阵营。他们自称自由共和党，并提名霍勒斯·格里利为总统候选人。格里利一直是最直言不讳地反对奴隶制的人之一。民主党找不到更好的候选人，于是他们也提名了格里利。但是，许多民主党人不愿意投票支持他。他们暂时脱离了自己的政党，提名了第三个总统候选人。所有这一切混乱的结果是格兰特再次当选。但是民主党这次获得了众议院的多数席位。

454. 公元1867—1877年，古巴叛乱——当其他西属美洲殖民地赢得独立的时候，古巴依然忠于西班牙。但是到了1867年，古巴人再也无法忍受西班牙的残暴统治了。他们发动了叛乱，并为获得自由战斗了十年。西班牙人认为一些村庄中有居民支持叛乱，因此就将那些村庄整个烧毁了。他们甚至威胁要杀死所有被发现逃离家园的古巴人。这些残酷行为激起了美国人的同情心。尽管美国政府竭力阻止人们去援助古巴人，可还是有远征军出海前往古巴。在这些前去援助古巴的船中，有一艘名为“弗吉纽斯号”。西班牙人俘获了它，将它带到了圣地亚哥，还杀死了船上的四十六名船员。这个事件险些引发了一场美国对西班牙的战争。但是，西班牙人向美国人道歉了，并向美国国旗致敬。1877年，格兰特总统坚定了他的想法，认为这场战争已经持续得够久了。他对西班牙说了狠话。于是，西班牙政府和叛乱者达成了协议，叛乱就此结束。

455. 政治生活中的丑闻——1872年，众议院对与太平洋铁路修建相关的贿赂的指控展开了一次调查。马萨诸塞州的奥克斯·埃姆斯（Oakes Ames，1804~1873）是一个名为“动产信托”的公司的首脑。这个公司是为了修建联邦太平洋铁路而组建起来的。由于害怕国会通过可能伤害这个企业的法律，埃姆斯将这个公司的股票赠送给了一些国会议员[①]。但是，众议院没有找到对任何一位议员不利的证据，于是此事就此作罢。格兰特的第二届任期开始后不久，许多邪恶的勾当就暴露出来了。其中之一就是“威士忌酒集团”，他们在一些政府官员的协助下以诈骗方式攫取了大量的政府资金[②]。格兰特希望进行一次彻底的调查，他还声称“不让任何一个有罪之人逃脱”。所有案件中最糟糕的或许就是和战争部长W. W. 贝尔纳普（William Worth Belknap，1829~1890）相关的案件。但是，他通过辞职逃脱

① 埃姆斯自己也是一位众议员，而涉嫌受贿的有十名众议员和四名参议员，其中包括当时的副总统斯凯勒·科尔费克斯和1880年当选为总统的詹姆斯·A. 加菲尔德。因为缺乏证据，结果埃姆斯甚至没有被逐出国会，只是受到了国会的谴责。

② 此案主要是财务部内部官员贪污国家对威士忌酒征收的税，涉案人员包括财务部长与格兰特的私人秘书。这项罪行持续了数年，该集团每年从中获得十万美元的赃款。直到1874年，新任财务部长才揭发了这项罪行。

了处罚。

456. 南方的无政府状态——与此同时，南方的重建进展并不顺利。在路易斯安那州、阿肯色州、南卡罗来纳州尤为如此。路易斯安那州——阿肯色州也一样——有两套行政机构和议会。小规模的内战仍在继续。在南卡罗来纳州，“提包客”与黑人夺取了控制权。他们四处偷窃。在其他的南方州，对黑人的暴行仍在继续。格兰特总统忧虑不已。“让我们拥有和平”是他衷心的希望。但是，尽管他知道北方的舆论已经转而和他敌对了，但他还是认为有必要让联邦军队继续驻守在南方。正是在这种情形下，1876年大选拉开了帷幕。

457. 公元1876年大选——共和党总统候选人是俄亥俄州的拉瑟福德·B. 海斯（Rutherford Birchard Hayes，1822~1893）。他是一位参加过内战的英勇军人，也是一位品格最为高尚的人。他的民主党对手是纽约州的塞缪尔·J. 蒂尔登（Samuel Jones Tilden，1814~1886）——一个因曾担任“帝国州”[①]州长而赢得声誉的精明律师。当总统选举人的投票结果送到国会时，来自南方的三个州各有两套总统选举人的投票结果，并且俄勒冈的投票结果也很可疑[②]。共和党把持着参议院，民主党把持着

拉瑟福德·伯查德·海斯
第十九任美国总统（1877~1881）

① “帝国州”是纽约州的别称。

② 所谓两组选票，其实是民主党和共和党各自扔掉了一部分选票得到的结果，而在俄亥俄州选举途中一名共和党选举人被换成了一名民主党选举人，从而产生一张重复的选票，因此其结果是“可疑的”。事实上，这一系列不正当的竞争，使得本来在普通选票上超过海斯，在选举人票数上只差一票即可当选的蒂尔登出人意料地遭遇了失败。

众议院。因为这两院不能就如何计票达成共识，他们便把这整件事交由一个总统选举人委员会去做。该委员会由五名参议员、五名众议员和五名联邦最高法院法官组成。他们中有八个共和党人，七个民主党人。他们以八比七裁定海斯当选，于是，1877年3月4日，海斯宣誓就职为总统。

**458. 从南方撤兵**——北方人民已经对南方无休止的政治动乱失去了兴趣。原来的南方领导人几乎重新掌控了南方所有的州。除了通过一场新的内战，没有别的办法让他们下台，而北方人民不愿再次卷入战争。唯一能做的其他事情就是撤出联邦军队，让南方人民尽其所能地自谋出路。海斯总统召回了军队，于是所有的南方州立即落到了民主党的掌控之中。

**459. 公元1877年，罢工与骚乱**——内战期间和内战结束后的几年间的挥霍无度和投机倒把以1873年的一场大恐慌而告终。在大恐慌之后到来的是“艰难时代”。生产量下降了，对劳动力的需求减少了。到处都在减薪。罢工成了常有的事，而骚乱也伴随着罢工而来。在宾夕法尼亚州西部的匹兹堡，骚乱者占领了铁路。他们烧毁了数以百计的火车车厢和火车头。他们毁坏了铁路建筑物。骚乱最终得以平息。但是在此之前，价值数百万美元的财产已经被毁了。

匹兹堡骚乱之后的废墟

詹姆斯·埃布拉姆·加菲尔德

第二十任美国总统（1881年3月~1881年9月）

**460. 公元1880年大选**——执政伊始，海斯就声明他不会再次参加竞选。那么谁应该成为共和党的旗手呢？格兰特的支持者们提议第三次提名他为总统候选人。这些主张格兰特应当第三次担任总统的政客们反对让詹姆斯·G. 布莱恩（James Gillespie Blaine，1830~1893）成为候选人。这些人被称为"坚定派共和党人"。在提名大会上，他们坚定而一致地投票支持格兰特。最终，他们的反对者们在"一切为了击败格兰特"的口号下突然转而支持了一个新人，他的名字之前一直少有人提及。这就是俄亥俄州的詹姆斯·A. 加菲尔德（James Abram Garfield，1831~1881）。他在内战中出名，并一直在国会中负责信贷方面的事务。对于副总统，共和党提名了切斯特·A. 阿瑟（Chester Alan Arthur，1829~1886），他是纽约的一位银行家。至于民主党，他们提名为总统候选人的是波托马克军中最杰出的、最受爱戴的军人之一——温费尔德·斯科特·汉考克将军（Winfield Scott Hancock，1824~1886）。竞选过程异常激烈。最后，加菲尔德赢得了竞选。

**461. 加菲尔德遇刺；公务员体制改革**——1881年3月4日，加菲尔德宣誓就职。7月2日，一个失望的官职索求者开枪击中了他的背部。加菲尔德忍受了数周巨大的痛苦。最后，这位备受折磨的总统于9月19日逝世。这时，政党分肥制的恶果终于引起了美国人民的注意。副总统阿瑟继任为总统。他全心全意投入到了改革的规划中。他不久就着手进行改革。但是，

切斯特·艾伦·阿瑟
第二十一任美国总统（1881~1885）

他发现进行任何持续的改革都是一件非常困难的事。宪法赋予了总统任命官员的权力，而对任命进行确认的权力则交给了参议院。未经总统同意，国会的任何立法都不得削弱宪法赋予总统的权力；而一位总统也不能约束继任他的总统。此外，任何改革方案都要耗费资金，这些资金也必须由国会每年投票决定。因此，每一位总统和每一届国会两院的同意是公务员体制改革持续下去的必要条件。尽管如此，到目前为止，公务员体制改革已经取得了稳步的进展。现在，绝大部分的行政部门都是基于功绩考核制度进行组织安排的。

462. 公元1884年大选——1884年，共和党提名缅因州的詹姆斯·G. 布莱恩为总统候选人。他的演讲具有吸引力，拥有众多支持者，但也树敌不少。许多共和党选民尤其不信任他。他们认为他曾利用自己的职位牟取私利，尽管他们没找到任何对他不利的证据。这些共和党人被称为“骑墙派”。他们拒绝支持本党的提名，转而去支持民主党候选人格罗弗·克利夫兰（Stephen Grover Cleveland，1837~1908）。他曾担任布法罗市的市长而且表现非常突出。他随后又以绝

斯蒂芬·格罗弗·克利夫兰
第二十二、二十四任美国总统（1885~1889；1893~1897）

对的优势当选为纽约州州长。1884年的竞选是以人身攻击的方式进行的。这让人想起1800年竞选和1828年竞选。克利夫兰赢得了四个北方大州和“可靠的南方”（Solid South）[①] 的支持，当选为总统。

463. 公元1885~1889年，克利夫兰政府——克利夫兰第一届任期内的最大纷争是一场关于关税的激烈斗争。政府在内战期间的资金短缺迫使国会以征收国内收入税的方式来募集了大量资金。这些税收反过来又给国外进口的商品关税税率带来了大幅的提高。尽管这时国内收入税几乎已经完全取消了，但是战时的关税事实上仍然有效。1887年，克利夫兰把这整个问题摆在了国会面前。有一阵子，国会似乎可能出台某些政策。但是，国会中的反对派非常积极而且非常强大。因此，这件事没有取得什么重大的结果。克利夫兰的第一届政府的真正意义在于这样一个事实，即重新允许南方人参与这个国家的管理。因此，它标志着美国人民再一次团结了起来。

## 【ORIGINAL TEXT】

**447. The Fifteenth Amendment.**—In February, 1869, just before Grant's inauguration, Congress proposed still another amendment, providing that neither the United States nor any state could abridge the rights of citizens of the United States on account of race, color, or previous condition of servitude. The state

① 又译为“坚固的南方”或“固若金汤的南方”。这个词含有浓厚的政治意味，因为南方各州从美国内战前就主要是民主党的势力范围，其选票一般固定地会投给民主党人，这也逐渐成为美国总统大选中民主党的一项固有优势，即“南方战略”。直到20世纪中后期，这种情况才逐渐有了改变。

legislatures hastened to accept this amendment, and it was declared in force in March, 1870.

**448. End of Reconstruction.**—Three states only were still unreconstructed. These were Virginia, Texas, and Mississippi. In 1869 Congress added to the conditions on which they could be readmitted to the Union the acceptance of the Fifteenth Amendment. Early in 1870 they all complied with the conditions and were readmitted. The Union was now again complete. Since 1860 four states had been added to the Union. These were Kansas, West Virginia, Nevada, and Nebraska. There were now thirty-seven states in all.

**449. The Southerners and the Negroes.**—The first result of the Congressional plan of reconstruction was to give the control of the Southern states to the freedmen and their white allies. Some of these white friends of the freedmen were men of character and ability, but most of them were adventurers who came from the North to make their fortunes. They were called the "carpetbaggers," because they usually carried their luggage in their hands. The few Southern whites who befriended the negroes were called "scalawags" by their white neighbors. Secret societies sprang into being. The most famous was the Ku-Klux-Klan. The object of these societies was to terrorize the freedmen and their white friends and to prevent their voting. This led to the passage of the Force Acts. These laws provided severe penalties for crimes of intimidation. They also provided that these cases should be tried in United States courts. Federal soldiers, stationed in the South, could be used to compel obedience to the law.

**450. The Alabama Claims.**—During the Civil War vessels built in British shipyards, or refitted and supplied with coal at British ports, had preyed upon American commerce. The most famous of these vessels was the Alabama. The claims for losses caused by these vessels which the United States presented to Great Britain were therefore called the "Alabama Claims." There also were disputes with Great Britain over the fisheries and over the western end of the Oregon boundary. In 1871 the United States and Great Britain made an arrangement called the Treaty of Washington. By this treaty all these points of dispute were referred to arbitration. The Oregon boundary was decided in favor of the United States, but the fishery dispute was decided in favor of Great Britain. The "Alabama Claims" were settled by five arbitrators who sat at Geneva in Switzerland. They decided that Great Britain had not used "due diligence" to prevent the abuse of her ports by the Confederates. They condemned her to pay fifteen and one-half million dollars damages to the United States.

**451. The Chicago Fire, 1871.**—Early one morning in October, 1871, a Chicago woman went to the barn to milk her cow. She carried a lighted kerosene lamp, for it was still dark. The cow kicked over the lamp. The barn was soon ablaze. A furious gale carried the burning sparks from one house to another. And so the fire went on spreading all that day and night and the next day. Nearly two hundred million dollars' worth of property was destroyed. The homes of nearly one hundred thousand persons were burned down. In a surprisingly short time the burnt district was rebuilt, and Chicago grew more rapidly than ever before.

**452. Corruption in Politics.**—New York City had no two hundred million dollar fire. But a "ring" of city officers stole more than one hundred and fifty million dollars of the city's money. In other cities also there was great corruption. Nor were the state governments free from bribery and thieving. Many officers in the national government were believed to be mixed up in schemes to defraud the people. The truth of the matter was that the Civil War had left behind it the habit of spending money freely. A desire to grow suddenly rich possessed the people. Men did not look closely to see where their money came from.

**453. Election of 1872.**—In fact, this condition of the public service made many persons doubtful of the wisdom of reelecting President Grant. There was not the slightest doubt as to Grant's personal honesty. There were grave doubts as to his judgment in making appointments. Reconstruction, too, did not seem to be restoring peace and prosperity to the South. For these reasons many voters left the Republican party. They called themselves Liberal Republicans and nominated Horace Greeley for President. He had been one of the most outspoken opponents of slavery. The Democrats could find no better candidate, so they, too, nominated Greeley. But many Democrats could not bring themselves to vote for him. They left their party for the moment and nominated a third candidate. The result of all this confusion was the reelection of Grant. But the Democrats elected a majority of the House of Representatives.

**454. The Cuban Rebellion, 1867~77.**—When the other Spanish-American colonies won their independence, Cuba remained true to Spain. But by 1867 the Cubans could no longer bear the hardships of Spanish rule. They rebelled and for ten years fought for freedom. The Spaniards burned whole villages because they thought the inhabitants favored the rebels. They even threatened to kill all Cuban men found away from their homes. This cruelty aroused the sympathy of the Americans. Expeditions sailed from the United States to help the Cubans, although the government did everything it could to prevent their departure. One of these vessels carrying aid to the Cubans was named the *Virginius*. The Spaniards captured her, carried her to Santiago, and killed forty-six of her crew. There came near being a war with Spain over this affair. But the Spaniards apologized and saluted the American flag. In 1877 President Grant made up his mind that the war had lasted long enough. He adopted a severe tone toward Spain. The Spanish government made terms with the rebels, and the rebellion came to an end.

**455. Scandals in Political Life.**—In 1872 the House of Representatives made a searching inquiry into the charges of bribery in connection with the building of the Pacific railroads. Oakes Ames of Massachusetts was the head of a company called the "Credit Mobilier." This company had been formed to build the Union Pacific Railway. Fearing that Congress would pass laws that might hurt the enterprise, Ames gave stock in the company to members of Congress. But nothing definite could be proved against any members, and the matter dropped. Soon after the beginning of Grant's second term, many evil things came to light. One of these was the Whiskey Ring, which defrauded the government of large sums of money with the aid of the government officials. Grant wished to have a thorough investigation, and said, "Let no guilty man escape." The worst case of all, perhaps, was that of W. W. Belknap, Secretary of War. But he escaped punishment by resigning.

**456. Anarchy in the South.**—Meantime reconstruction was not working well in the South. This was especially true of Louisiana, Arkansas, and South Carolina. In Louisiana, and in Arkansas also, there were two sets of governors and legislatures, and civil war on a small scale was going on. In South Carolina the carpetbaggers and the negroes had gained control. They stole right and left. In other Southern states there were continued outrages on the negroes. President Grant was greatly troubled. "Let us have peace," was his heartfelt wish. But he felt it necessary to keep Federal soldiers in the South, although he knew that public opinion in the North was turning against their employment. It was under these circumstances that the election of 1876 was held.

**457. Election of 1876.**—The Republican candidate was Rutherford B. Hayes of Ohio. He was a gallant soldier of the Civil War, and was a man of the highest personal character. His Democratic opponent was Samuel J. Tilden of New

York—a shrewd lawyer who had won distinction as governor of the Empire State. When the electoral returns were brought in, there appeared two sets of returns from each of three Southern states, and the vote of Oregon was doubtful. The Senate was Republican, and the House was Democratic. As the two houses could not agree as to how these returns should be counted, they referred the whole matter to an electoral commission. This commission was made up of five Senators, five Representatives, and five justices of the Supreme Court. Eight of them were Republicans and seven were Democrats. They decided by eight seven that Hayes was elected, and he was inaugurated President on March 4, 1877.

**458. Withdrawal of the Soldiers from the South.**—The People of the North were weary of the ceaseless political agitation in the South. The old Southern leaders had regained control of nearly all the Southern states. They could not be turned out except by a new civil war, and the Northern people were not willing to go to war again. The only other thing that could be done was to withdraw the Federal soldiers and let the Southern people work out their own salvation as well as they could. President Hayes recalled the troops, and all the Southern states at once passed into the control of the Democrats.

**459. Strikes and Riots, 1877.**—The extravagance and speculation of the Civil War, and the years following its close, ended in a great panic in 1873. After the panic came the "hard times." Production fell off. The demand for labor diminished. Wages were everywhere reduced. Strikes became frequent, and riots followed the strikes. At Pittsburg, in western Pennsylvania, the rioters seized the railroad. They burned hundreds of railroad cars and locomotives. They destroyed the railroad buildings. At last the riot came to an end, but not until millions of dollars' worth of property had been destroyed.

**460. Election of 1880.**—At the beginning of his administration Hayes had declared that he would not be a candidate for reëlection. Who should be the Republican standard bearer? Grant's friends proposed to nominate him for a third term. The politicians who advocated a third term for Grant were opposed to the candidacy of James G. Blaine. They were called the Stalwart Republicans. In the convention they voted steadily and solidly for Grant. Finally their opponents, with the cry of "Anything to beat Grant," suddenly turned to an entirely new man, whose name had been little mentioned. This was James A. Garfield of Ohio. He had won distinction in the Civil War and had served with credit in Congress. For Vice-President the Republicans nominated Chester A. Arthur, a New York banker. The Democrats, on their part, nominated one of the most brilliant and popular soldiers of the Army of the Potomac, General Winfield Scott Hancock. The campaign was very hotly contested. In the end Garfield won.

**461. Garfield murdered; Civil Service Reform.**—President Garfield took the oath of office on March 4, 1881. On July 2 he was shot in the back by a disappointed office-seeker. Week after week he endured terrible agony. At length, on September 19, the martyred President died. Now at last the evils of the "Spoils System" were brought to the attention of the American people. Vice-President Arthur became President and entered heartily into projects of reform. A beginning was soon made. But it was found to be a very difficult thing to bring about any lasting reform. The Constitution gives the President the appointment of officers, subject to the confirmation of the Senate. No act of Congress can diminish the constitutional powers of the President except so far as he consents, and one President cannot bind succeeding Presidents. Any scheme of reform also costs money, which must be voted annually by Congress. It follows, therefore, that the consent of every President and of both Houses of every Congress is necessary to make the reform of the civil service permanent. Nevertheless the reform has made steady progress until now by far the greater part of the civil service is organized on the merit system.

**462. Election of 1884.**—In 1884 the Republicans nominated James G. Blaine of Maine for President. He was a man of magnetic address and had made many friends, but he also had made many enemies. Especially many Republican voters distrusted him. They felt that he had used his position for private gain, although nothing was proved against him. These Republicans were called "Mugwumps." They "bolted" the nomination and supported the Democratic candidate, Grover Cleveland. As mayor of Buffalo, Cleveland had done very well. He had then been elected governor of New York by a very large majority. The campaign of 1884 was conducted on lines of personal abuse that recall the campaigns of 1800 and of 1828. Cleveland carried four large Northern states and the "solid South" and was elected.

**463. Cleveland's Administration, 1885~89.**—The great contest of Cleveland's first term was a fierce struggle over the tariff. The government's need of money during the Civil War had compelled Congress to raise large sums by means of internal revenue taxes. These taxes in turn had brought about a great increase in the tariff rates on goods imported from foreign countries. The internal revenue taxes had been almost entirely removed, but the war tariff substantially remained in force. In 1887 Cleveland laid the whole question before Congress. For a time it seemed probable that something would be done. But the opposition in Congress was very active and very strong. It fell out, therefore, that nothing important was done. The real significance of Cleveland's first administration lay in the fact that the Southerners were once again admitted to a share in the government of the nation. It marked, therefore, the reunion of the American people.

# QUESTIONS AND TOPICS
# 问题与论题

## CHAPTER 42

§§ 437,438.—a. Explain carefully Lincoln's plan for reconstruction. How was it affected by his death?

b. What was Johnson's attitude toward reconstruction? Precisely what is meant by "reconstruction"?

§§ 439-441.—a. What was the force of the Emancipation Proclamation? How was the institution of slavery abolished?

b. Explain the reasons for the establishment of the freedmen's bureau. What do you think of the provision relating to the use of the army?

c. How was Congress able to pass a bill over the President's veto?

d. Explain carefully the Fourteenth Amendment. What do you think of the provision as to debts?

§§ 442, 443.—a. Why were the elections of 1866 important?

b. What was the force of the Tenure of Office Act, and why was it passed?

c. Describe the actual process of reconstruction.

d. Why was Johnson impeached? Why did the impeachment fail?

§§ 444, 445.—a. How did this act of Napoleon's set the Monroe Doctrine at defiance?

b. What action did the government take? With what result?

c. What advantage has Alaska been to the United States?

§ 446.—a. What were the issues in the campaign of 1868?

b. What had Blair done for the Union?

c. What did the election of Grant show?

## CHAPTER 43

§§ 447-449.—a. What were the provisions of the Fifteenth Amendment?

b. Under what conditions were the remaining seceded states readmitted?

c. What was the Force Act? Why was it passed?

§ 450.—a. How was the injury to our shipping during the Civil War connected with Great Britain?

b. What is meant by "arbitration"? Is it better to settle disputes by arbitration or by war?

§§ 451-452.—a. Describe the Chicago fire and its results.

b. Why was there so much bribery and corruption at this time?

c. Should city governments be conducted as business enterprises?

§ 453.—a. Why was there so much opposition to Grant's reëlection?

b. Why did the Democrats nominate Greeley? What was the result of the election?

§ 454.—a. What trouble broke out in Cuba? Why?

b. Describe the Virginius affair. How did the Cuban rebellion come to an end?

§§ 455, 456.—a. What scandal arose in connection with the Union Pacific Railway?

b. What was the "Whiskey Ring"? What was Grant's wish?

c. What troubles arose in the South? Could they have been avoided?

§§ 457, 458.—a. Why was there a dispute about the election of 1876? How was it settled?

b. Was it wise to let the Southerners work out their questions for themselves or not? Why?

§§ 459,460.—a. Compare the panic of 1873 with that of 1877 explaining the likenesses and differences.

b. Why was opposition to the nomination of Grant so strong?

c. Who were nominated? Who was elected?

§ 461.—a. What was the cause of Garfield's murder?

b. Why is Civil Service Reform so difficult?

c. What is meant by the "Merit System"? Do you consider such a system better or worse than the Spoils System? Why?

§§ 462, 463.—a. Why was Blaine so strongly opposed? Who were the "Mugwumps"? How did their action influence the election?

b. What is the difference between internal revenue taxes and customs duties?

c. What was the real significance of Cleveland's first election?

## GENERAL QUESTIONS
## 综合性问题

a. Give all the treaties with Great Britain, with dates, reason for the treaty, and results.

b. Why were there no executions for treason at the close of the Civil War?

c. What two methods does the Constitution provide for its amendment? Which method has always been followed?

d. What were the chief difficulties in the way of reconstruction?

e. What are the important duties of citizens? Why do you select these?

# SUGGESTIONS TO THE TEACHER
# 给教师的建议

The importance of the topics treated in Part XIV can hardly be overestimated. The opportunities to impress the pupils with their public duties are many and important. Reconstruction should be broadly treated and not discussed in a partisan spirit. It is better to dwell on our duties to the negroes than to seek out Northern blunders and Southern mistakes. In connection with the amendments the whole question of the suffrage can be discussed in the responsibility devolving upon the voter fully set forth. Questions of municipal organizations also arise and can be illustrated by local experience.

# 第十五篇
# PART XV

## 1889—1900年，国家发展
## NATIONAL DEVELOPMENT, 1889-1900

## Books for Study and Reading

## 研究和阅读用书

**References.**—Scribner's *Popular History*, V, 579-659; McMaster's *School History*, chs. xxxiv, xxxv.

**Home Readings.**—Any short, attractive account of the Spanish War.

CHAPTER 44

# 政治混乱

## CONFUSION IN POLITICS

464. 公元1888年，本杰明·哈里逊当选总统——1888年，民主党推举克利夫兰作为他们的总统候选人。共和党则提名了印第安纳州的本杰明·哈里逊（Benjamin Harrison，1833~1901）。与海斯和加菲尔德一样，哈里逊也是在内战中出名的，是一个拥有极高声望和公认的才能的人。原来的南方领袖在民主党政府中的突显，以及北方商业利益的被忽略，迫使许多曾投票支持克利夫兰的北方共和党人返回了共和党阵营。结果哈里逊当选，共和党获得了众议院的多数席位。

本杰明·哈里逊

第二十三任美国总统（1889~1893）

465. 公元1890年，《麦金莱关税法》——1888年竞选中争论最激烈的问题之一就是关税的改革。看来已经出现了两派改革者。一派改革者提议通过尽可能多地削减关税来改革关税。另一派改革者则提议重新调整关税以使保护性制度更有连贯性且更完善。在威廉·麦金莱（William McKinley，1843~1901）的领导下，共和党按照后者的思路开始改革关税。他们以普遍提高保护性商品的关税来实现这一点。《麦金莱

威廉·麦金莱

第二十五任美国总统（1897~1901）

关税法》还为那些支持美国商品的国家提供互惠政策。举例来说，如果阿根廷政府愿意给美国商品提供比它从其他国家进口类似商品更好的条件的话，那么这个政策就将生效，从而降低从阿根廷进口的商品的关税。

**466. 公元1890年，《谢尔曼白银法》**——内战期间，金银退出了流通市场。但是战争结束后，硬币支付又逐渐恢复。在殖民地时代，与黄金的需求量相比，白银的需求量大于供给。结果，与黄金相比，白银常常会变得更有价值。在19世纪，白银的供给已经远大于需求，结果，与黄金相比，白银又大幅度地贬值。1871年，政府决定只用白银制造小硬币，而且不允许将白银用在金额超过五美元的支付上。这被称为“白银非货币化”。1878年，一小群白银自由铸币的热心倡导者促使国会通过了一项每月铸造200万美元银币的法案。[①]这些一美元银币所含白银的价值只相当于六十至九十美分金币所含黄金的价值。1890年，俄亥俄州的参议员约翰·谢尔曼（John Sherman，1823~1900）提出了一个增加一美元银币铸造量的法案[②]。而这些一美元银币的价值到1894年只相当于四十九美分的金币了。

约翰·谢尔曼

**467. 公元1892年大选**——大量增加银币铸造的结果之一就是让全国

① 该法案即《布兰迪-埃里森法》（Bland-Allison Act），它其实并没有让自由银元的支持者满意，因为它只是规定政府财政部每月需要购买一定的银元，却没有放开铸币的限制。

② 该法案又被称为《谢尔曼白银购买法》（Sherman Silver Purchase Act），它与《布兰迪-埃里森法》同样要求政府每月购买银元，但是购买量达到了450万美元，这几乎就是当时美国白银的月总产量。因为这个法案还规定允许将债券兑换成金银货币，结果导致美国金银储备在1893年跌破1亿美元，这一事实使得国会批准通过了克利夫兰总统的提案，于当年废除了《谢尔曼白银购买法》。

位于华盛顿的国会大厦

商人陷入了恐慌。商业持续衰退。每个人都在尽可能地节省开支。作坊主和铁路经营者解雇了他们的工人或者削减了工人的薪水。哈里逊和克利夫兰再次分别成为共和党和民主党的总统候选人。和往常一样，执政的政党被认为必须对不景气的时期负责。有足够多的选民转而投票支持克利夫兰，于是，克利夫兰第二次就任总统（1893年3月4日）。

**468. 白银与关税**——1893年夏，金银货币非常匮乏。数以千计的民众从银行中取出了他们能够取出的所有钱，并把它们锁到了安全的地方。但是，国会这时废除了《谢尔曼白银法》，于是也结束了强制性的白银购买和银元铸造。这逐渐恢复了人民的信心。民主党再次彻底改革了关税。在西弗吉尼亚州的众议员威尔逊（William Lyne Wilson，1843~1900）的领导下，他们通过了一部关税法案，由此降低了部分关税并把许多商品[①]加入到免税名单中。

威廉·莱恩·威尔逊

① 主要是铁矿石、煤炭、木材和羊毛等制造业的原材料。这些商品在1897年的《丁利关税法》中又被规定需要缴税。

芝加哥世界博览会上展出的渔业设施

469. 公元1893年，芝加哥博览会——1892年10月是哥伦布发现美洲的400周年纪念。人们准备在芝加哥举办一次大型纪念性博览会。但是把一切都筹备妥当要花费很长时间，因此这个博览会直到1893年夏天才得以举行。人们用价格低廉但令人满意的材料建起了漂亮的大楼。它们的设计极富品位，里面布满了豪华展品，显示出了美国人的技术和财力。里面也有来自外国的产品。成千上万人从全国各地赶来，他们以愉悦的心情参观了这次博览会并且很有收获。过去从不曾有过这样出色或成功的博览会。

威廉·詹宁斯·布莱恩

470. 公元1896年大选——1896年，共和党在圣路易斯举行了大会并在会上提名俄亥俄州的威廉·麦金莱为总统候选人。他们声称，除非与其他国家达成某项关于金银货币标准的协议，否则他们支持金本位制。他们还宣称将保护国内工业。民主党的提名大会在芝加哥举行。克利夫兰的支持者们发现自己成了一个孤立无援的少数派。内布拉斯加州的威廉·詹宁斯·布莱恩（William Jennings Bryan，1860~1925）被提名为总统候选人。他们在执政纲领中提倡白银自由铸币制，并将以社会主义为指导方向对法律做出许多调整。平民党人① 和"白银"共和党人② 也接受布莱恩作为他们的候选人。这时，关于采用金本位还是银本位的问题终于完全摆在了选民面前。他们以选举麦金莱和让共和党占众议院的多数席位对这个问题做出了回应。

**471. 公元1897年，《丁利关税法》**——再次控制了政府的共和党开始着手改革关税以利于加强保护性政策。缅因州众议员丁利（Nelson Dingley, Jr.，1832~1899）是众议院起草这个新法案的委员会主席，因此这项法案最终是以他的名字命名获得通过的。该法案提高了某些种类的商品的税，并对许多迄今为止一直免税的商品征税。它还特别提高了制造业的某些特定原材料的税，目的是鼓励合众国生产这些原材料。《麦金莱关税法》所强调的互惠性政策也在这部法案中得以恢复。

## 【ORIGINAL TEXT】

**464. Benjamin Harrison elected President, 1888.**—In 1888 the Democrats put forward Cleveland as their candidate for President. The Republicans nominated Benjamin Harrison of Indiana. Like Hayes and Garfield, he had won renown

① 又译为"人民党"。该党派主要由工人、小农场主、商贩等"平民"群体组成。其纲领除了提倡自由铸币，还包括反对铁路垄断、降低贷款利率、实行八小时工作制以及直接选举参议员等。

② 即支持白银自由铸币的、提倡银本位的共和党人。

in the Civil War and was a man of the highest honor and of proved ability. The prominence of the old Southern leaders in the Democratic administration, and the neglect of the business interests of the North, compelled many Northern Republicans who had voted for Cleveland to return to the Republican party. The result was the election of Harrison and of a Republican majority in the House of Representatives.

**465. The McKinley Tariff, 1890.**—One of the questions most discussed in the campaign of 1888 was the reform of the tariff. There seem to have been two sets of tariff reformers. One set of reformers proposed to reform the tariff by doing away with as much of it as possible. The other set of reformers proposed to readjust the tariff duties so as to make the protective system more consistent and more perfect. Led by William McKinley, the Republicans set to work to reform the tariff in this latter sense. This they did by generally raising the duties on protected goods. The McKinley Tariff Act also offered reciprocity to countries which would favor American goods. This offer was in effect to lower certain duties on goods imported from Argentina, for instance, if the Argentine government would admit certain American goods to Argentina on better terms than similar goods imported from other countries.

**466. The Sherman Silver Law, 1890.**—In the Civil War gold and silver had disappeared from circulation. But after the close of the war a gradual return was made to specie payments. In the colonial days the demand for silver, as compared with the demand for gold, outran the supply. The consequence was that silver was constantly becoming worth more in comparison with gold. In the nineteenth century the supply of silver has greatly outstripped the demand, with the result that silver has greatly declined in value as compared with gold. In 1871 the government decided to use silver for small coins only, and not to allow silver to be offered in payment of a larger sum than five dollars. This was called the "demonetization of silver." In 1878 a small but earnest band of advocates of the free coinage of silver secured the passage of an act of Congress for the coinage of two million silver dollars each month. The silver in each one of these dollars was only worth in gold from ninety to sixty cents. In 1890, Senator John Sherman of Ohio brought in a bill to increase the coinage of these silver dollars which, in 1894, were worth only forty nine cents on the dollar in gold.

**467. Election of 1892.**—One result of this great increase in the silver coinage was to alarm business men throughout the country. Business constantly declined. Every one who could lessened his expenses as much as possible. Mill owners and railroad managers discharged their workers or reduced their wages. Harrison and Cleveland were again the Republican and Democratic candidates for the presidency. As is always the case, the party in power was held to be responsible for the hard times. Enough voters turned to Cleveland to elect him, and he was inaugurated President for the second time (March 4, 1893).

**468. Silver and the Tariff.**—In the summer of 1893 there was a great scarcity of money. Thousands of people withdrew all the money they could from the banks and locked it up in places of security. But Congress repealed the Sherman Silver Law and put an end to the compulsory purchase of silver and the coinage of silver dollars. This tended to restore confidence. The Democrats once more overhauled the tariff. Under the lead of Representative Wilson of West Virginia they passed a tariff act, lowering some duties and placing many articles on the free list.

**469. The Chicago Exhibition, 1893.**—The four hundredth anniversary of the Columbian discovery of America occurred in October, 1892. Preparations were made for holding a great commemorative exhibition at Chicago. But it took so long to get everything ready that the exhibition was not held until the summer of

1893. Beautiful buildings were erected of a cheap but satisfactory material. They were designed with the greatest taste, and were filled with splendid exhibits that showed the skill and resources of Americans, and also with the products of foreign countries. Hundreds of thousands of persons from all parts of the country visited the exhibition with pleasure and great profit. No more beautiful or successful exhibition has ever been held.

**470. Election of 1896.**—In 1896 the Republicans held their convention at St. Louis and nominated William McKinley of Ohio for President. They declared in favor of the gold standard, unless some arrangement with other nations for a standard of gold and silver could be made. They also declared for protection to home industries. The Democrats held their convention at Chicago. The men who had stood by Cleveland found themselves in a helpless minority. William Jennings Bryan of Nebraska was nominated for President on a platform advocating the free coinage of silver and many changes in the laws in the direction of socialism. The Populists and the Silver Republicans also adopted Bryan as their candidate. Now, at last, the question of the gold standard or the silver standard was fairly before the voters. They responded by electing McKinley and a Republican House of Representatives.

**471. The Dingley Tariff, 1897.**—The Republicans, once more in control of the government, set to work to reform the tariff in favor of high protection. Representative Dingley of Maine was chairman of the committee of the House that drew up the new bill, and the act as finally passed goes by his name. It raised the duties on some classes of goods and taxed many things that hitherto had come in free. Especially were duties increased on certain raw materials for manufactures, with a view to encourage the production of such materials in the United States. The reciprocity features of the McKinley tariff were also restored.

CHAPTER 45

# 1898年，西班牙战争

## THE SPANISH WAR, 1898

472. 公元1894~1898年，古巴叛乱——古巴人在1877年放下了武器，因为他们相信了西班牙人做出的更好的政府承诺。但是，这些承诺并没有兑现。古巴人依然年复一年地忍受着压迫。但是，他们终于忍无可忍。1894年，他们再次发动叛乱。西班牙人派了一支军队来镇压他们。不久，关于西班牙人残酷行径的传闻就传到了合众国。最后，西班牙总督维勒将军采用了一项残酷的措施：把老人、妇女和儿童从村子里赶了出来，把他们集中到沿海的镇上。这些可怜的人没有钱，没有食物，只有少量的栖身之所，吃尽了苦头。他们中有数千人就这样死去。美国民众给他们送去了救济品，但这对他们没有太多帮助。古巴人还在美国港口装备了一些远征军向叛军运送武器和给养。政府用尽了办法来阻止这些远征军，但是合众国的海岸线太长了，不可能把他们全部拦下来，尤其在大量美国民众对古巴人怀有深切同情的情况下。和西班牙关于古巴问题的争论自然而然地不断产生。这也同时引起了合众国和西班牙国内人民的愤怒。

473. 公元1898年，宣战——1898年1月5日，美国军舰“缅因号”停在了哈瓦那港。2月15日，它因一场爆炸而被毁，舰上的253名船员与它一同沉入海底。一个最具有法律资格的调查法庭被任命调查此事。调查报告说，“缅因号”的爆炸是由外部引起的。调查法庭的报告被送到西班牙政府，以期西班牙政府能道歉并给予赔偿。但是，西班牙政府只是提议通过仲裁解决此事。[①]古巴人的处境这时很惨。几名参议员和众议员造访了古巴。他们报告说，古巴人的处境是令人震惊的。总统把这整件事交由国会做出决断。1898年4月19日，国会承认了古巴人民的独立，并要求西班牙从该岛撤离。国会还授予总统强迫西班牙人撤走的权力，并声明合众国无意吞并古巴，而是将把该岛交由它的常住居民来管理。在这些条款正式呈递给西班牙政府之前，西班牙政府就已下令让美国公使离开了西班牙。

"缅因号"

**474. 西班牙太平洋舰队的覆灭**——海军上将杜威（George Dewey，1837~1917）当时负责指挥美国驻亚洲基地的分舰队，他这时已将他所有的军舰都聚集到了香港，因为他相信战争一触即发。当然，一旦宣战他便不能留在香港。他唯一能做的事情就是摧毁西班牙舰队，并把西班牙港口作为一个海军基地来用。西班牙舰队当时驻守在马尼拉湾。于是杜威率领

① 事实上，美国的调查结果并不明确，它只是指出"缅因号"的爆炸来自于外部，从而暗示有可能是被西班牙的水雷引发的。而西班牙随即也对此事展开了调查，其结果却正好相反——爆炸来自内部。因对此事质疑者众多，美国后于1911年再次展开调查，其结果更倾向于认为爆炸来自内部。无论真相如何，"缅因号"事件在当时成了一个导火索，美国舆论因此强烈要求对西班牙宣战，导致一直力图避免发动战争的麦金莱总统改变了态度，对西班牙宣战。

舰队向那里进发。在5月1日清晨，天还没亮，杜威通过了海湾入口处的西班牙要塞。西班牙舰队停泊在海军兵工厂附近，离马尼拉市有数英里远。天一亮，杜威就向西班牙人开了火。很快，一艘西班牙军舰就着了火，随后又是一艘，接着是第三艘。有一阵子，杜威率领舰队驶出了敌舰射程，以便让他的战士休息并吃早饭。随后他再次率领舰队驶入马尼拉湾，然后彻底消灭了敌人的舰队。没有一艘美国军舰严重受损，也没有一名美国军人战死。对西班牙而言，这场胜仗让美国获得了太平洋和亚洲海域的控制权。它解除了合众国的太平洋海岸受到攻击的所有忧虑。它使得向马尼拉运送士兵和给养成为可能，而不用担心在途中受到袭击。运送士兵也是必要的，因为杜威尽管在水上所向披靡，也能轻而易举地迫使马尼拉城投降，但是他没法在占据这个城镇后完全控制住它。

杜威的旗舰“奥林匹亚号”

**475. 大西洋海岸与封锁**——战争刚有爆发迹象的时候，大西洋沿岸的人民就对西班牙军舰产生了一种莫名的恐惧。因为西班牙人有一些新式的快速舰。主要港口的入口都布置了水雷和鱼雷。政府购买了各种各样的商船，在沿海建立了一支巡逻舰队。它也封锁了一些相对重要的古巴海港。但是古巴的海岸线太长了，根本无法全部封锁。不过即便如此，也让西班牙在古巴的陆军主力吃了不少苦头。

**476. 大西洋舰队**——不久，一支由四艘新式快速装甲巡洋舰和三艘大型远洋鱼雷快艇驱逐舰组成的西班牙舰队就出现在了西印度群岛。西班牙的舰队司令似乎不知道具体该向哪里进军。但是，在加勒比海徘徊了一段时间后，他把舰队停在了圣地亚哥港——停靠在古巴南部的海岸。美国海军只拥有“纽约号”和“布鲁克林号”这两艘快速装甲巡洋舰。在海军上将桑普森（William Thomas Sampson，1840~1902）的率领下，它们和五艘战列舰——“俄勒冈号”“爱荷华号”“印第安纳号”“马萨诸塞号”和“得克萨斯号”——以及若干相对较小的军舰被一同派往圣地亚哥。另一支由远洋低舷炮塔装甲舰（sea-going monitors）[①]和非装甲巡洋舰组成的舰队则继续维持对古巴的封锁。

**477. “俄勒冈号”的远航**——在“缅因号”被摧毁时，“俄勒冈号”正驻守在西北海岸的皮吉特湾。它这时立即受命全速开往大西洋海岸。这艘巨大的战列舰平稳地沿着北美洲、中美洲、南美洲的太平洋海岸线向南航行。它穿过了麦哲伦海峡，沿南美洲东部的海岸线北上。达到西印度群岛时，有人曾担心它会遇到整个西班牙舰队。但是它从未看到过它们。它以最佳状态到达了佛罗里达，并立即加入了桑普森的舰队。

**478. 封锁西班牙舰队**——圣地亚哥港似乎是专门为走投无路的舰队设计的避难所。它狭窄蜿蜒的入口由筑有坚固的防御工事的巨大山脉把守着。这些山脉之间的海峡布满了水雷和鱼雷。美国舰队进不去。但是，绝不能让西班牙舰队在未经察觉的情况下跑出来。于是，霍布森中尉（Richmond Pearson Hobson，1870~1937）接到命令，他要把运煤船“梅里马克号”开进那个狭窄的入口，并将它横着沉入海峡的最窄处。他做了最

① 这种战舰直译即为“远洋莫尼特”，它由内战时期的著名装甲舰“莫尼特号”发展而来，具有低舷、装甲、旋转炮塔这三个特点，因此其在机动性、防御性以及火力输出上都很优秀。虽然它名为“远洋”，实际上更适合在沿海地区作战。因此这时美国海军主要用它来封锁古巴的海岸。它是今天的浅水重炮舰的雏形。

谨慎的准备。但是，“梅里马克号”在下沉之前就被打得失去了行动力，但它还是在沉没前坚持漂到了海峡的最窄处。西班牙的海军上将被这一英雄主义的尝试深深打动了，于是派遣了一艘小船前往美国舰队，向他们保证说霍布森和他的六个勇敢的同伴已经获救。

霍布森中尉和他的船员正在撤离“梅里马克号”

**479. 西班牙舰队的覆灭**——既然美国舰队无法进入圣地亚哥港去把停泊在那里的西班牙舰队击沉，那么向圣地亚哥派遣一支陆军就变得有必要了。但是，西班牙人不会坐等美军攻陷圣地亚哥。星期天早上，即7月3日，西班牙舰队突然驶出了海港。“马萨诸塞号”那时为补充煤而离开了，“纽约号”也载着桑普森上将去和沙夫特将军（William Rufus Shafter, 1835~1906）进行一次会议。但是，还是有足够多的军舰留在那里。西班牙人过来了。美国军舰朝他们冲过去。西班牙舰队掉头西行，试图沿着海岸逃走。很快，一艘西班牙军舰就被美国炮弹击中并起火。为了免于沉没，它向海岸驶去。随即，第二艘西班牙军舰步其后尘，接着是第三艘。鱼雷快艇驱逐舰队也都在距离海港入口不远处被击沉。但是还有一艘西班牙军舰仍然漂浮在海上。它也很快被追上并投降。在数小时之内，整个西班牙舰队就被消灭了。几百名西班牙海员被杀死、受伤或溺水而亡，还有1600名西班牙士兵被俘。美国的损失是一人战死，两人受伤。美国舰队几乎可以随时去消灭另一支西班牙舰队——要是有这么一支舰队出现在攻击范围内的话。在马尼拉海湾和圣地亚哥附近的美国舰队比敌人的舰队先进。但是，它们的惊人战绩很大程度上归功于美国舰船一直都得到了最好的保养，尤其要归功于战士们精准的射击和过人的勇气。数年的和平没有在任何方面让美国海军战士耀眼的本领失去光芒。

480. 美国陆军——与此同时，位于圣地亚哥海岸的美国士兵在进军中遭遇了巨大的挫折，但他们表现出的英勇与顽强将永远令后人折服。海军低调而高效地成长为一支秩序井然的军队，相比而言，陆军的运作起初并没有海军那么好。兵力是充足的。从东到西，从南到北，从平原上的牧场到知名大学的教室——身处联邦各地的爱国者们响应了祖国的召唤，从四面八方赶来奉献自己的生命。但是，陆军非常缺乏有序的管理。士兵中间爆发了疾病。志愿军团的装备是老式步枪。把一个军团从一个地方调到另一个地方而不引起极度的混乱似乎非常困难。当西班牙舰队被封锁在圣地亚哥港时，沙夫特将军奉命率领的一支一万五千人的军队前去攻占圣地亚哥城，以使圣地亚哥港无法继续庇护西班牙舰队。

481. 远征圣地亚哥——6月22日和23日，远征军在圣地亚哥港入口东面不远的地方登陆。陡峭而高耸的群山守卫着这部分海岸。但是，美军的登陆没有受到任何阻挠。正规军步行骑兵部队和罗斯福（Theodore

Roosevelt，Jr.，1858~1919）率领的“莽骑兵”① ——他们也是步行部队——立即向圣地亚哥挺进。在拉瓜西马斯，西班牙人试图阻止他们。但是正规军和“莽骑兵”赶走了他们，随后继续前行。到6月28日，这支军队到达了离圣地亚哥只有几英里的据点。西班牙人在圣胡安和凯尼占据了两

圣胡安的一间木屋，上面可以看到战斗留下的弹痕

圣胡安山战役之后，伤员被送往部队医院

处非常有利的阵地。7月1日，他们被美军赶出了这两个阵地。正规军和志愿军表现出了最伟大的勇气和英雄主义。他们冒着西班牙人新式步枪的炮火穿越了许多长距离的开阔地。这时下起了雨，美军的处境变得更加糟糕了。7月3日，西班牙舰队驶出了港口，去迎接美国军舰的炮火给它带来的毁灭。沙夫特得到了增援，重炮被拖上了山路并设置在可以打到敌军战线的位置。西班牙人投降了，于是美军于7月17日进入了这座被攻占的城市。

① 其正式名称是“第一美国志愿骑兵团”（the 1st United States Volunteer Cavalry），它虽然被当成一个骑兵单位，实际上却是以步行的方式作战的。它的第一任团长伦纳德·伍德因此将其称为“伍德的疲惫步行者”（Wood's Weary Walkers），而第二任团长罗斯福将其改名为“罗斯福的莽骑兵”（Roosevelt's Rough Riders）。这个兵团主要是由矿工、农场主、西部牛仔和大学运动员等志愿者组成。罗斯福在1899年曾出版《莽骑兵》一书以讲述他在古巴的作战经历。

482. 波多黎各战役——在美洲还剩下另一个仍被西班牙控制的重要殖民地，那就是波多黎各。尼尔森·A. 迈尔斯将军（Nelson Appleton Miles，1839~1925）率领一支大军前去征服它。虽然圣胡安是海岸地区唯一的设有强大防御工事的据点，但迈尔斯将军没有选择在它附近的北部海岸登陆，相反，他率军在庞塞附近的南部海岸登陆。当地居民们以最大的热情欢迎美军的到来。这一天是8月1日。随后，美军开始横穿这座岛屿。但是他们还没有走得很远，就传来了战争结束的消息。

尼尔森·阿普尔顿·迈尔斯

483. 马尼拉的陷落——当杜威获胜的消息传到合众国时，政府派军队去援助他。但是这需要时间，因为从旧金山到菲律宾的路程非常远，而且在太平洋沿岸不容易取得适合用来运输的船只。韦斯利·梅里特将军（Wesley Merritt，1836~1910）负责指挥地面部队。与此同时，杜威和他的舰队从水上封锁了马尼拉数月，而菲律宾叛乱者则从陆路封锁了马尼拉。外国船只，尤其是德国船只嫉妒地注视着美国舰队的举动，并严重考验着杜威的耐心。8月17日，梅里特觉得已经强大到足以攻打马尼拉城。马尼拉立即向他投降了。

韦斯利·梅里特

484. 战争结束——西班牙大西洋舰队的覆灭和圣地亚哥的沦陷让西班牙人相信进一步的抵抗是徒劳的。于是，它同意停止战斗。这是1898年7

月。但是，实际的和平条约直到这一年的12月才得以签订。停战条件是：西班牙放弃古巴，并把波多黎各、菲律宾和一些相对较小的岛屿割让给合众国，而合众国要向西班牙支付两千万美元。多年以来，美国的传教士、商人

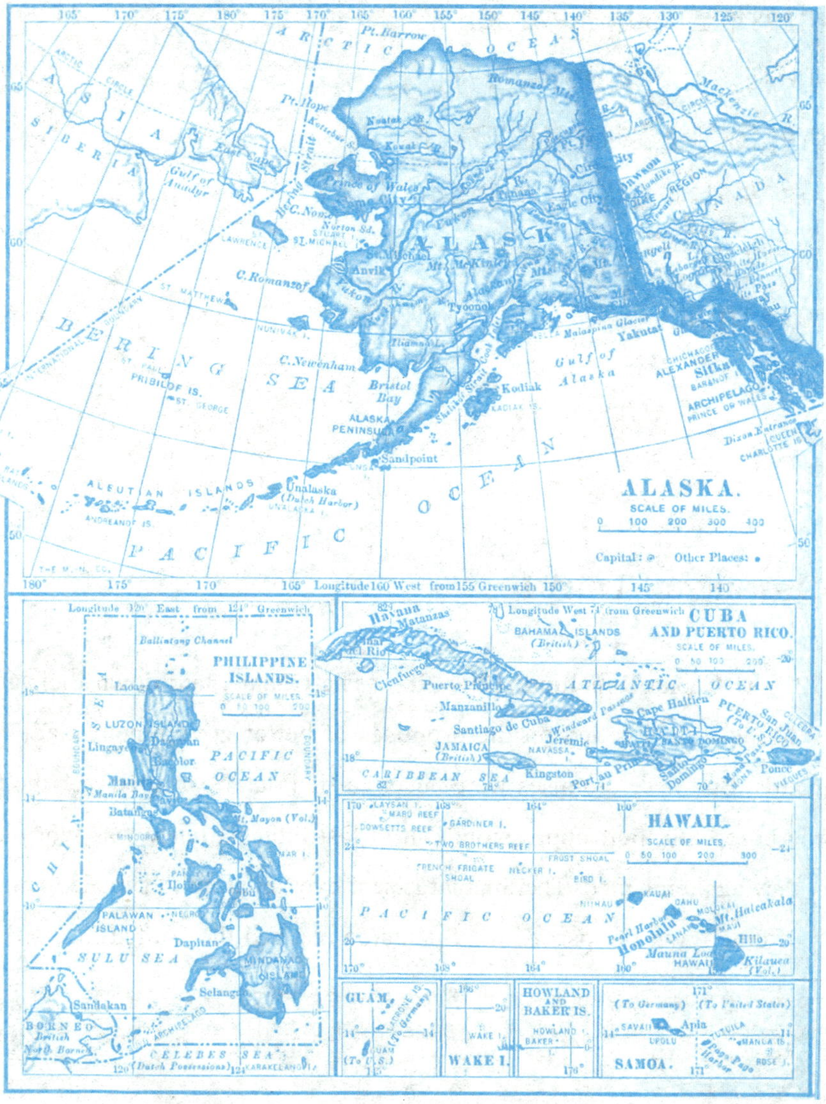


1900年附属于美国的国家和地区（阿拉斯加、菲律宾、古巴和夏威夷群岛）

和种植园主一直都对夏威夷群岛感兴趣。这场战争证明了这些岛屿作为一个军事和海军基地对美国的重要性，于是它们被附加到了条约中。

485. 繁荣——对美国人民来说，1898年至1900年是一个无比繁荣的时期。对外贸易大幅增长，美国的制成品也逐渐在其他国家打开销路。一场叛乱[①]一直在菲律宾进行，但是它似乎也在逐渐平息（1900年2月）。

如今（1900年）的国旗

## 【ORIGINAL TEXT】

**472. The Cuban Rebellion, 1894~98.**—The Cubans laid down their arms in 1877 because they relied on the promises of better government made by the Spaniards. But these promises were never carried out. Year after year the Cuban people bore with their oppression. But at last their patience was worn out. In 1894 they again rebelled. The Spaniards sent over an army to subdue them. Soon tales of cruelty on the part of the Spaniards reached the United States. Finally

① 这股所谓的叛乱势力其实就是在美西战争中曾包围马尼拉的埃米利奥·阿吉纳尔多领导的菲律宾革命军。当梅里特的援军赶来之前，杜威曾对阿吉纳尔多表示美国将像支持古巴独立一样支持菲律宾独立，因此阿吉纳尔多这时与美军是合作关系。但当梅里特赶到之后，杜威与梅里特一方面让阿吉纳尔多暂时继续包围马尼拉，一方面又私下与西班牙驻马尼拉的总督交涉，令其向美军投降，条件是不让菲律宾人参加受降仪式。得知美军的背叛之举后，阿吉纳尔多退守马尼拉以北的马洛洛镇，宣布成立菲律宾共和国。

the Spanish governor, General Weyler, adopted the cruel measure of driving the old men, the women, and the children from the country villages and huddling them together in the seaboard towns. Without money, without food, with scant shelter, these poor people endured every hardship. They died by thousands. The American people, sent relief, but little could be done to help them. The Cubans also fitted out expeditions in American ports to carry arms and supplies to the rebels. The government did everything in its power to stop these expeditions, but the coast line of the United States is so long that it was impossible to stop them all, especially as large numbers of the American people heartily sympathized with the Cubans. Constant disputes with Spain over the Cuban question naturally came up and gave rise to irritation in the United States and in Spain.

**473. The Declaration of War, 1898.**—On January 5, 1898, the American battleship *Maine* anchored in Havana harbor. On February 15 she was destroyed by an explosion and sank with two hundred and fifty-three of her crew. A most competent Court of Inquiry was appointed. It reported that the *Maine* had been blown up from the outside. The report of the Court of Inquiry was communicated to the Spanish government in the hope that some kind of apology and reparation might be made. But all the Spanish government did was to propose that the matter should be referred to arbitration. The condition of the Cubans was now dreadful. Several Senators and Representatives visited Cuba. They reported that the condition of the Cubans was shocking. The President laid the whole matter before Congress for its determination. On April 19, 1898, Congress recognized the independence of the Cuban people and demanded the withdrawal of the Spaniards from the island. Congress also authorized the President to compel Spain's withdrawal and stated that the United States did not intend to annex Cuba, but to leave the government of the island to its inhabitants. Before these terms could be formally laid before the Spanish government, it ordered the American minister to leave Spain.

**474. The Destruction of the Spanish Pacific Fleet.**—Admiral Dewey, commanding the American squadron on the Asiatic station, had concentrated all his vessels at Hong Kong, in the belief that war was at hand. Of course he could not stay at Hong Kong after the declaration of war. The only thing that he could do was to destroy the Spanish fleet and use Spanish ports as a naval base. The Spanish fleet was in Manila Bay. Thither sailed Dewey. In the darkness of the early morning of May 1, Dewey passed the Spanish forts at the entrance of the bay. The fleet was at anchor near the naval arsenal, a few miles from the city of Manila. As soon as it was light Dewey opened fire on the Spaniards. Soon one Spanish ship caught fire, then another, and another. Dewey drew off out of range for a time while his men rested and ate their breakfasts. He then steamed in again and completed the destruction of the enemy's fleet. Not an American ship was seriously injured. Not one American sailor was killed. This victory gave the Americans the control of the Pacific Ocean and the Asiatic waters, as far as Spain was concerned. It relieved the Pacific seacoast of the United States of all fear of attack. It made it possible to send soldiers and supplies to Manila, without fear of attack while on the way. And it was necessary to send soldiers because Dewey, while he was supreme on the water and could easily compel the surrender of Manila, could not properly police the town after its capture.

**475. The Atlantic Seacoast and the Blockade.**—No sooner did war seem probable than the people on the Atlantic seacoast were seized with an unreasoning fear of the Spanish fleets. For the Spaniards had a few new fast ships. The mouths of the principal harbors were blocked with mines and torpedoes. The government bought merchant vessels of all kinds and established a patrol along the coast. It also blockaded the more important Cuban seaports. But the Cuban coast was so long that it was impossible to blockade it all. As it was, great suffering was inflicted on the principal Spanish armies in Cuba.

**476. The Atlantic Fleets.**—Before long a Spanish fleet of four new, fast armored cruisers and three large sea-going torpedo-boat destroyers appeared in the West Indies. The Spanish admiral did not seem to know exactly where to go. But after sailing around the Caribbean Sea for a time, he anchored in Santiago harbor—on the southern coast of Cuba. In the American navy there were only two fast armored cruisers, the *New York* and the *Brooklyn*. These with five battleships—the *Oregon*, *Iowa*, *Indiana*, *Massachusetts*, and *Texas*—and a number of smaller vessels were placed under the command of Admiral Sampson and sent to Santiago. Another fleet of sea-going monitors and unarmored cruisers maintained the Cuban blockade.

**477. The Oregon's Great Voyage.**—When the Maine was destroyed, the Oregon was at Puget Sound on the northwest coast. She was at once ordered to sail to the Atlantic coast at her utmost speed. Steadily the great battleship sped southward along the Pacific coast of North America, Central America, and South America. She passed through Magellan Straits and made her way up the eastern coast of South America. As she approached the West Indies, it was feared that she might meet the whole Spanish fleet. But she never sighted them. She reached Florida in splendid condition and at once joined Sampson's squadron.

**478. The Blockade of the Spanish Fleet.**—Santiago harbor seemed to have been designed as a place of refuge for a hard-pressed fleet. Its narrow winding entrance was guarded by huge mountains strongly fortified. The channel between these mountains was filled with mines and torpedoes. The American fleet could not go in. The Spanish fleet must not be allowed to come out unseen. Lieutenant Hobson was ordered to take the collier *Merrimac* into the narrow entrance and sink her across the channel at the narrowest part. He made the most careful preparations. But the *Merrimac* was disabled and drifted by the narrowest part of the channel before she sank. The Spanish admiral was so impressed by the heroism of this attempt that he sent a boat off to the American squadron to assure them that Hobson and his six brave companions were safe.

**479. Destruction of the Spanish Fleet.**—As the American vessels could not enter Santiago harbor to sink the Spanish ships at their anchors, it became necessary to send an army to Santiago. But the Spaniards did not wait for the soldiers to capture the city. On Sunday morning, July 3, the Spanish fleet suddenly appeared steaming out of the harbor. The *Massachusetts* was away at the time, getting a supply of coal, and the *New York* was steaming away to take Admiral Sampson to a conference with General Shafter. But there were enough vessels left. On came the Spaniards. The American ships rushed toward them. The Spaniards turned westward and tried to escape along the coast. Soon one of them was set on fire by the American shells. She was run on shore to prevent her sinking. Then another followed her, and then a third. The torpedo-boat destroyers were sunk off the entrance to the harbor. But one ship now remained afloat. Speedily, she, too, was overtaken and surrendered. In a few hours the whole Spanish fleet was destroyed; hundreds of Spanish seamen were killed, wounded, or drowned, and sixteen hundred Spanish sailors captured. The American loss was one man killed and two wounded. The American ships were practically ready to destroy another Spanish fleet had one been within reach. At Manila Bay and off Santiago the American fleets were superior to the enemy's fleets. But the astounding results of their actions were due mainly to the splendid manner in which the American ships had been cared for and, above all, to the magnificent training and courage of the men behind the guns. Years of peace had not in any way dimmed the splendid qualities of the American sea-fighters.

**480. The American Army.**—Meantime the American soldiers on shore at Santiago were doing their work under great discouragement, but with a valor and stubbornness that will always compel admiration. While the navy was silently and efficiently increased to be a well-ordered force, the army was not so well managed at first. Soldiers there were in plenty. From all parts of the Union, from the South and from the North, from the West and from the East, from the cattle ranches of the plains and the classrooms of the great universities, patriots offered their lives at their country's call. But there was great lack of order in the management of the army. Sickness broke out among the soldiers. Volunteer regiments were supplied with old-fashioned rifles. It seemed to be difficult to move one regiment from one place to another without dire confusion. When the Spanish fleet was shut up in Santiago harbor, a force of fifteen thousand soldiers under General Shafter was sent to capture Santiago itself and make the harbor unsafe for the ships.

**481. The Santiago Expedition.**—On June 22 and 23 the expedition landed not far to the east of the entrance to Santiago harbor. Steep and high mountains guard this part of the coast. But no attempt was made to prevent the landing of the Americans. Dismounted cavalrymen of the regular army and Roosevelt's Rough Riders, also on foot, at once pushed on toward Santiago. At La Guasimas the Spaniards tried to stop them. But the regulars and the Rough Riders drove them away, and the army pushed on. By June 28 it had reached a point within a few miles of the city. The Spaniards occupied two very strong positions at San Juan (San Huan) and Caney. On July 1 they were driven from them. The regulars and the volunteers showed the greatest courage and heroism. They crossed long open spaces in the face of a terrible fire from the Spaniards, who were armed with modem rifles. The rains now set in, and the sufferings of the troops became terrible. On July 3 the Spanish fleet sailed out of the harbor to meet its doom from the guns of the American warships. Reinforcements were sent to Shafter, and heavy guns were dragged over the mountain roads and placed in positions commanding the enemy's lines. The Spaniards surrendered, and on July 17 the Americans entered the captured city.

**482. The Porto Rico Campaign.**—The only other important colony still remaining to Spain in America was Porto Rico. General Nelson A. Miles led a strong force to its conquest. Instead of landing on the northern coast near San Juan, the only strongly fortified position on the seacoast, General Miles landed his men on the southern coast near Ponce (Pon-tha). The inhabitants received the Americans with the heartiest welcome. This was on August 1. The American army then set out to cross the island. But before they had gone very far news came of the ending of the hostilities.

**483. Fall of Manila.**—When the news of Dewey's victory reached the United States, soldiers were sent to his aid. But this took time, for it was a very long way from San Francisco to the Philippines and vessels suitable for transports were not easily procured on the Pacific coast. General Wesley Merritt was given command of the land forces. Meantime, for months Dewey with his fleet blockaded Manila from the water side, while Philippine insurgents blockaded it from the land side. Foreign vessels, especially the German vessels, jealously watched the operations of the American fleet and severely taxed Dewey's patience. On August 17 Merritt felt strong enough to attack the city. It was at once surrendered to him.

**484. End of the War.**—The destruction of the Spanish Atlantic fleet and the fall of Santiago convinced the Spaniards that further resistance was useless. So it was agreed that the fight should be stopped. This was in July, 1898. But the actual treaty of peace was not made until the following December. The conditions were that Spain should abandon Cuba, should cede to the United States Porto Rico, the Philippines, and some smaller islands, and should receive from the United

States twenty million dollars. For many years American missionaries, merchants, and planters had been interested in the Hawaiian Islands. The war showed the importance of these islands to the United States as a military and naval station, and they were annexed.

**485. Prosperity.**—The years 1898~1900 have been a period of unbounded prosperity for the American people. Foreign trade has increased enormously, and the manufactures of the United States are finding a ready market in other countries. A rebellion has been going on in the Philippines, but it seems to be slowly dying out (February, 1900).

# QUESTIONS AND TOPICS
# 问题与论题

## CHAPTER 44

§§ 464, 465.—a. Why was Harrison chosen President?

b. What is "tariff reform"? What is "reciprocity"? Do you consider such a method wise or not? Why?

§§ 466, 467.—a. Why was silver demonetized? What is meant by the word "demonetization"?

b. What was the Sherman Silver Law? What effect did it have upon business?

c. Was there any reason for the fear on the part of business men?

d. Why was Harrison defeated in 1892?

§§ 468, 469.—a. Why did money become scarce in the summer of 1893?

b. How did the repeal of the Sherman Law affect confidence in the future of business?

c. Describe the Chicago Exhibition. What is the advantage of such an exhibition?

§§ 470, 471.—a. Who were the leading candidates for the presidency in 1896? What principles did they stand for?

b. Explain the provisions of the Dingley Tariff.

c. Ask some business man what he thinks of the wisdom of changing the tariff very often.

## CHAPTER 45

§§ 472, 473.—a. What promises had the Spaniards made to the Cubans and how had they kept them?

b. What do you think of Weyler's policy?

c. Could the Spanish war have been avoided?

§ 474.—a. Why could not Admiral Dewey remain at Hong Kong?

b. Describe the battle of Manila Bay. What were the results of this action?

§§ 475-477.—a. Why were the American people on the Atlantic seacoast alarmed? Were the harbors well defended?

b. Compare the American and the Spanish Atlantic fleets. Why was the voyage of the *Oregon* important?

§§ 478, 479.—a. Describe the harbor of Santiago. What advantages did it possess for the Spaniards?

b. How did Hobson try to prevent the escape of the Spanish fleet?

c. Describe the encounter between the two fleets.

d. To what was this great success due?

§§ 480-482.—a. From what parts of the country did the volunteers come?

b. Why was there so much confusion in the army?

c. Describe the Santiago campaign and the suffering of the soldiers.

d. Describe the Porto Rico expedition. Why did General Miles land on the southern coast?

§§ 483-485.—a. Why were the soldiers needed after Dewey's victory?

b. Give the conditions of peace. Exactly what was the condition as to Cuba?

c. Why are the Hawaiian islands important to the United States?

## GENERAL QUESTIONS
## 综合性问题

a. What are the advantages and disadvantages of a tariff?

b. What important matters have been definitely settled during the past one hundred year?

c. What are some of the problems now before the American people?

d. Should the United States be a "world power"?

## SUGGESTIONS TO THE TEACHER
## 给教师的建议

Interesting constitutional questions will inevitably arise in teaching this section, but the events are too recent to admit of dogmatizing on lines of policy. The Spanish War and the Philippine trouble are too near to be properly judged, and the facts only should be taught. The duties and responsibilities resting upon the United States through its closer connection with all parts of the world can, however, be emphasized without the display of partisan spirit. Furthermore, the causes of present prosperity and the industrial advantages of the United States may well demand attention. Throughout every part of this section, also, the importance of good citizenship, in the broadest sense of the word, should receive special emphasis.

# 附录

APPENDIX

# 独立宣言

于大陆会议，1776年7月4日

**美洲十三盟邦的一致宣言**

在人类事务的进程中，当一个民族必须解除其与另一个民族之间迄今存在的政治联系，并在世界各国之间接受自然之律法与自然之神性所授予的独立与平等的地位时，一种对人类舆论应有的尊重，要求他们将迫使其独立之原因予以宣布。

我们认为这些真理是不证自明的：人人生而平等，他们都从其造物主那里被赋予某些不可让与的权利，其中包括生命权、自由权和追求幸福的权利。为使这些权利得到保障，人类才在他们中间建立政府，而政府之正当权力，则来自于被治者的同意。当任何形式的政府对这些目标变得具有破坏性时，其人民便有权利去改变或废除它，并建立一个新的政府；对于其人民来说，奠定此新政府基础的原则与组织其权力的方式，须看来最可能使其获得安全与幸福。诚然，为慎重起见，设立已久的政府不应由于轻微和暂时的原因而予以变更。而过去的一切经验也都已表明，只要恶行尚可被容忍，人类都宁愿容忍，也不愿为了自身的权利便将他们已习惯了的政府形式废除。然而，当一系列对权力的滥用与僭越——它们自始至终都是为了同一个目的——表明了一种企图，即将他们束缚于绝对的专制之下，那么他们就有权利，也有义务去推翻这样一个政府，并为他们未来的安全筹备新的保障——这就是这些殖民地一直以来的逆来顺受，也是迫使他们改变他们以往的政府体系的必要缘由。现任之大不列颠国王的历史，是一部接连不断的侵害与侵犯的历史，这些行为的直接目的，就是在这些邦国建立一个绝对的专制暴政。为了证明所言属实，现在将事实呈递于公正的世界之前：

他拒绝批准对公众利益最有益、最必要的法律。

他禁止他的总督们通过紧急且迫切重要的法律，抑或是推迟它们的生效，等待他的同意；而一旦这些法律被推迟生效，他就对它们完全置之不理。

他拒绝通过其他的使广大地区供人民居住的法律，除非那些人民情愿放弃自己在立法机构中的代表权；此项权利对他们来说是无价的，而只有对暴君来说才是可怕的。

他把各邦立法团体召集到异常的、不便的、远离其公共档案存放处的地方去开会，其唯一目的就在使他们疲于奔命，从而遵守他的法令。

他屡次解散各邦立法机构，因为它们以无畏的坚定反对他侵犯人民的权利。

他在解散各邦立法机构之后，又长期拒绝另选新议会，由此，那无法取消的立法权便回到了广大人民之手，交由他们来行使；然而与此同时，各邦仍暴露在外侵之忧和内乱之患的一切威胁之下。

他竭力抑制各邦增加人口；为此目的，他妨碍通过《外籍人归化法》，拒绝通过其他的鼓励外籍人移民至此的法律，并提高了新的土地分配的条件。

他拒绝批准设置司法权力机构的法律，以此妨碍司法的行政化管理。

他通过控制法官的任期、薪金数额及其支付，以使他们完全受制于他个人的意志。

他设立了大量的新官职，还派遣了大批军官到此，以侵扰我们的人民，并耗尽他们的资财。

他在和平时期，未经我们的立法机关同意，就在我们中间驻屯常备军。

他力图使军队独立于且凌驾于公民权力。

他联合了其他人，要使我们屈服于一个与我们的体制格格不入，且不为我们的法律所承认的权力的管辖；他还对那些人号称为法律的法案授予许可，这些法案是为了达到以下目的：

在让大批武装部队驻扎在我们中间；

用虚假的审判来保护他们，使他们对我们各邦居民犯下的任何谋杀都可以免受处罚；

切断我们同世界各地间的贸易；

未得到我们的同意便向我们强行征税；

在许多案件中剥夺我们由陪审团审理的权益；

以莫须有的罪名押送我们到海外去受审；

在一个相邻地区废除保障自由的英国法律体系，在那里建立一个专制政府，并扩大其边界，以使其立即成为一个先例和准备手段，以便进而向这里的各殖民地推行同样的专制统治；

取消我们的特许状，废除我们最宝贵的法律，并从根本上改变我们各邦政府的形式；

废止我们自己的立法机构，并宣称他们自己被授权就一切事宜为我们立法。

他宣布我们已不受他的保护，并对我们开战，从而放弃了在这里的政务。

他在劫掠我们的船舶，蹂躏我们的海滨，烧毁我们的城镇，并残害我们人民的生命。

他此刻正在运派大批外国雇佣军，来完成这些带来死亡、废墟和专制的暴行。这些暴行已经以残忍与不义的事实作为开始，其残忍与不义之甚，即使在最野蛮的时代都罕有其匹，而且与一个文明国度的元首毫不相称。

他强迫我们的那些在公海上被俘的同胞拿起武器来对抗他们的祖国，成为残杀自己亲人和朋友的刽子手，或是死于自己的亲人和朋友之手。

他在我们中间引发内乱，并竭力唆使我们边疆上的居民、那些毫无怜悯之心的印第安蛮族来犯；而印第安人众所周知的作战方式是不论敌人的年龄、性别和身份，一律格杀勿论。

在这些压迫行为的每一个阶段中，我们都曾以最谦卑的言辞申诉请愿，但我们的连番请愿所得到的答复却只有连番的侮辱。一位君主，其品性已由其行为彰显，而其每一行为皆可由此确定其为一暴君，这样的君主，实不配为一个自由民族的统治者。

我们并非不曾顾念我们的英国弟兄。我们已经不时地警告过他们不要企图用他们的立法机构，把一种无法解释的管辖权强加到我们的头上。我们已经提醒他们，应注意到我们在这里移民和定居的情形。我们已经向他们呼吁，希望唤起他们天生的正义感和宽宏大量，我们已经恳求过他们，希望他们念在同种同宗的份上，不要拒绝为这些侵害行为承担责任，这些行为势必将影响我们彼此的关系和来往。然而，他们对于这种正义的、血肉之亲的呼声，也同样置若罔闻。因此，我们不得不勉为其难地承认宣告我们的分离之必要，而我们也不得不以对待世界上其他民族一样的态度来对待他们：在对抗时为敌人，在和平时为朋友。

因此，我们这些大会中的北美盟邦的代表们集合于此，以这些殖民地的善良人民的名义，并经他们授权，为了向全世界呼吁，对我们的意向之公正做出至高无上的判断，特此庄严宣布并昭告：这些联合殖民地从此成为，而且依照法律和道义的要求理应成为自由且独立的国家；它们解除了一切对英王效忠的义务，而它们与大不列颠国之间的一切政治关系亦已经且应当完全断绝；作为自由且独立的国家，它们享有全权去发动战争、议定合约、缔结同盟、建立商贸关系以及进行独立国家依照法律和道义的要求有权进行的一切其他行动与事宜。怀着对上帝福佑的坚定信念，我们谨以我们的生命、我们的财产和我们神圣的名誉彼此宣誓，拥护此宣言。

## 以大陆会议的命令和名义签署

主　席：约翰·汉考克（John Hancock）

新罕布什尔：

乔塞亚·巴特利特（Josiah Bartlett）

威廉·惠普尔（Wm. Whipple）

马修·桑顿（Matthew Thornton）

马萨诸塞湾：

塞缪尔·亚当斯（Saml. Adams）

约翰·亚当斯（John Adams）

罗伯特·特里特·佩因（Robt. Treat Paine）

埃尔布里奇·格里（Elbridge Gerry）

罗得岛：

斯蒂芬·霍普金斯（Step. Hopkins）

威廉·埃勒里（William Ellery）

康涅狄格：

罗杰·谢尔曼（Roger Sherman）

塞缪尔·亨廷顿（Saml. Huntington）

威廉·威廉姆斯（Wm. Williams）

奥利弗·沃尔考特（Oliver Wolcott）

纽 约：

威廉·弗洛伊德（Wm. Floyd）

菲利普·利文斯顿（Phil. Livingston）

弗朗西斯·莱维斯（Frans. Lewis）

刘易斯·莫里斯（Lewis Morris）

新泽西：

理查德·斯托克顿（Richd. Stockton）

约翰·威瑟斯庞（Jno. Witherspoon）

弗朗西斯·霍普金森（Fras. Hopkinson）

约翰·哈特（John Hart）

亚伯拉罕·克拉克（Abra. Clark）

宾夕法尼亚：

罗伯特·莫里斯（Robt. Morris）

本杰明·拉什（Benjamin Rush）

本杰明·富兰克林（Benja. Franklin）

约翰·莫顿（John Morton）

乔治·克莱默（Geo. Clymer）

詹姆斯·史密斯（Jas. Smith）

乔治·泰勒（Geo. Taylor）

詹姆斯·威尔森（James Wilson）

乔·罗斯（Geo Ross）

特拉华：

凯撒·罗德尼（Caesar Rodney）

乔治·里德（Geo. Read）

托马斯·麦基恩（Tho. M'Kean）

马里兰：

塞缪尔·蔡斯（Samuel Chase）

威廉·帕卡（Wm. Paca）

托马斯·斯通（Thos. Stone）

卡罗敦的查尔斯·卡罗尔（Charles Carroll of Carrollton）

弗吉尼亚：

乔治·威斯（George Wythe）

理查德·亨利·李（Richard Henry Lee）

托马斯·杰斐逊（Ths. Jefferson）

本杰明·哈里森（Benja. Harrison）

小托马斯·尼尔森（Thos. Nelson，Jr. ）

弗朗西斯·莱特福特·李（Francis Lightfoot Lee）

卡特·布拉克斯顿（Carter Braxton）

北卡罗来纳：

威廉·胡珀（Wm. Hooper）

约瑟夫·休斯（Joseph Hewes）

约翰·佩恩（John Penn）

南卡罗来纳：

爱德华·拉特利奇（Edward Rutledge）

小托马斯·海沃德（Thos Heyward，junr. ）

小托马斯·林奇（Thomas Lynch，junr. ）

亚瑟·米德尔顿（Arthur Middleton）

佐治亚：

巴顿·格威内特（Button Gwinnett）

莱曼·霍尔（Lyman Hall）

乔治·沃尔顿（Geo. Walton）

证明人：书记官查尔斯·汤姆森（Charles Thomson）

# DECLARATION OF INDEPENDENCE

*In Congress, July 4, 1776,*

**The unanimous Declaration of the thirteen united States of America,**

When in the Course of human events, it becomes necessary for one people to dissolve the political bands which have connected them with another, and to assume among the Powers of the earth, the separate and equal station to which the Laws of Nature and of Nature's God entitle them, a decent respect to the opinions of mankind requires that they should declare the causes which impel them to the separation.

We hold these truths to be self-evident, that all men are created equal, that they are endowed by their Creator with certain unalienable Rights, that among these are Life, Liberty and the pursuit of Happiness. That to secure these rights, Governments are instituted among Men, deriving their just powers from the consent of the governed, That whenever any Form of Government becomes destructive of these ends, it is the Right of the People to alter or to abolish it, and to institute new Government, laying its foundation on such principles and organizing its powers in such form, as to them shall seem most likely to effect their Safety and Happiness. Prudence, indeed, will dictate that Governments long established should not be changed for light and transient causes; and accordingly all experience hath shown, that mankind are more disposed to suffer, while evils are sufferable, than to right themselves by abolishing the forms to which they are accustomed. But when a long train of abuses and usurpations, pursuing invariably the same Object evinces a design to reduce them under absolute Despotism, it is their right, it is their duty, to throw off such Government, and to provide new Guards for their future security.—Such has been the patient sufferance of these

Colonies; and such is now the necessity which constrains them to alter their former Systems of Government. The history of the present King of Great Britain is a history of repeated injuries and usurpations, all having in direct object the establishment of an absolute Tyranny over these States. To prove this, let Facts be submitted to a candid world.

He has refused his Assent to Laws, the most wholesome and necessary for the public good.

He has forbidden his Governors to pass Laws of immediate and pressing importance, unless suspended in their operation till his Assent should be obtained; and when so suspended, he has utterly neglected to attend to them.

He has refused to pass other Laws for the accommodation of large districts of people, unless those people would relinquish the right of Representation in the Legislature, a right inestimable to them and formidable to tyrants only.

He has called together legislative bodies at places unusual, uncomfortable, and distant from the depository of their Public Records, for the sole purpose of fatiguing them into compliance with his measures.

He has dissolved Representative Houses repeatedly, for opposing with manly firmness his invasions on the rights of the people.

He has refused for a long time, after such dissolutions, to cause others to be elected; whereby the Legislative Powers, incapable of Annihilation, have returned to the People at large for their exercise; the State remaining in the mean time exposed to all the dangers of invasion from without, and convulsions within.

He has endeavoured to prevent the population of these States; for that purpose obstructing the Laws of Naturalization of Foreigners; refusing to pass others to encourage their migration hither, and raising the conditions of new Appropriations of Lands.

He has obstructed the Administration of Justice, by refusing his Assent to Laws for establishing Judiciary Powers.

He has made Judges dependent on his Will alone, for the tenure of their offices, and the amount and payment of their salaries.

He has erected a multitude of New Offices, and sent hither swarms of Officers to harass our People, and eat out their substance.

He has kept among us, in times of peace, Standing Armies without the Consent of our legislature.

He has affected to render the Military independent of and superior to the Civil Power.

He has combined with others to subject us to a jurisdiction foreign to our constitution, and unacknowledged by our laws; giving his Assent to their acts of pretended legislation:

For quartering large bodies of armed troops among us:

For protecting them, by a mock Trial, from Punishment for any Murders which they should commit on the Inhabitants of these States:

For cutting off our Trade with all parts of the world:

For imposing taxes on us without our Consent:

For depriving us in many cases, of the benefits of Trial by Jury:

For transporting us beyond Seas to be tried for pretended offences:

For abolishing the free System of English Laws in a neighbouring Province, establishing therein an Arbitrary government, and enlarging its Boundaries so as to render it at once an example and fit instrument for introducing the same absolute rule into these Colonies:

For taking away our Charters, abolishing our most valuable Laws, and altering fundamentally the Forms of our Governments:

For suspending our own Legislature, and declaring themselves invested with Power to legislate for us in all cases whatsoever.

He has abdicated Government here, by declaring us out of his Protection and waging War against us.

He has plundered our seas, ravaged our Coasts, burnt our towns, and destroyed the lives of our people.

He is at this time transporting large armies of foreign mercenaries to compleat the works of death, desolation and tyranny, already begun with circumstances of Cruelty & perfidy scarcely paralleled in the most barbarous ages, and totally unworthy the Head of a civilized nation.

He has constrained our fellow Citizens taken Captive on the high Seas to bear Arms against their Country, to become the executioners of their friends and Brethren, or to fall themselves by their Hands.

He has excited domestic insurrections amongst us, and has endeavoured to bring on the inhabitants of our frontiers, the merciless Indian Savages, whose known rule of warfare, is an undistinguished destruction of all ages, sexes and conditions.

In every stage of these Oppressions We have Petitioned for Redress in the most humble terms: Our repeated Petitions have been answered only by repeated injury. A Prince, whose character is thus marked by every act which may define a Tyrant, is unfit to be the ruler of a free People.

Nor have We been wanting in attention to our British brethren. We have warned them from time to time of attempts by their legislature to extend an unwarrantable jurisdiction over us. We have reminded them of the circumstances of our emigration and settlement here. We have appealed to their native justice and magnanimity, and we have conjured them by the ties of our common kindred to disavow these usurpations, which, would inevitably interrupt our connections and correspondence. They too have been deaf to the voice of justice and of consanguinity. We must, therefore, acquiesce in the necessity, which denounces our Separation, and hold them, as we hold the rest of mankind, Enemies in War, in Peace Friends.

We, therefore, the Representatives of the united States of America, in General

Congress, Assembled, appealing to the Supreme Judge of the world for the rectitude of our intentions, do in the Name, and by Authority of the good People of these Colonies, solemnly publish and declare, That these United Colonies are, and of Right ought to be Free and Independent States; that they are Absolved from all Allegiance to the British Crown, and that all political connection between them and the State of Great Britain, is and ought to be totally dissolved; and that as Free and Independent States, they have full Power to levy War, conclude Peace, contract Alliances, establish Commerce, and to do all other Acts and Things which Independent States may of right do. And for the support of this Declaration, with a firm reliance on the Protection of Divine Providence, we mutually pledge to each other our Lives, our Fortunes and our sacred Honor.

JOHN HANCOCK.

New Hampshire—JOSIAH BARTLETT, WM. WHIPPLE, MATTHEW THORNTON.

Massachusetts Bay—SAML. ADAMS, JOHN ADAMS, ROBT. TREAT PAINE, ELBRIDGE GERRY.

Rhode Island—STEP. HOPKINS, WILLIAM ELLERY.

Connecticut—ROGER SHERMAN, SAM'EL HUNTINGTON, WM. WILLIAMS, OLIVER WOLCOTT.

New York—WM. FLOYD, PHIL. LIVINGSTON, FRANS. LEWIS, LEWIS MORRIS.

New Jersey—RICHD. STOCKTON, JNO. WITHERSPOON, FRAS. HOPKINSON, JOHN HART, ABRA. CLARK.

Pennsylvania—ROBT. MORRIS, BENJAMIN RUSH, BENJA. FRANKLIN, JOHN MORTON,

GEO. CLYMER, JAS. SMITH, GEO. TAYLOR, JAMES WILSON,

GEO. ROSS.

Delaware—CAESAR RODNEY, GEO. READ, THO. M'KEAN.

Maryland—SAMUEL CHASE, WM. PACA, THOS. STONE,

CHARLES CARROLL of Carrollton.

Virginia—GEORGE WYTHE, RICHARD HENRY LEE, TH. JEFFERSON,

BENJA. HARRISON, THOS. NELSON, jr., FRANCIS LIGHTFOOT LEE,

CARTER BRAXTON.

North Carolina__WM. HOOPER, JOSEPH HEWES, JOHN PENN.

South Carolina—EDWARD RUTLEDGE, THOS. HEYWARD, Junr.,

THOMAS LYNCH, Junr., ARTHUR MIDDLETON.

Georgia—BUTTON GWINNETT, LYMAN HALL, GEO. WALTON.

CHARLES THOMSON.

# 美利坚合众国宪法

我合众国之人民，为形成一个更完善之联盟，树立正义，确保国内之安宁，筹设共同之防务，促进公共之福利，并为我们自身及后代谋求自由之福祉，特为美利坚合众国制定并确立此宪法。

## 第一条

### 第一款

由本宪法所授予的全部立法权，均属于由一个参议院和一个众议院组成的合众国国会。

### 第二款

众议院由众议员组成，众议员由各州人民每两年选举一次。各州的选举人须具备该州州议会人数最多一院选举人所必需之资格。

凡年龄不满25岁，或成为合众国公民不满7年，或在一州当选时却非该州常住居民者，均不得担任众议员。

众议员之名额及直接税之税额，均须按本联邦内各州人口比例进行分配。各州人口数，按自由人口总数加上所有其他人口数的五分之三予以确定。自由人包括须服一定年限劳役之人，但不包括未被征税之印第安人。人口的实际统计在合众国国会第一次会议后三年内完成，并于此后每十年依法律规定之方式进行一次。每三万人选出的众议员人数不得超过一名，但各州须至少各有一名众议员；在上述人口统计完成以前，各州有权选出的众议员人数如下：新罕布什尔三名，马萨诸塞八名，罗得岛与普罗维登斯种植园一名，康涅狄格五名，纽约六名，新泽西四名，宾夕法尼亚八名，特拉华一名，马里兰六名，弗吉尼亚十名，北卡罗来纳五名，南卡罗来纳五名，佐治亚三名。

当任一州代表名额出现空缺时，该州行政当局须发布选举令以填补此空缺。

众议院须选出本院议长及其他官员；且众议院拥有提出弹劾之专属权。

**第三款**

合众国的参议院由参议员组成，参议员由各州州议会选出，每两年选一次，每次两名，每名参议员的任期为六年；每名参议员有一票表决权。

参议员在因第一次当选而集合之后，须立即分为人数尽可能相等的三组。第一组参议员席位于第二年年终时空出，第二组参议员席位于第四年年终时空出，第三组参议员席位于第六年年终时空出，以使三分之一的参议员每两年改选一次。在任何一州州议会休会期间，该州参议员名额如因辞职或其他原因而出现空缺时，该州行政当局须在州议会下次集会前任命临时参议员，以填补此空缺。

凡年龄不满30岁，或成为合众国公民不满9年，或在一州当选时非该州常住居民者，均不得担任参议员。

合众国副总统任参议院议长，但除非参议员投票时赞成票和反对票相等，否则议长无表决权。

参议院须选出本院其他官员，并在没有副总统或副总统行使合众国总统职权时，选举一名临时议长。

参议院拥有审理所有弹劾案之专属权。一旦为此目的而开庭，全体参议员皆须凭圣经或道德宣誓 。合众国总统受审时，须由最高法院首席大法官主持审判。无论何人，若非经出席参议员的三分之二的同意，皆不得被定罪。

弹劾案之判决，不得超出令被定罪者免职和剥夺其担任并享有合众国属下有荣誉、有责任或有薪酬的任何官职的资格。然而被定罪的人仍可依法受到起诉、审判、判决和惩罚。

**第四款**

各州进行参议员和众议员选举的时间、地点及方式由该州议会规定。但除选举参议员的地点外，国会亦可随时通过法律做出或改变这些规定。

国会每年须至少开会一次，若非国会以法律另订日期，此会议须在十二月第一个星期一举行。

**第五款**

两院分别是其各自议员的选举、选举结果报告和议员资格的裁判者。各院议员出席人数过半即构成可进行议事的法定人数；而不足法定人数时，须逐日延期开会，且各院有权按本院规定的方式及处罚办法强迫缺席议员出席会议。

各院可规定本院议事规则，惩罚本院议员的违纪行为，并可经三分之二议员的同意开除一名议员。

各院须有本院会议记录，并时常予以公布，但本院认为需要保密的部分除外。在五分之一的出席议员的请求下，各院议员对于任何问题的赞成票与反对票须载入会议记录。

在国会开会期间，任何一院，未经另一院同意，不得休会达三日以上，亦不得到非两院开会的任何地方休会。

## 第六款

参议员和众议员须得到服务的报酬，该报酬须由法律确定，并从合众国国库支付。两院议员在一切情况下——犯叛国罪、重罪和妨害治安罪除外——都享有在出席各自议院会议期间和往返于各自议院途中不受逮捕的特权。他们亦不得因在任一议院进行的演说或论辩而在任何其他地方受到审讯。

参议员或众议员在当选任期内，不得被任命担任在此期间设置或增薪的合众国政府授权的任何文官职务。凡在合众国政府供职者，在继续任职期间不得担任任何一院议员。

## 第七款

一切征税议案须首先在众议院提出，而参议院须像处理其他议案一样，以修正案的方式提出建议或表示赞同。

每一项由众议院和参议院通过的议案，在成为法律前须送交合众国总统。若总统赞成该议案，须予以签署批准；若不赞成，则须将该议案连同其反对意见退回至最初提出该议案的议院。该院须将此反对意见详细载入本院会议记录并对此进行复议。经复议后，若该院三分之二议员同意通过该议案，则将该议案连同反对意见一并送交至另一议院。该院须同样对此议案进行复议，若该院三分之二议员赞同，则该议案成为法律。在所有这类情况下，两院的表决都由赞成票和反对票所决定：对该议案投赞成票和反对票的议员的姓名须分别载入各议院的会议记录。任何议案若在送交总统后十日内（星期日除外）未经总统退回，则该议案等同于已被总统签署，即成为法律；但因国会休会而使该议案不能退回的情况除外，在此种情况下，该议案不得成为法律。

凡必须由参众两院一致同意的命令、决议或表决（关于休会的问题除外），均须送交合众国总统。该项命令、决议或表决须由总统赞成后才可生效；若总统不赞成，则必须按照关于议案所规定的规则和限制，由参议院和众议院各以三分之二的多数表决重新通过。

**第八款**

国会有权：规定并征收直接税、间接税、关税及消费税，以偿付国债、筹备合众国共同防务与公共福利。但所征的所有间接税、关税与消费税须全国统一；

以合众国之信用借款；

管制同外国的、各州之间的以及同各印第安部落的贸易；

在全国范围内统一制定一个归化条例以及各项涉及破产的法律；

铸造货币，厘定其与外国货币的价值，并确定度量衡的标准；

规定有关伪造合众国债券和通行货币的罚则；

设立邮政局并修建邮政道路；

通过保障作家和发明家对其著作和发明在一定限定期限内的专有权利以促进知识和有用技术的进步；

在最高法院之下设立各级法院；

界定并惩罚在公海上所犯的海盗罪和重罪以及违反国际法的犯罪行为；

宣战，颁发捕拿许可状，制定关于陆上和水上捕获的条例；

招募并供给陆军，但此项用途的拨款期限不得超过两年；

装备并维持一支海军；

制定管控陆军与海军的条例；

规定征召民兵，以执行联邦法律、镇压叛乱和抵御入侵；

规定民兵的组织、装备和纪律，规定服役于合众国的民兵的管理，但各州保留民兵军官的任命和按国会规定的纪律训练民兵的权力；

在由某些州让出、经国会接受而成为合众国政府所在地的地区（不得超过10平方英里）的一切事项中行使独有的立法权；在所有经州议会同意、由合众国在该州购买的用于建造要塞、弹药库、兵工厂、船厂以及其他必要建筑物的地方行使同样的权力；

为执行上述各项权力和由本宪法授予合众国政府或其任何部门及官员的一切其他权力制定必要且适当的一切法律。

**第九款**

在1808年以前，对既存任何一州认为当准予其迁移或入境之人的迁移或入境，国会不得加以禁止，但对每个此类人的入境，可向其征收不超过10美元的直接税或关税。

人身保护令之特权不得被终止，除非发生内乱或外患时公共安全要求中止此项特权。

不得通过剥夺公民权利的法案或追溯既往的法律。

除非依本宪法上文所规定的人口普查或统计的比例，不得征收人头税或其他直接税。

对于从任何一州出口的货物，均不得征收直接税或关税。

任何商业或税收条例，都不得给予一州港口以优于其他州港口的待遇，亦不得强迫开往或来自某一州的船只在另一州办理入关、出关手续或交纳关税。

除根据法律规定的拨款外，不得从国库提取款项。一份关于所有公款收支的定期的报告及账目，应不时予以公布。

合众国不得授予贵族爵位。凡在合众国政府担任任何有酬或有责的职务的人，未经国会同意，不得从任何国王、亲王或外国政权接受任何礼物、薪酬、官职或任何一种爵位。

### 第十款

任何一州皆不得：缔结条约，参加同盟或邦联；颁发捕拿许可状；铸造货币；发行纸币；使用金银币以外的物品作为偿还债务的货币；通过剥夺公民权利的法案、追溯既往的法律或损害契约义务的法律；授予贵族爵位。

任何一州，未经国会同意，不得对进出口货物征收关税，但为执行本州检查法所绝对必需者除外。任何一州对进出口货物所征全部关税纯收益均应充作合众国国库之用；所有这类法律须由国会加以修正和控制。

任何一州，未经国会同意，不得征收船舶吨税，不得在和平时期保有军队或战舰，不得与他州或外国缔结协定或盟约；除非遭到实际入侵或遇刻不容缓的紧迫危险，否则不得参加战争。

## 第二条

### 第一款

行政权属于美利坚合众国总统。总统的任期为四年，副总统的任期与总统的任期相同。总统与副总统均按以下程序进行选举：

各州按照本州议会所定方式选派数名选举人，其数目与该州在国会应有的参议员和众议员总人数相等。但参议员和众议员，以及在合众国政府担任有责或有酬之职务的人，均不得被选派为选举人。

选举人须在各自州内进行集会并投票选举出两人，其中须至少有一人不是选举人本州的常住居民。选举人须开列名单，写明所有被选人姓名及其所得票数，并在该名单上签名作证，然后将封印后的名单送至合众国政府所在地，交给参议院议长。参议院议长须在参议院和众议院全体议员面前开拆所有证明书，随后计算票数。得票最多之人，若其所得票数超过所选派选举人总数的半数，即为总统。若得票数过半者不止一人，且得票相等，众议院须立即投票选举其中一人为总统。若无人得票数过半，则众议院须以同样方式从名单上得票最多的五人中选举一人为总统。而选举总统时，以州为单位计票，每州全体代表有一票表决权；三分之二的州各有一名或多名众议员出席，即构成选举总统的法定人数。当选总统需要获得将所有州都计算在内的过半数票。在任何情况下，总统选出后，得选举人票最多者，即为副总统。但若有两人或两人以上得票相等，参议院应投票选举其中一人为副总统。

国会须确定选出选举人的时间和选举人投票日期，且该日期须全国一致。

无论何人，若非本土出生的公民，或本宪法采用时非合众国公民，则不得当选为总统；凡年龄不满35岁、在合众国境内居住不满14年者，亦不得当选为总统。

当总统免职、死亡、辞职或丧失履行总统职务之权力和责任的能力时，总统职务之权力和责任须移交给副总统。当总统和副总统皆免职、死亡、辞职或丧失任职能力时，国会须以法律规定宣布代理总统的官员。该官员须代行总统职务之权力和责任直到总统恢复任职能力或新总统选出为止。

总统须在规定时间内得到其服务之薪酬，此薪酬在其担任总统任期内不得增加或减少。总统在任期内不得从合众国或任何一州接受任何其他的薪酬。

总统在就任前，须凭圣经或道德作如下宣誓：“我庄严宣誓，我一定忠实执行合众国总统职务，并竭尽全力维持、保护和捍卫合众国宪法。”

### 第二款

总统为合众国陆军、海军及征调为合众国服役的各州民兵的总司令。他可要求各行政部门长官就其各自职责有关的任何事项提出了书面意见。他有权对危害合众国的违法行为发布缓刑令和赦免令，但弹劾案除外。

总统在经咨询参议院并取得其同意，且出席参议员总数三分之二对此批准的前提下，有权缔结条约。他须提名大使、公使和领事、最高法院法官以及未在本宪法中另行规定但依法所设立的合众国所有其他官职的任命，经咨询参议院并取得其同意后任命生效。但当国会认为适当时，可依法将此类低级官员的任命权授予总统、法院或各部部长。

总统有权委任人员填补在参议院休会期间可能出现的官员空缺，此项委任在参议院下期会议结束时满期。

### 第三款

总统须不时向国会报告联邦情况，并向国会提出他认为必要且妥当的措施供国会审议。在非常情况下。总统可召集两院或任何一院开会。如遇两院对休会时间有意见分歧时，他可令两院休会至他认为适当的时间。他须接见大使和其他公使；他须负责使法律切实执行，并委任合众国的所有武官。

### 第四款

总统、副总统和合众国的所有文职官员，因叛国、贿赂或其他重罪与轻罪而受弹劾并被定罪时，皆须予以免职。

# 第三条

## 第一款

合众国的司法权属于一个最高法院以及由国会随时规定并设立的下级法院。最高法院和下级法院的法官如行为端正，则须继续任职，并须在规定时间内得到其服务之薪酬，此薪酬在其任职期间不得减少。

## 第二款

司法权的适用范围包括：一切由本宪法、合众国法律和根据合众国权力已订立或将订立的条约而产生的涉及普通法与衡平法的案件；一切涉及大使、公使和领事的案件；一切关于海事法和海事管辖权的案件；合众国为一方当事者的诉讼；州之间的诉讼；一州与他州公民之间的诉讼；不同州公民之间的诉讼；同州公民之间对不同州转让土地的所有权的诉讼；一州或其公民同外国政府、公民或臣民之间的诉讼。

对于一切涉及大使、公使和领事以及一州为一方当事者的案件，最高法院有初审管辖权。对上述所有其他案件，不论法律方面还是事实方面，最高法院皆具有上诉裁决权，但由国会规定为例外及另有处理条例者除外。

除弹劾案外，一切罪行皆由陪审团审判，且此类审判须在该罪行发生的州内举行；但若该罪行不发生在任何一州之内，审判须在国会以法律规定的一个或几个地点举行。

## 第三款

唯向合众国宣战，或依附、帮助和慰劳合众国之敌人者，方构成叛国罪。无论何人，除根据两名证人对其同一公开行为的作证或其本人在公开法庭上的供认，不得被定为叛国罪。

国会有权宣告对叛国罪的惩罚，但不得在因叛国罪而剥夺其公民权之外进而剥夺其继承人之继承权，亦不得在被剥夺公民权者在世期间之外没收其财产。

## 第四条

### 第一款

对于其他州的公共法律、文件和司法程序，各州应给予充分的信任和尊重。国会须以一般法律规定此类法律、文件和司法程序如何证明其效力以及其具有何等效力。

### 第二款

每个州的公民享有各州公民的所有特权与豁免权。

在任何一州被指控犯有叛国罪、重罪或其他罪行的人，如畏罪潜逃出该州而在他州被寻获时，须根据其所逃出之州行政当局的要求将他交出，以解送其至对其犯罪行为有管辖权的州。根据一州法律须在该州服劳役或劳动的人，若逃至他州，不得因他州之法律或规章而免除此种劳役或劳动，而应根据有权得此劳役或劳动之当事人的要求将其交出。

### 第三款

新州可由国会接纳加入本联邦；但不得在任何其他州的管辖区域内组成或建立新州；未经相关州的议会和国会同意，亦不得将两个或两个以上的州合并、或将几个州的一部分合并组成新州。

对于属于合众国的领土或其他资产，国会有权处置和制定一切必要的条例和规章。对本宪法之条文不得作有损于合众国或任何一州之任何权利的解释。

### 第四款

合众国须保证本联邦各州实行共和政体，保护各州免遭入侵，并须应州议会——在州议会不能召开时，应该州行政长官——之请求平定内乱。

## 第五条

国会在两院各有三分之二议员认为必要时，须提出本宪法的修正案，或根据各州三分之二州议会的请求，召开制宪会议提出修正案。不论哪种方式提出的修正案，经各州四分之三州议会或四分之三州制宪大会的批准，即实际成为本宪法的一部分并生效；采用何种批准方式，可由国会提出建议。但在1808年以前制定的修正案，均不得以任何形式影响本宪法第一条第九款的第一项和第四项；任何一州，未经其同意，不得被剥夺其在参议院的平等投票权。

## 第六条

本宪法被采用前订立的一切债务和应承担义务的一切条约，对于实行本宪法的合众国同邦联时期的合众国一样有效。

本宪法与依本宪法所制定的合众国法律，以及根据合众国的权力已订立或将订立的一切协定，皆为全国之最高法律；各州法官皆受其约束，即使该州宪法和法律中有与之相抵触的内容。

上述参议员、众议员、各州州议会议员，以及合众国和各州所有行政和司法官员，应凭圣经或道德宣誓拥护本宪法；但不得以宗教标准作为担任合众国政府任何官职或公职之条件。

## 第七条

经九个州全州大会的批准，即足以使本宪法在各批准其通过的州成立。

本宪法于公元1787年，即美利坚合众国独立之后第十二年的9月17日，经出席制宪大会的各州在会上一致同意后制定。我们谨在此签名作证。

# CONSTITUTION OF THE UNITED STATES OF AMERICA

WE THE PEOPLE of the United States, in Order to form a more perfect Union, establish Justice, insure domestic Tranquility, provide for the common defence, promote the general Welfare, and secure the Blessings of Liberty to ourselves and our Posterity, do ordain and establish this CONSTITUTION for the United States of America.

## ARTICLE I.

SECTION 1. All legislative Powers herein granted shall be vested in a Congress of the United States, which shall consist of a Senate and House of Representatives.

SECTION 2. The House of Representatives shall be composed of Members chosen every second Year by the People of the several States, and the Electors in each State shall have the Qualifications requisite for Electors of the most numerous Branch of the State Legislature.

No Person shall be a Representative who shall not have attained to the Age of twenty five Years, and been seven Years a Citizen of the United States, and who shall not, when elected, be an Inhabitant of that State in which he shall be chosen.

Representatives and direct Taxes shall be apportioned among the several States which may be included within this Union, according to their respective Numbers, which shall be determined by adding to the whole Number of free Persons, including those bound to Service for a Term of Years, and excluding Indians not taxed, three fifths of all other Persons. The actual Enumeration shall be made within three Years after the first Meeting of the Congress of the United States, and within every subsequent Term of ten Years, in such Manner as they shall by Law direct. The Number of Representatives shall not exceed one for every thirty Thousand, but each State shall have at Least one Representative; and until such enumeration shall be made, the State of New Hampshire shall be entitled to chuse three, Massachusetts eight, Rhode-Island and Providence Plantations one, Connecticut five, New-York six, New Jersey four, Pennsylvania eight, Delaware one, Maryland six, Virginia ten, North Carolina five, South Carolina five, and Georgia three.

When vacancies happen in the Representation from any State, the Executive Authority thereof shall issue Writs of Election to fill such Vacancies.

The House of Representatives shall choose their Speaker and other Officers; and shall have the sole Power of Impeachment.

SECTION 3. The Senate of the United States shall be composed of two Senators from each State, chosen by the Legislature thereof for six Years; and each Senator shall have one Vote.

Immediately after they shall be assembled in Consequence of the first Election, they shall be divided as equally as may be into three Classes. The Seats of the Senators of the first Class shall be vacated at the Expiration of the second Year, of the second Class at the Expiration of the fourth Year, and of the third Class at the Expiration of the sixth Year, so that one third may be chosen every second Year; and if Vacancies happen by Resignation, or otherwise, during the Recess of the Legislature of any State, the Executive thereof may make temporary Appointments until the next Meeting of the Legislature, which shall then fill such Vacancies.

No Person shall be a Senator who shall not have attained to the Age of thirty Years, and been nine Years a Citizen of the United States, and who shall not, when elected, be an Inhabitant of that State for which he shall be chosen.

The Vice President of the United States shall be President of the Senate, but shall have no Vote, unless they be equally divided.

The Senate shall chuse their other Officers, and also a President pro tempore, in the Absence of the Vice President, or when he shall exercise the Office of President of the United States.

The Senate shall have the sole Power to try all Impeachments. When sitting for that Purpose, they shall be on Oath or Affirmation. When the President of the United States is tried, the Chief Justice shall preside: And no Person shall be convicted without the Concurrence of two thirds of the Members present.

Judgment in Cases of Impeachment shall not extend further than to removal from Office, and disqualification to hold and enjoy any Office of honor, Trust or Profit under the United States: but the Party convicted shall nevertheless be liable and subject to Indictment, Trial, Judgment and Punishment, according to Law.

SECTION 4. The Times, Places and Manner of holding Elections for Senators and Representatives, shall be prescribed in each State by the Legislature thereof; but the Congress may at any time by Law make or alter such Regulations, except as to the Places of chusing Senators.

The Congress shall assemble at least once in every Year, and such Meeting shall be on the first Monday in December, unless they shall by Law appoint a different Day.

SECTION 5. Each House shall be the Judge of the Elections, Returns and Qualifications of its own Members, and a Majority of each shall constitute a Quorum to do Business; but a smaller Number may adjourn from day to day, and may be authorized to compel the Attendance of absent Members, in such Manner, and under such Penalties as each House may provide.

Each House may determine the Rules of its Proceedings, punish its Members for disorderly Behaviour, and, with the Concurrence of two thirds, expel a Member.

Each House shall keep a Journal of its Proceedings, and from time to time publish the same, excepting such Parts as may in their Judgment require Secrecy; and the Yeas and Nays of the Members of either House on any question shall, at the Desire of one fifth of those Present, be entered on the Journal.

Neither House, during the Session of Congress, shall, without the Consent of the other, adjourn for more than three days, nor to any other Place than that in which the two Houses shall be sitting

SECTION 6. The Senators and Representatives shall receive a Compensation for their Services, to be ascertained by Law, and paid out of the Treasury of the United States. They shall in all Cases, except Treason, Felony and Breach of the Peace, be privileged from Arrest during their Attendance at the Session of their respective Houses, and in going to and returning from the same; and for any Speech or Debate in either House, they shall not be questioned in any other Place.

No Senator or Representative shall, during the Time for which he was elected, be appointed to any civil Office under the Authority of the United States, which shall have been created, or the Emoluments whereof shall have been increased during such time; and no Person holding any Office under the United States, shall be a Member of either House during his Continuance in Office.

SECTION 7. All Bills for raising Revenue shall originate in the House of Representatives; but the Senate may propose or concur with Amendments as on other Bills.

Every Bill which shall have passed the House of Representatives and the Senate, shall, before it become a Law, be presented to the President of the United States;If he approve he shall sign it, but if not he shall return it, with his Objections to that House in which it shall have originated, who shall enter the Objections at large on their Journal, and proceed to reconsider it. If after such Reconsideration two thirds of that House shall agree to pass the Bill, it shall be sent, together with the Objections, to the other House, by which it shall likewise be reconsidered, and if approved by two thirds of that House, it shall become a Law. But in all such Cases the Votes of both Houses shall be determined by yeas and Nays, and the Names of the Persons voting for and against the Bill shall be entered on the Journal of each House respectively. If any Bill shall not be returned by the President within ten Days (Sundays excepted) after it shall have been presented to him, the Same shall be a Law, in like Manner as if he had signed it, unless the Congress by their Adjournment prevent its Return, in which Case it shall not be a Law.

Every Order, Resolution, or Vote to which the Concurrence of the Senate and House of Representatives may be necessary (except on a question of Adjournment) shall be presented to the President of the United States; and before the Same shall take Effect, shall be approved by him, or being disapproved by him, shall be repassed by two thirds of the Senate and House of Representatives, according to the Rules and Limitations prescribed in the Case of a Bill.

SECTION 8. The Congress shall have Power To lay and collect Taxes, Duties, Imposts and Excises, to pay the Debts and provide for the common Defence and general Welfare of the United States; but all Duties, Imposts and Excises shall be uniform throughout the United States;

To borrow Money on the credit of the United States;

To regulate Commerce with foreign Nations, and among the several States, and with the Indian Tribes;

To establish an uniform Rule of Naturalization, and uniform Laws on the subject of Bankruptcies throughout the United States;

To coin Money, regulate the Value thereof, and of foreign Coin, and fix the Standard of Weights and Measures;

To provide for the Punishment of counterfeiting the Securities and current Coin of the United States;

To establish Post Offices and post Roads;

To promote the Progress of Science and useful Arts, by securing for limited Times to Authors and Inventors the exclusive Right to their respective Writings and Discoveries;

To constitute Tribunals inferior to the supreme Court;

To define and punish Piracies and Felonies committed on the high Seas, and Offences against the Law of Nations;

To declare War, grant Letters of Marque and Reprisal, and make Rules concerning Captures on Land and Water;

To raise and support Armies, but no Appropriation of Money to that Use shall be for a longer Term than two Years;

To provide and maintain a Navy;

To make Rules for the Government and Regulation of the land and naval Forces;

To provide for calling forth the Militia to execute the Laws of the Union, suppress Insurrections and repel Invasions;

To provide for organizing, arming, and disciplining, the Militia, and for governing such Part of them as may be employed in the Service of the United States, reserving to the States respectively, the Appointment of the Officers, and the Authority of training the Militia according to the discipline prescribed by Congress;

To exercise exclusive Legislation in all Cases whatsoever, over such District (not exceeding ten Miles square) as may, by Cession of particular States, and the Acceptance of Congress, become the Seat of the Government of the United States, and to exercise like Authority over all Places purchased by the Consent of the Legislature of the State in which the Same shall be, for the Erection of Forts, Magazines, Arsenals, dock-Yards, and other needful Buildings;–And

To make all Laws which shall be necessary and proper for carrying into Execution the foregoing Powers, and all other Powers vested by this Constitution in the Government of the United States, or in any Department or Officer thereof.

SECTION 9. The Migration or Importation of such Persons as any of the States now existing shall think proper to admit, shall not be prohibited by the Congress prior to the Year one thousand eight hundred and eight, but a Tax or duty may be imposed on such Importation, not exceeding ten dollars for each Person.

The Privilege of the Writ of Habeas Corpus shall not be suspended, unless when in Cases of Rebellion or Invasion the public Safety may require it.

No Bill of Attainder or ex post facto Law shall be passed.

No Capitation, or other direct, Tax shall be laid, unless in Proportion to the Census or enumeration herein before directed to be taken.

No Tax or Duty shall be laid on Articles exported from any State.

No Preference shall be given by any Regulation of Commerce or Revenue to the Ports of one State over those of another; nor shall Vessels bound to, or from, one State, be obliged to enter, clear, or pay Duties in another.

No Money shall be drawn from the Treasury, but in Consequence of Appropriations made by Law; and a regular Statement and Account of the Receipts and Expenditures of all public Money shall be published from time to time.

No Title of Nobility shall be granted by the United States: And no Person holding any Office of Profit or Trust under them, shall, without the Consent of the Congress, accept of any present, Emolument, Office, or Title, of any kind whatever, from any King, Prince, or foreign State.

SECTION 10. No State shall enter into any Treaty, Alliance, or Confederation; grant Letters of Marque and Reprisal; coin Money; emit Bills of Credit; make any Thing but gold and silver Coin a Tender in Payment of Debts; pass any Bill of Attainder, ex post facto Law, or Law impairing the Obligation of Contracts, or grant any Title of Nobility.

No State shall, without the Consent of the Congress, lay any Imposts or Duties on Imports or Exports, except what may be absolutely necessary for executing it's inspection Laws: and the net Produce of all Duties and Imposts, laid by any State on Imports or Exports, shall be for the Use of the Treasury of the United States; and all such Laws shall be subject to the Revision and Control of the Congress.

No State shall, without the Consent of Congress, lay any Duty of Tonnage, keep Troops, or Ships of War in time of Peace, enter into any Agreement or Compact with another State, or with a foreign Power, or engage in War, unless actually invaded, or in such imminent Danger as will not admit of delay.

## ARTICLE II.

SECTION 1. The executive Power shall be vested in a President of the United States of America. He shall hold his Office during the Term of four Years, and, together with the Vice President, chosen for the same Term, be elected, as follows:

Each State shall appoint, in such Manner as the Legislature thereof may direct, a Number of Electors, equal to the whole Number of Senators and Representatives to which the State may be entitled in the Congress: but no Senator or Representative, or Person holding an Office of Trust or Profit under the United States, shall be appointed an Elector.

The Electors shall meet in their respective States, and vote by Ballot for two Persons, of whom one at least shall not be an Inhabitant of the same State with themselves. And they shall make a List of all the Persons voted for, and of the Number of Votes for each; which List they shall sign and certify, and transmit sealed to the Seat of the Government of the United States, directed to the President of the Senate. The President of the Senate shall, in the Presence of the Senate and House of Representatives, open all the Certificates, and the Votes shall then be counted. The Person having the greatest Number of Votes shall be the President, if such Number be a Majority of the whole Number of Electors appointed; and if there be more than one who have such Majority, and have an equal Number of Votes, then the House of Representatives shall immediately chuse by Ballot one of them for President; and if no Person have a Majority, then from the five highest on the List the said House shall in like Manner chusing the President. But in chusing the President, the Votes shall be taken by States, the Representation from each State having one Vote; A quorum for this purpose shall consist of a Member or Members from two thirds of the States, and a Majority of all the States shall be necessary to a Choice. In every Case, after the Choice of the President, the Person having the greatest Number of Votes of the Electors shall be the Vice President. But if there should remain two or more who have equal Votes, the Senate shall chuse from them by Ballot the Vice President.

The Congress may determine the Time of chusing the Electors, and the Day on which they shall give their Votes; which Day shall be the same throughout the United States.

No Person except a natural born Citizen, or a Citizen of the United States, at the time of the Adoption of this Constitution, shall be eligible to the Office of President; neither shall any Person be eligible to that Office who shall not have attained to the Age of thirty five Years, and been fourteen Years a Resident within the United States.

In Case of the Removal of the President from Office, or of his Death, Resignation, or Inability to discharge the Powers and Duties of the said Office, the Same shall devolve on the Vice President, and the Congress may by Law provide for the Case of Removal, Death, Resignation or Inability, both of the President and Vice President, declaring what Officer shall then act as President, and such Officer shall act accordingly, until the Disability be removed, or a President shall be elected.

The President shall, at stated Times, receive for his Services, a Compensation, which shall neither be increased nor diminished during the Period for which he shall have been elected, and he shall not receive within that Period any other Emolument from the United States, or any of them.

Before he enter on the Execution of his Office, he shall take the following Oath or Affirmation:—"I do solemnly swear (or affirm) that I will faithfully execute the Office of President of the United States, and will to the best of my Ability, preserve, protect and defend the Constitution of the United States."

SECTION 2. The President shall be Commander in Chief of the Army and Navy of the United States, and of the Militia of the several States, when called into the actual Service of the United States; he may require the Opinion, in writing, of the principal Officer in each of the executive Departments, upon any Subject relating to the Duties of their respective Offices, and he shall have Power to grant Reprieves and Pardons for Offences against the United States, except in Cases of Impeachment.

He shall have Power, by and with the Advice and Consent of the Senate, to make Treaties, provided two thirds of the Senators present concur; and he shall nominate, and by and with the Advice and Consent of the Senate, shall appoint Ambassadors, other public Ministers and Consuls, Judges of the supreme Court, and all other Officers of the United States, whose Appointments are not herein otherwise provided for, and which shall be established by Law: but the Congress may by Law vest the Appointment of such inferior Officers, as they think proper, in the President alone, in the Courts of Law, or in the Heads of Departments.

The President shall have Power to fill up all Vacancies that may happen during the Recess of the Senate, by granting Commissions which shall expire at the End of their next Session.

SECTION 3. He shall from time to time give to the Congress Information of the State of the Union, and recommend to their Consideration such Measures as he shall judge necessary and expedient; he may, on extraordinary Occasions, convene both Houses, or either of them, and in Case of Disagreement between them, with

Respect to the Time of Adjournment, he may adjourn them to such Time as he shall think proper; he shall receive Ambassadors and other public Ministers; he shall take Care that the Laws be faithfully executed, and shall Commission all the Officers of the United States.

SECTION 4. The President, Vice President and all civil Officers of the United States, shall be removed from Office on Impeachment for, and Conviction of, Treason, Bribery, or other high Crimes and Misdemeanors.

## ARTICLE III.

SECTION 1. The judicial Power of the United States shall be vested in one supreme Court, and in such inferior Courts as the Congress may from time to time ordain and establish. The Judges, both of the supreme and inferior Courts, shall hold their Offices during good Behaviour, and shall, at stated Times, receive for their Services a Compensation, which shall not be diminished during their Continuance in Office.

SECTION 2. The judicial Power shall extend to all Cases, in Law and Equity, arising under this Constitution, the Laws of the United States, and Treaties made, or which shall be made, under their Authority;–to all Cases affecting Ambassadors, other public Ministers and Consuls;–to all Cases of admiralty and maritime Jurisdiction;–to Controversies to which the United States shall be a Party;–to Controversies between two or more States;– between a State and Citizens of another State,–between Citizens of different States,–between Citizens of the same State claiming Lands under Grants of different States, and between a State, or the Citizens thereof, and foreign States, Citizens or Subjects.

In all Cases affecting Ambassadors, other public Ministers and Consuls, and those in which a State shall be Party, the supreme Court shall have original Jurisdiction. In all the other Cases before mentioned, the supreme Court shall have appellate Jurisdiction, both as to Law and Fact, with such Exceptions, and under such Regulations as the Congress shall make.

The Trial of all Crimes, except in Cases of Impeachment, shall be by Jury; and such Trial shall be held in the State where the said Crimes shall have been committed; but when not committed within any State, the Trial shall be at such Place or Places as the Congress may by Law have directed.

SECTION 3. Treason against the United States, shall consist only in levying War against them, or in adhering to their Enemies, giving them Aid and Comfort. No Person shall be convicted of Treason unless on the Testimony of two Witnesses to the same overt Act, or on Confession in open Court.

The Congress shall have Power to declare the Punishment of Treason, but no Attainder of Treason shall work Corruption of Blood, or Forfeiture except during the Life of the Person attainted.

## ARTICLE IV.

SECTION 1. Full Faith and Credit shall be given in each State to the public Acts, Records, and judicial Proceedings of every other State. And the Congress may by general Laws prescribe the Manner in which such Acts, Records and Proceedings shall be proved, and the Effect thereof.

SECTION 2. The Citizens of each State shall be entitled to all Privileges and Immunities of Citizens in the several States.

A Person charged in any State with Treason, Felony, or other Crime, who shall flee from Justice, and be found in another State, shall on Demand of the executive Authority of the State from which he fled, be delivered up, to be removed to the State having Jurisdiction of the Crime.

No Person held to Service or Labour in one State, under the Laws thereof, escaping into another, shall, in Consequence of any Law or Regulation therein, be discharged from such Service or Labour, but shall be delivered up on Claim of the Party to whom such Service or Labour may be due.

SECTION 3. New States may be admitted by the Congress into this Union; but no new State shall be formed or erected within the Jurisdiction of any other State; nor any State be formed by the Junction of two or more States, or Parts of States, without the Consent of the Legislatures of the States concerned as well as of the Congress.

The Congress shall have Power to dispose of and make all needful Rules and Regulations respecting the Territory or other Property belonging to the United States; and nothing in this Constitution shall be so construed as to Prejudice any Claims of the United States, or of any particular State.

SECTION 4. The United States shall guarantee to every State in this Union a Republican Form of Government, and shall protect each of them against Invasion; and on Application of the Legislature, or of the Executive (when the Legislature cannot be convened), against domestic Violence.

## ARTICLE V.

The Congress, whenever two thirds of both Houses shall deem it necessary, shall propose Amendments to this Constitution, or, on the Application of the Legislatures of two thirds of the several States, shall call a Convention for proposing Amendments, which, in either Case, shall be valid to all Intents and Purposes, as Part of this Constitution, when ratified by the Legislatures of three fourths of the several States, or by Conventions in three fourths thereof, as the one or the other Mode of Ratification may be proposed by the Congress; Provided that no Amendment which may be made prior to the Year One thousand eight hundred and eight shall in any Manner affect the first and fourth Clauses in the Ninth Section of the first Article; and that no State, without its Consent, shall be deprived of its equal Suffrage in the Senate.

## ARTICLE VI.

All Debts contracted and Engagements entered into, before the Adoption of this Constitution, shall be as valid against the United States under this Constitution, as under the Confederation.

This Constitution, and the Laws of the United States which shall be made in Pursuance thereof; and all Treaties made, or which shall be made, under the Authority of the United States, shall be the supreme Law of the Land; and the Judges in every State shall be bound thereby, any Thing in the Constitution or Laws of any State to the Contrary notwithstanding.

The Senators and Representatives before mentioned, and the Members of the several State Legislatures, and all executive and judicial Officers, both of the United States and of the several States, shall be bound by Oath or Affirmation, to support this Constitution; but no religious Test shall ever be required as a Qualification to any Office or public Trust under the United States.

## ARTICLE VII.

The Ratification of the Conventions of nine States, shall be sufficient for the Establishment of this Constitution between the States so ratifying the Same.

# 美利坚合众国宪法修正案

## 第一条

国会不得就下列事项制定法律：确立宗教或禁止宗教自由；剥夺人民的言论自由或出版自由；剥夺人民和平集会以及为纠正不平而向政府请愿申诉的权利。

## 第二条

一个完备的民兵组织是保障一个自由州安全所必需的，因此人民持有并携带武器的权利不得予以侵犯。

## 第三条

任何士兵，在和平时期，若未经屋主之许可，不得进驻任何民房；在战争时期，若未依法律所规定之方式，亦不得如此。

## 第四条

人民有保护其人身、住所、文件与财产不受无理搜查与扣押之权利，不得予以侵犯；不得颁发搜查、拘捕或扣押等行为之授权令，除非有合理之缘由，以凭圣经或道德进行的宣誓为保证，并详述指定搜索之地、拘捕之人或扣押之物。

## 第五条

任何人，在无大陪审团的报告或起诉书的前提下，不受可判死罪或其他可判不名誉罪的指控，但发生于战争或公共危险时期服现役的陆、海军或民兵组织中的案件除外；任何人，不得因同一罪行而两次受到性命或身体上的损害；任何人，不得在任何刑事案件中被迫做不利于自己的证明，亦不得未经正当法律程序被剥夺生命、自由或财产；任何人，若无对其的合理补偿，其私人财产不得被充作公用。

## 第六条

在一切刑事诉讼中，被告人均享受下列之权利：由发生罪案之州或地区——该地区须先经过法律确认——的一个公正的陪审团予以迅速且公开的审判；被告知所受指控的性质与理由；与指证其罪行的证人当面对质；以强制程序获得对于自己有利的证据，并拥有在法律上为其辩护之人的协助。

## 第七条

依据普通法提出的诉讼，若所争议之物的价额超过20美元，则其受陪审团审判之权利须受到保护，由一个陪审团判决之事实，除依照普通法之规则外，不得于合众国的任何法院中再加审理。

## 第八条

不得要求额外保释金，或处以过重之罚金，或施加残酷且异常之刑。

## 第九条

宪法对某些权利的列举，不得被解释为对其他保留给人民之权利的否定或减损。

## 第十条

宪法所未授予合众国，亦未禁止各州行使之权力，皆由各州或其人民保留之。

## 第十一条

在普通法或衡平法上，凡他州人民或外国人民控诉合众国任何一州之案件，不得由合众国法院受理。

合众国的司法权不得被解释为延伸到根据普通法或衡平法，合众国任何一州所受另一州之公民，以及任何外国公民或臣民发起或提出控诉之案件上。

## 第十二条

选举人须在其各自州内集合，投票选举总统与副总统，两者中至少有一人不得与选举人同为一州之常住居民。选举人须在其选举票上写明选为总统者之姓名，并在另一选票上写明选为副总统者之姓名；他们还须分别列出投票给其所选之总统与副总统的选举人的名单，每份名单上还须写明其得票数，并在该名单上签名作证，然后将封印后的名单送至合众国政府所在地，交给参议院议长。参议院议长须在参议院和众议院全体议员面前开拆所有证明书，随后计算票数。得总统选票最多者，若其所得票数超过所选派选举人总数的半数，即为总统；若无人得票数过半，则众议院须从被选为总统之名单上得票最多之人——不得超过三名——中立即投票选举其中一人为总统。而选举总统时，以州为单位计票，每州全体代表有一票表决权。选举总统之法定人数由三分之二的州各选出之一名或多名众议员组成，而当选所需票数为所有州半数以上。当需要众议院选举总统而众议院在次年3月4日之前尚未选出总统时，则副总统应有如总统遭遇死亡或其他宪法所规定之失去履行总统职责之情况，代行总统之职。得副总统选票最多者，若其所得票数超过所选派选举人总数的半数，即当选为副总统；若无人得票数过半，则参议院须从被选为副总统之名单上得票最多之两人中投票选举出其中一人为副总统。选举副总统之法定人数为参议员的三分之二，而当选票数为全体参议员之半数以上。但宪法规定无被选为合众国总统之资格者，亦不得当选为合众国副总统。

# 第十三条

## 第一款

在合众国境内或受合众国管辖的任何地区内，皆不得有奴役或强制劳役存在，但作为对被依法判处有罪者之罪行的惩罚除外。

## 第二款

国会有权通过适当的立法以实施本条法律。

# 第十四条

## 第一款

凡在合众国出生或加入合众国国籍并受其管辖之人，皆为合众国及其居住州之公民。各州皆不得制定或施行剥夺合众国公民之特权或豁免权的法律；未经正当法律程序，各州亦不得剥夺任何人之生命、自由或财产；各州亦不得拒绝承认任何人在其辖内受法律的平等保护。

## 第二款

各州众议员名额应按其各自的全部人口予以分配，但不被征税的印第安人除外。但当选举合众国总统与副总统之选举人、国会议员、一州之行政官与司法官或该州州议会议员之权利被拒绝给予该州年满21岁且为合众国公民之男性常住居民，或此类公民的此类权利被以任何方式进行削减——因叛国罪或其他罪行除外——时，则该州代表之基数须予以减少，减少的比例为此类男性公民在该州年满21岁的男性公民所占的人口比例。

## 第三款

凡曾宣誓成为一名国会议员，或一名合众国军官，或任何州的一名州议会议员，或任何州的一名行政官或司法官，并以此拥护合众国宪法者，若有参与反抗合众国的暴乱或叛乱，或对合众国之敌人给予援助或支持，则不得担任国会的参议员或众议员，不得担任总统与副总统之选举人，不得在合众国政府或任何一州州政府下任文武官职。但国会可在两院皆以三分之二票数表决通过的前提下撤销此项限制。

**第四款**

凡经法律审定的合众国公共债务，包括因支付有功于平定内乱或叛乱者之养老金与奖励金所产生之债务在内，其有效性不容置疑。但合众国或任何一州皆不得承担或偿付任何因资助反抗合众国的暴动或叛乱所产生之债务或承付款项，或任何因失去或解放任何一名奴隶所要求之赔偿。所有此类债务、承付款项或赔偿要求，皆非法且无效。

**第五款**

国会有权通过适当的立法以实施本条法律。

## 第十五条

**第一款**

合众国或其任何一州，对于合众国公民之投票权，不得因其种族、肤色或曾为奴隶而拒绝承认或予以剥夺。

**第二款**

国会有权通过适当的立法以实施本条法律中的各项规定。

# THE AMENDMENTS

## I.

Congress shall make no law respecting an establishment of religion, or prohibiting the free exercise thereof; or abridging the freedom of speech, or of the press; or the right of the people peaceably to assemble, and to petition the Government for a redress of grievances.

## II.

A well regulated Militia, being necessary to the security of a free State, the right of the people to keep and bear Arms, shall not be infringed.

## III.

No Soldier shall, in time of peace be quartered in any house, without the consent of the Owner, nor in time of war, but in a manner to be prescribed by law.

## IV.

The right of the people to be secure in their persons, houses, papers, and effects, against unreasonable searches and seizures, shall not be violated, and no Warrants shall issue, but upon probable cause, supported by Oath or affirmation, and particularly describing the place to be searched, and the persons or things to be seized.

V.

No person shall be held to answer for a capital, or otherwise infamous crime, unless on a presentment or indictment of a Grand Jury, except in cases arising in the land or naval forces, or in the Militia, when in actual service in time of War or public danger; nor shall any person be subject for the same offence to be twice put in jeopardy of life or limb; nor shall be compelled in any criminal case to be a witness against himself, nor be deprived of life, liberty, or property, without due process of law; nor shall private property be taken for public use, without just compensation.

VI.

In all criminal prosecutions, the accused shall enjoy the right to a speedy and public trial, by an impartial jury of the State and district wherein the crime shall have been committed, which district shall have been previously ascertained by law, and to be informed of the nature and cause of the accusation; to be confronted with the witnesses against him; to have compulsory process for obtaining witnesses in his favor, and to have the Assistance of Counsel for his defence.

VII.

In Suits at common law, where the value in controversy shall exceed twenty dollars, the right of trial by jury shall be preserved, and no fact tried by a jury, shall be otherwise re-examined in any Court of the United States, than according to the rules of the common law.

VIII.

Excessive bail shall not be required, nor excessive fines imposed, nor cruel and unusual punishments inflicted.

IX.

The enumeration in the Constitution, of certain rights, shall not be construed to deny or disparage others retained by the people.

X.

The powers not delegated to the United States by thc Constitution, nor prohibited by it to the States, are reserved to the States respectively, or to the people.

XI.

The Judicial power of the United States shall not be construed to extend to any suit in law or equity, commenced or prosecuted against one of the United States by Citizens of another State, or by Citizens or Subjects of any Foreign State.

XII.

The Electors shall meet in their respective states and vote by ballot for President and Vice-President, one of whom, at least, shall not be an inhabitant of the same state with themselves; they shall name in their ballots the person voted for as President, and in distinct ballots the person voted for as Vice-President, and they shall make distinct lists of all persons voted for as President, and of all persons voted for as Vice-President, and of the number of votes for each, which lists they shall sign and certify, and transmit sealed to the seat of the government of the United States, directed to the President of the Senate; — the President of the Senate shall, in the presence of the Senate and House of Representatives, open all the certificates and the votes shall then be counted; — The person having the greatest number of votes for President, shall be the President, if such number be a majority of the whole number of Electors appointed; and if no person have such majority, then from the persons having the highest numbers not exceeding three on the list of those voted for as President, the House of Representatives shall choose immediately, by ballot, the President. But in choosing the President, the votes shall be taken by states, the representation from each state having one vote; a quorum for this purpose shall consist of a member or members from two-thirds of the states, and a majority of all the states shall be necessary to a choice. And if the House of Representatives shall not choose a President whenever the right of choice shall devolve upon them, before the fourth day of March next following, then the Vice-President shall act as President, as in the case of the death or other constitutional disability of the President. The person having the greatest number of votes as Vice-President, shall be the Vice-President, if such number be a majority of the whole number of Electors appointed, and if no person have a majority, then from the two highest numbers on the list, the Senate shall choose the Vice-President; a quorum for the purpose shall consist of two-thirds of the whole number of Senators, and a majority of the whole number shall be necessary to a choice. But no person constitutionally ineligible to the office of President shall be eligible to that of Vice-President of the United States.

## XIII.

SECTION 1. Neither slavery nor involuntary servitude, except as a punishment for crime whereof the party shall have been duly convicted, shall exist within the United States, or any place subject to their jurisdiction.

SECTION 2. Congress shall have power to enforce this article by appropriate legislation.

## XIV.

SECTION 1. All persons born or naturalized in the United States, and subject to the jurisdiction thereof, are citizens of the United States and of the State wherein they reside. No State shall make or enforce any law which shall abridge the privileges or immunities of citizens of the United States; nor shall any State deprive any person of life, liberty, or property, without due process of law; nor deny to any person within its jurisdiction the equal protection of the laws.

SECTION 2. Representatives shall be apportioned among the several States according to their respective numbers, counting the whole number of persons in each State, excluding Indians not taxed. But when the right to vote at any election for the choice of electors for President and Vice-President of the United States, Representatives in Congress, the Executive and Judicial officers of a State, or the members of the Legislature thereof, is denied to any of the male inhabitants of such State, being twenty-one years of age, and citizens of the United States, or in any way abridged, except for participation in rebellion, or other crime, the basis of representation therein shall be reduced in the proportion which the number of such male citizens shall bear to the whole number of male citizens twenty-one years of age in such State.

SECTION 3. No person shall be a Senator or Representative in Congress, or elector of President and Vice-President, or hold any office, civil or military, under the United States, or under any State, who, having previously taken an oath, as a member of Congress, or as an officer of the United States, or as a member of any

State legislature, or as an executive or judicial officer of any State, to support the Constitution of the United States, shall have engaged in insurrection or rebellion against the same, or given aid or comfort to the enemies thereof. But Congress may by a vote of two-thirds of each House, remove such disability.

SECTION 4. The validity of the public debt of the United States, authorized by law, including debts incurred for payment of pensions and bounties for services in suppressing insurrection or rebellion, shall not be questioned. But neither the United States nor any State shall assume or pay any debt or obligation incurred in aid of insurrection or rebellion against the United States, or any claim for the loss or emancipation of any slave; but all such debts, obligations and claims shall be held illegal and void.

SECTION 5. The Congress shall have the power to enforce, by appropriate legislation, the provisions of this article.

## XV.

SECTION 1. The right of citizens of the United States to vote shall not be denied or abridged by the United States or by any State on account of race, color, or previous condition of servitude.

SECTION 2. The Congress shall have the power to enforce this article by appropriate legislation.

# 美利坚合众国历届总统（1789~1900）

THE PRESIDENTS OF THE UNITED STATES

| | 肖像 | 姓名与生卒年 | 就任日期 | 离任日期 | 所属党派 | 就任前的职位 |
|---|---|---|---|---|---|---|
| 1 |  | 乔治・华盛顿<br>George Washington<br>1732~1799 | 1789年<br>4月30日 | 1797年<br>3月4日 | 无党派 | 大陆军<br>总司令 |
| 2 |  | 约翰・亚当斯<br>John Adams<br>1735~1826 | 1797年<br>3月4日 | 1801年<br>3月4日 | 联邦党 | 副总统 |
| 3 |  | 托马斯・杰斐逊<br>Thomas Jefferson<br>1743~1826 | 1801年<br>3月4日 | 1809年<br>3月4日 | 民主<br>共和党 | 副总统 |
| 4 |  | 詹姆斯・麦迪逊<br>James Madison<br>1751~1836 | 1809年<br>3月4日 | 1817年<br>3月4日 | 民主<br>共和党 | 国务卿 |
| 5 |  | 詹姆斯・门罗<br>James Monroe<br>1758~1831 | 1817年<br>3月4日 | 1825年<br>3月4日 | 民主<br>共和党 | 国务卿 |

| | 肖像 | 姓名与生卒年 | 就任日期 | 离任日期 | 所属党派 | 就任前的职位 |
|---|---|---|---|---|---|---|
| 6 |  | 约翰·昆西·亚当斯<br>John Quincy Adams<br>1767~1848 | 1825年<br>3月4日 | 1829年<br>3月4日 | 民主<br>共和党 | 国务卿 |
| 7 |  | 安德鲁·杰克逊<br>Andrew Jackson<br>1767~1845 | 1829年<br>3月4日 | 1837年<br>3月4日 | 民主党 | 田纳西州<br>参议员 |
| 8 |  | 马丁·范布伦<br>Martin Van Buren<br>1782~1862 | 1837年<br>3月4日 | 1841年<br>3月4日 | 民主党 | 副总统 |
| 9 |  | 威廉·H. 哈里逊<br>William H. Harrison<br>1773~1841 | 1841年<br>3月4日 | 1841年<br>4月4日 | 辉格党 | 美国驻<br>哥伦比亚<br>公使 |
| 10 |  | 约翰·泰勒<br>John Tyler<br>1790~1862 | 1841年<br>4月4日 | 1845年<br>3月4日 | 辉格党 | 副总统 |
| 11 |  | 詹姆斯·K. 波尔克<br>James Knox Polk<br>1795~1849 | 1845年<br>3月4日 | 1849年<br>3月4日 | 民主党 | 田纳西州<br>州长 |

| | 肖像 | 姓名与生卒年 | 就任日期 | 离任日期 | 所属党派 | 就任前的职位 |
|---|---|---|---|---|---|---|
| 12 |  | 扎卡里·泰勒<br>Zachary Taylor<br>1784~1850 | 1849年<br>3月4日 | 1850年<br>9月9日 | 辉格党 | 美国陆军<br>第一步兵团<br>少将 |
| 13 |  | 米勒德·菲尔莫尔<br>Millard Fillmore<br>1800~1874 | 1850年<br>9月9日 | 1853年<br>3月4日 | 辉格党 | 副总统 |
| 14 |  | 富兰克林·皮尔斯<br>Franklin Pierce<br>1804~1869 | 1853年<br>3月4日 | 1857年<br>3月4日 | 民主党 | 美国陆军<br>第九步兵团<br>准将 |
| 15 |  | 詹姆斯·布坎南<br>James Buchanan<br>1791~1868 | 1857年<br>3月4日 | 1861年<br>3月4日 | 民主党 | 美国<br>驻英国<br>公使 |
| 16 |  | 亚伯拉罕·林肯<br>Abraham Lincoln<br>1809~1865 | 1861年<br>3月4日 | 1865年<br>4月15日 | 共和党 | 伊利诺伊州<br>众议员 |

| | 肖像 | 姓名与生卒年 | 就任日期 | 离任日期 | 所属党派 | 就任前的职位 |
|---|---|---|---|---|---|---|
| 17 |  | 安德鲁·约翰逊<br>Andrew Johnson<br>1808~1875 | 1865年<br>4月15日 | 1869年<br>3月4日 | 民主党 | 副总统 |
| 18 |  | 尤利塞斯·S. 格兰特<br>Ulysses S. Grant<br>1822~1885 | 1869年<br>3月4日 | 1877年<br>3月4日 | 共和党 | 美国陆军总司令 |
| 19 |  | 拉瑟福德·B. 海斯<br>Rutherford B. Hayes<br>1822~1893 | 1877年<br>3月4日 | 1881年<br>3月4日 | 共和党 | 俄亥俄州州长 |
| 20 |  | 詹姆斯·A. 加菲尔德<br>James A. Garfield<br>1831~1881 | 1881年<br>3月4日 | 1881年<br>9月19日 | 共和党 | 俄亥俄州众议员 |
| 21 |  | 切斯特·A. 阿瑟<br>Chester A. Arthur<br>1829~1886 | 1881年<br>9月19日 | 1885年<br>3月4日 | 共和党 | 副总统 |
| 22 |  | 格罗弗·克利夫兰<br>Grover Cleveland<br>1837~1908 | 1885年<br>3月4日 | 1889年<br>3月4日 | 民主党 | 纽约州州长 |

| 肖像 | | 姓名与生卒年 | 就任日期 | 离任日期 | 所属党派 | 就任前的职位 |
|---|---|---|---|---|---|---|
| 23 |  | 本杰明·哈里逊<br>Benjamin Harrison<br>1833~1901 | 1889年<br>3月4日 | 1893年<br>3月4日 | 共和党 | 印第安纳州<br>参议员 |
| 24 |  | 格罗弗·克利夫兰<br>Grover Cleveland<br>1837~1908 | 1893年<br>3月4日 | 1897年<br>3月4日 | 民主党 | 总统 |
| 25 |  | 威廉·麦金莱<br>William McKinley<br>1843~1901 | 1897年<br>3月4日 | 1901年<br>9月14日 | 共和党 | 俄亥俄州<br>州长 |

# 大事年表

# CHRONOLOGY

1000年，北欧人利夫发现美洲。

1492年，意大利人哥伦布率西班牙船队抵达美洲。

1497年，意大利人约翰·卡伯特率英国船队探索美洲。

1513年，西班牙人德·里昂探索佛罗里达。

1524年，意大利人维拉扎诺率法国船队探索北美海岸。

1534~1536年，法国人卡迪尔探索圣劳伦斯河。

1539年，西班牙人德·索托从佛罗里达出发开始探索美洲。

1540年，西班牙人科罗纳多从墨西哥出发开始探索美洲。

1562年，法国人里博探索卡罗来纳海岸。

1565年，法国殖民地被西班牙人摧毁。

1577~1578年，英国人德雷克到达加利福尼亚海岸。

1604年，法国人在罗亚尔港建立阿卡迪亚殖民地。

1607年，英国的伦敦弗吉尼亚公司在弗吉尼亚建立詹姆斯敦殖民地。

1608年，法国人尚普兰在魁北克建立殖民地。

1609年，尚普兰发现五大湖；亨利·哈德逊发现哈德逊河。

1619年，第一批黑人奴隶运到美洲；弗吉尼亚建立美洲第一个议会。

1620年，英国清教徒乘“五月花号”到达普利茅斯，并订立《“五月花号”公约》。

1621年，荷兰西印度公司成立，并在美洲建立新阿姆斯特丹和新尼德兰。

1624年，弗吉尼亚公司被解散，弗吉尼亚变成英国皇家行省。

1630年，英国人建立马萨诸塞殖民地。

1632年，巴尔的摩勋爵获得马里兰殖民地。

1635~1636年，部分英国人离开马萨诸塞，建立康涅狄格殖民地。

1636年，罗杰·威廉姆斯被逐出马萨诸塞，并建立普罗维登斯殖民地。

1637年，哈钦森夫人及其追随者被逐出马萨诸塞，并定居于罗得岛。

1638年，部分英国人离开马萨诸塞，建立纽黑文殖民地。

1638~1639年，康涅狄格殖民地制定了美洲第一部成文宪法。

1643年，新英格兰同盟成立。

1649年，巴尔的摩勋爵在马里兰实行《宗教信仰自由法》。

1663年，英国人建立卡罗来纳殖民地。

1664年，英国征服新尼德兰，并建立纽约和新泽西殖民地。

1681年，法国人拉萨尔勘探密西西比河。

1682年，英国人威廉·佩恩建立宾夕法尼亚殖民地。

1699年，拉萨尔建立路易斯安那殖民地。

1732年，英国人詹姆斯·爱德华·奥格尔索普建立佐治亚殖民地。

1754年，英法之间爆发战争；同年，殖民地代表大会在奥尔巴尼召开，本杰明·富兰克林提出组建殖民地大议会方案，未被采纳。

1761年，詹姆斯·奥蒂斯反对《援助令》。

1763年，战争结束，英法签订《巴黎和约》，法国人退出美洲。

1765年，弗吉尼亚殖民地发生反《印花税法》暴动；同年10月，殖民地代表大会在纽约召开，大会起草了《殖民者的权利和不满的宣言书》。

1766年，《印花税法》被废止；《公告法》获得通过。

1767年，《汤森法》获得通过。

1768年，各殖民地议会反对《汤森法》，遭到英国政府的解散。

1769年，弗吉尼亚议会通过《1769年弗吉尼亚决议案》，遭到英国政府解散；被解散的议会成员签署了华盛顿提出的《抵制进口协定》；英国政府取消了《汤森法》中茶税以外的关税；弗吉尼亚成立殖民地通信委员会。

1770年3月5日，波士顿惨案。

1773年，波士顿倾茶事件。

1774年，惩罚马萨诸塞殖民地的系列法案获得通过；《魁北克法》获得通过。

1774年9月，第一届大陆会议在费城召开。美洲同盟成立。

1775年4月19日，爱国者在列克星敦与康科德打响了独立战争的第一枪。

1775年6月17日，邦克山之战，美军撤退，英军伤亡过半。

1775年7月，第二届大陆会议在费城召开。华盛顿担任大陆军司令。

1775~1776年，美军入侵加拿大，结果战败。

1776年，英军撤离波士顿；同年6月，英军进攻莫尔特里堡，结果战败。

1776年7月4日，《独立宣言》获得通过。

1776年8月2日，大陆会议全体成员在《独立宣言》上签名。

1776年12月，美军防守纽约失败，大陆会议撤离费城，华盛顿被授予大陆军唯一指挥权。

1777年夏，布兰迪万河之战，美军败，英军攻占费城；华盛顿奇袭日耳曼敦失败，退守福吉谷。

1777年，萨拉托加之战。10月17日，英军指挥官伯戈因向美军投降。

1778年，法国承认美国独立，并与美国签订同盟条约；同年，英军撤离费城。

1778~1779年，乔治·罗杰斯·克拉克讨伐了西北地区的英军。

1780年，查尔斯顿沦陷；盖茨兵败卡姆登。

1781年，格林接替盖茨担任南部战区司令，并收复了大部分南部地区。

1781年9月，美法联军包围约克敦。10月17日，英军指挥官康沃利斯向联军投降。

1783年9月，英国与美国签订和约，承认美国独立。

1787年，《1787年法令》获得通过。

1787年5月，联邦制宪大会在费城召开。

1787年9月，《美利坚合众国宪法》获得通过。

1789年4月30日，乔治·华盛顿就任美国第一任总统。

1789年，国会通过美国第一部关税法。

1790年，合众国第一银行成立。

1791年，美国进行第一次人口普查；定都华盛顿市；接纳佛蒙特州；前十条宪法修正案获得通过。

1792年，接纳肯塔基州。

1793年，华盛顿发表《中立宣言》，声明美国将不参与欧洲的冲突。

1793年，伊莱·惠特尼发明了轧棉机。

1794年，威士忌暴动被镇压。

1795年，美英签订《杰伊条约》；美法签订条约；第十一条宪法修正案获得通过。

1797年3月4日，联邦党人约翰·亚当斯就任美国第二任总统。

1797~1798年，X.Y.Z事件，美法交恶。

1798~1799年，美法之间发生了小规模海战。

1799年，乔治·华盛顿逝世。

1800年，美法签订合约。

1801年3月4日，共和党人托马斯·杰斐逊就任美国第三任总统。

1803年，美国以1500万美元向法国购得路易斯安那。

1804年，第十二条宪法修正案获得通过。

1804~1806年，刘易斯和克拉克进行西部勘探。

1807年，罗伯特·尔顿发明的蒸汽船投入使用；《禁运法》获得通过；英国强行征用“切萨皮克号”上的美国船员。

1809年3月4日，共和党人詹姆斯·麦迪逊就任美国第四任总统。

1809年，《互不通商法》获得通过。

1811年，蒂珀卡努之战，美军胜，英国收留了逃亡的印第安首领特库姆斯。

1812年，美国对英宣战；赫尔在底特律向英军投降。

1813年，伊利湖与泰晤士河之战，美军胜。

1814年，普拉茨堡之战，美军胜；英军攻占华盛顿市，放火后撤离；美军获得新奥尔良保卫战的胜利；美英停战，签订《根特条约》。

1816年，接纳印第安纳州；合众国第二银行成立。

1817年3月4日，共和党人詹姆斯·门罗就任美国第五任总统。

1817年，接纳密西西比州。

1818年，接纳伊利诺伊州。

1819年，接纳亚拉巴马州；美国以500万美元向西班牙购得佛罗里达。

1820年，《密苏里妥协案》获得通过；接纳缅因州和密苏里州。

1822年，门罗发表《门罗宣言》。

1825年3月4日，共和党人约翰·昆西·亚当斯就任美国第六任总统。

1825年，伊利运河通航。

1829年3月4日，共和党人安德鲁·杰克逊就任美国第七任总统。

1830年，蒸汽火车头问世；罗伯特·杨·海恩与丹尼尔·韦伯斯特在国会进行辩论。

1831年，塞勒斯·霍尔·麦考密克发明马拉收割机；纳特·特纳叛乱。

1833年，南卡罗来纳州拒绝执行联邦法律；《强制法案》获得通过。

1835年，波士顿反废奴主义者暴动。

1836年，杰克逊发布《使用金属通货公告》；德克萨斯共和国成立，申请加入联邦。

1837年3月4日，共和党人马丁·范布伦就任美国第八任总统。

1840年，《独立国库法》获得通过。

1841年3月4日，辉格党人威廉·亨利·哈里逊就任美国第九任总统。同年4月4日，哈里逊去世，同为辉格党人的副总统约翰·泰勒就任美国第十任总统。

1842年，美英签订《韦伯斯特–阿什伯顿条约》，确定美加边界。

1844年，第一条电报线路开通。

1845年3月4日，民主党人詹姆斯·诺克斯·波尔克就任美国第十一任总统。

1845年，接纳德克萨斯。

1846年，美国向墨西哥宣战；加利福尼亚“熊共和国”成立；美国与英国签订《俄勒冈条约》。

1847年，布埃纳维斯塔之战，美军胜；美军攻占墨西哥城。

1848年，美墨签订和约；人们在加利福尼亚发现黄金。

1849年3月4日，辉格党人扎卡里·泰勒就任美国第十二任总统。

1849年，加利福尼亚申请作为自由准州加入联邦。

1850年，克莱提出妥协案；新的《逃亡奴隶法》获得通过。

1850年9月9日，扎卡里·泰勒去世，同为辉格党人的副总统米勒德·菲尔莫尔就任美国第十三任总统。

1853年3月4日，民主党人富兰克林·皮尔斯就任美国第十四任总统。

1853年，加兹登购地案。

1854年，斯蒂芬·阿诺德·道格拉斯提出《堪萨斯-内布拉斯加法案》。

1857年3月4日，民主党人詹姆斯·布坎南就任美国第十五任总统。

1857年，联邦最高法院对德雷德·斯科特案做出判决。

1860年，南卡罗来纳州退出联邦。

1861年3月4日，共和党人亚伯拉罕·林肯就任美国第十六任总统。

1861年4月19日，内战爆发。

1861年7月，第一次布尔溪之战，联邦军败。

1861年9月，联邦军攻占凯罗市。

1862年，联邦组建波托马克军；南部邦联组建北弗吉尼亚军。

1862年1月，密尔斯普林斯之战，联邦军胜。

1862年2月，联邦军攻陷亨利堡与多纳尔森堡。

1862年4月，联邦军攻占新奥尔良；夏洛伊之战，联邦军胜。

1862年5月，科林斯湾之战，南部联邦军胜；半岛战役，双方皆损失惨重。

1862年8月，第二次布尔溪之战，联邦军败。

1862年9月，安蒂特姆之战，联邦军失利。

1862年9月23日，林肯发表《初步解放宣言》。

1862年11月，默夫里斯伯勒之战，联邦军胜。

1862年12月，弗雷德里克斯堡之战，联邦军失利。

1863年1月1日，林肯发表《解放宣言》。

1863年5月，钱瑟勒斯维尔之战，联邦军失利。

1863年7月，葛底斯堡之战，联邦军胜。

1863年7月4日，联邦军攻陷维克斯堡。

1863年9月，奇克莫加河之战，联邦军撤退到查塔努加。

1863年11月，查塔努加之战，联邦军胜。

1864年3月，尤利塞斯·辛普森·格兰特担任联邦陆军总司令。

1864年5月，亚特兰大之战。9月，南部邦联军弃守亚特兰大。

1864年5月至6月，荒野之战、斯波特斯凡尼亚之战、冷港之战，联邦军皆不利并撤退。

1864年7月，南部邦联军奇袭华盛顿市未果，撤退到谢南多厄河谷。

1864年10月，谢南多厄河谷之战，联邦军胜。

1864年11月，富兰克林之战，联邦军撤退至纳什维尔。

1864年12月，纳什维尔之战，联邦军胜。

1865年4月9日，南部邦联军在阿波马托克斯投降。内战结束。

1865年4月15日，林肯遇刺身亡，身为民主党人的副总统安德鲁·约翰逊就任美国第十七任总统。

1865年12月，第十三条宪法修正案获得通过，奴隶制在美国境内被废除。

1866年，《民权法案》在总统反对的情况下获得通过；同年7月，第十四条宪法修正案获得通过。

1867年，《官职任期法》和《重建法》在总统反对的情况下获得通过；美国以700万美元向俄国购得阿拉斯加。

1868年，众议院弹劾约翰逊总统，但经投票表决，弹劾不成立。

1869年3月4日，共和党人尤利塞斯·辛普森·格兰特就任美国第十八任总统。

1870年2月，第十四条宪法修正案获得通过。

1871年，美英就亚拉巴马索赔案签订《华盛顿条约》；同年10月，芝加哥发生大火。

1877年，格兰特向西班牙政府施压，使其与叛乱者达成协议，结束了长达十年的古巴叛乱。

1877年3月4日，共和党人拉瑟福德·伯查德·海斯就任美国第十九任总统。

1880年3月4日，共和党人詹姆斯·埃布拉姆·加菲尔德就任美国第二十任总统。

1881年9月19日，加菲尔德遇刺身亡，同为共和党人的副总统切斯特·艾伦·阿瑟就任美国第二十一任总统。

1885年3月4日，民主党人斯蒂芬·格罗弗·克利夫兰就任美国第二十二任总统。

1889年3月4日，共和党人本杰明·哈里逊就任美国第二十三任总统。

1890年，《麦金莱关税法》获得通过。

1893年3月4日，斯蒂芬·格罗弗·克利夫兰再次当选，就任美国第二十四任总统。

1897年3月4日，共和党人威廉·麦金莱就任美国第二十五任总统。

1897年，《丁利关税法》获得通过。

1894年，古巴再度发生叛乱。

1898年2月，“缅因号”被毁。

1898年4月，美国承认古巴独立，并向西班牙宣战。

1898年5月1日，马尼拉湾海战，西班牙太平洋舰队覆灭。

1898年7月，美西战争结束

1898年12月，美西签订和约。